A WARDEN'S GUIDE to health care in sheltered housing

2nd edition

Dr Anne Roberts

ACE BOOKS

© 1993 Dr Anne Roberts MB, BS, MRCP
2nd Edition
Published by Age Concern England
1268 London Road
London SW16 4ER

Editor Gillian Clarke
Production Marion Peat
Design and typesetting Eugenie Dodd
Printed in Great Britain by Bell & Bain Ltd, Glasgow.

A catalogue record for this book is available from the British Library.

ISBN 0–86242–113–6

Contents

About the Author 4
Acknowledgements 5
How to Use this Book 6
Introduction 7

1   Good Health in Old Age 20

2   Common Illnesses in Later Life 49

3   Residents and their Medicines 83

4   What to do in an Emergency 111

5   When Older People become Frail 140

6   Terminal Illness and Bereavement 190

7   Getting Help from Other Agencies 202

Useful Addresses 220
Further Reading 225
About Age Concern 229
Publications from ACE Books 230

Index 234

About the Author

Anne Roberts is a doctor specialising in geriatric medicine. Her main current interest is in teaching those who look after older people, especially wardens of sheltered housing, staff of residential homes, home care assistants and control centre operators. Her previous books include *Keeping Well – A Guide to Health in Retirement* (Faber & Faber), *Health and Illness in Sheltered Housing – A Case Study Approach* (Centre for Sheltered Housing Studies) and the health section in *The Time of Your Life* for Help the Aged. She has also written numerous articles on health-related topics, and produces a regular feature for *Nursing Times*.

She is on the Board of Management of Anchor Housing Association, is an almshouse trustee and advises many organisations connected with health and housing for older people. She lives in London with her child-psychiatrist husband and two sons.

Acknowledgements

The author would like to thank:

- Gillian Clarke, Marion Peat and the Publishing Department at Age Concern for their help and patience.
- Evelyn McEwen and staff of the Information Department, who were kind enough to check the typescript.
- Her ever-tolerant family, Eric, Thomas and Paul Taylor.

Anne Roberts
September 1993

How to Use this Book

This book is intended for wardens of standard Category 2 sheltered housing, the various types of special schemes for frailer people, for those working in almshouses and for mobile wardens.

To find your way around it, use the Index on page 234, as different aspects of a subject are discussed in different chapters. For example, basic information about a disease is covered in Chapter 2, 'Common Illnesses in Later Life', while notes on the medicines used to treat it are in Chapter 3. Directions on coping with urgent situations can be found in Chapter 4, 'What to do in an Emergency'. Suggestions on making the most of life while living with a disability make up Chapter 5, 'When Older People become Frail', while advice on getting the best out of health and social services can be found in Chapter 7, 'Getting Help from Other Agencies'. Care of terminally ill people and bereavement are covered in Chapter 6. The book ends with a list of addresses of helpful organisations mentioned in the text, and a list of suggestions for further reading.

The word 'warden' is used as a general term for people with several different job titles. In the same way, the occupants of sheltered housing are described as 'residents', to include tenants, owner-occupiers and licensees.

Wardens work in many different ways, in a variety of work settings. As you read the book and think about the topics discussed, you will need to modify the suggestions for action according to your particular work pattern.

Introduction

AGEING IS NATURAL; ILLNESS ISN'T

Ill health and disability are very common among older people, but are not due to the effects of ageing alone. They happen because something has gone wrong, and there is therefore a chance of putting things right. Often, physical, mental and social factors interact to produce disability; a resident's reluctance to go out, for instance, may result from a combination of problems such as arthritis, depression and lack of money.

Though elderly people have considerable potential for recovery, they require prompt attention for it to be complete. This may be difficult to achieve when a serious illness seems undramatic; a heart attack, for instance, may be painless.

Elderly people often do not receive the medical help they need, despite the serious impact of illness on their lives. This may happen because they do not realise that anything can be done for them. Ill-informed carers may fob them off with, 'What do you expect at your age?' They often find health and social services difficult to use, they may have no telephone or car, and also lack the assertiveness necessary to 'work with the system'. Good health care may not seem the prime need of your elderly residents. Nevertheless, poor health matters, because it often prevents older people from enjoying an independent and fulfilling old age.

WHAT SHELTERED HOUSING IS

Sheltered housing is designed to give the people who live in it secure independence. Though every scheme is unique, there are some broad groupings, and it is important for wardens to understand the jargon terms used to describe them. 'Category 1' schemes are collections of flats or bungalows which have been specially designed so that older people can run them easily; in Scotland this is called 'amenity housing'. Most residents of Category 1 schemes have no access to a warden, but a few are linked by an alarm system to a control centre. If residents call for help, the central control operators may organise it themselves. Alternatively, the operator may alert a mobile warden, who will visit the caller, assess the need and then send for whatever sort of help seems necessary.

Category 2 schemes

'Category 2' schemes are what most people understand by sheltered housing. They usually have a warden, and more special design features than Category 1 accommodation. If the scheme is on more than one level, there will usually be a lift, and some communal rooms are often provided. These may include laundry and hairdressing rooms, guest rooms where visiting friends or relatives can stay and a room where residents can meet for social activities. An increasingly useful addition is a bath or shower room fitted with equipment to help residents to keep clean despite having disabilities.

Housing for frailer residents

Some sheltered housing is designed to meet the needs of frailer old people. The idea is that residents can keep their independence, privacy and control over their lives, while still getting any extra help they need. Residents may live in small flats or in bedsitters, with private toilet facilities, basic cooking equipment and, ideally, their own front door. Some or all meals will usually be taken in a communal dining room. The amount and the type of care given are often flexible and can therefore respond to the residents' changing requirements from day to day. In some areas a number of home care assistants or care attendants are allocated to the scheme as a whole. What is on offer varies a good deal from one scheme to another.

These schemes may be called 'Housing with Care', 'Very Sheltered Housing', 'Extra Care Schemes' or 'Category 2½'. Sometimes only a proportion of their residents need extra care, while the remainder are more able and independent.

THE WARDEN'S CHANGING ROLE

Most wardens work in Category 2 schemes. Their role has often been poorly defined, and has varied considerably from one employer to another. The original idea was often of the warden as 'good neighbour': wardens were expected to keep a friendly eye on residents and to mobilise help if and when things went wrong. A few wardens also provided some personal care or domestic help. Apart from care duties, the job also involved overseeing the structure and running of the building and reporting when repairs or maintenance became necessary.

Over the years wardens have found that their work has changed from what it was when the original job was planned. Their residents have become older and frailer, and have gradually required more and more help to get on with their daily lives. As time has gone by, wardens have become more and more involved in direct hands-on care – tasks such as helping with washing and dressing, cooking the occasional meal or supervising the taking of medicines. Some were pleased to be involved in this way and jumped at the chance to do so, but more often the situation came about because there seemed to be no one else to do the job, and the resident's need was urgent.

Various problems followed. The first was the prospect of an enormous increase in the warden's workload: no one person could give this sort of extra care to 30–40 residents, and in fairness they all had to be treated the same. Another was the attitude of health and social services staff: never having been very clear about what the warden's role entailed, and increasingly hard pressed by the difficulty in matching dwindling services to swelling demand, they welcomed the evidence that wardens would fill in gaps in care with tired sighs of relief. A third problem arose for wardens who were helping their residents in ways their employers had specifically forbidden: giving out medicines to a resident was the commonest example. There seemed to be no alternative to what they were doing, but suppose the resident they had helped became suddenly ill after taking the medicines, and their action was blamed? Not unreasonably, wardens in this position felt vulnerable to criticism, disciplinary action or dismissal by their employers and even legal action by relatives or others.

Increasing frailty of residents

Why are sheltered housing residents frailer than they were? There are two main reasons. The first is that there are more very old people in the retired population: while ill health is not normal at any age, it does become more common as the years pass. People over 80 years old and, even more so, people over 85, tend to need more help and care than those between 60 and 80. As sheltered housing residents are drawn from the retired population, they too tend to be older and frailer than used to be the case.

The second reason is the enactment of community care legislation, designed to enable people to stay at home in the community as long as they wish and are able to do so. This means that, if sheltered housing residents become frail, they are less likely to move into a residential home and more likely to stay where they are, needing extra care.

Population studies show that there will be a large number of very old people well into the next century, while 'community care' has come so far that it is unlikely – and perhaps impossible – that the changes producing it will be reversed. This means that the increased frailty of sheltered housing residents is a long-term trend; the problems arising from it will not go away. If the warden's job is to go on being useful and workable, his or her role must alter to mirror the changing needs of the residents.

Planning for change

Some housing providers have thought carefully about how their sheltered schemes will run in these new circumstances. One housing association has extended the job description of its wardens far beyond the traditional 'good neighbour' model. Once they have received appropriate training, wardens will be expected to:

- Assess the care needs of potential residents and those already in the scheme and help plan their care, making appropriate referrals when necessary.

- Undertake direct hands-on support in emergencies for a short while, usually for less than 48 hours. This might include help with transferring between bed, chair and lavatory and helping with dressing, toileting and keeping clean.

- Note and report on whether the care and support services that come into the scheme meld together into a system that works well. In effect, wardens are acting as care managers.

The warden as residents' advocate

In addition, the wardens will sometimes need to act as 'residents' advocate'. Older people are often well able to put their own case forward, but some who are frail, unwell or less assertive by nature may sometimes find this difficult to do. When residents are unable or unwilling to make their wishes known – for instance, to a care provider or at a case conference – it may be appropriate for the warden to do this on their behalf.

In some areas it may be possible to find someone from a local advocacy service who is completely detached from the situation to represent the resident's interests in this way. This can be especially useful at times when the warden has to give an opinion based on professional judgement; someone who has to fill the two roles of warden and resident's advocate simultaneously may find themselves putting a strong case on the resident's behalf and immediately contradicting it on their own.

The warden and residents from ethnic minority groups

The warden's advocacy role is especially important in schemes containing a number of residents from ethnic minority groups: here the warden may have to act as translator and also explain the special cultural requirements of the residents to those who provide their care. You may well know more about the way of life of your ethnic minority residents than do visiting professionals such as doctors and nurses. People from all groups vary in how strictly they follow cultural customs or religious practices, so you may need to make tactful enquiries as to what foods a particular person finds unacceptable, for instance. Older people from ethnic minority communities, especially those with language difficulties, may agree with what a doctor or other 'authority figure' says out of politeness and respect. They may do this even when the advice is culturally unacceptable or when they do not understand what is said. It will be very helpful for you to do what you can to clarify matters in these sensitive circumstances.

Older people from ethnic minorities prefer to consult doctors and pharmacists who share their language and culture, but may not know how to go about finding them; you may be able to help with this. Careful spoken instructions that the older listener can understand are particularly important for the resident who cannot read.

Equipping yourself for the future – knowledge and training

Let us look a little more closely at what this new role for wardens entails. First, it is obviously important that wardens should know exactly what their duties are and exactly what is expected of them. For instance, when wardens provide short-term care themselves, they should know how long a 'short term' is, how to find alternatives and what to do if care providers seem to expect them to continue indefinitely rather than to fill unavoidable gaps.

Next, further training will be needed, in addition to that which some but not all wardens already receive. Depending on circumstances, necessary topics may include some or all of the following:

- General health and welfare issues – in particular, how to recognise when things have gone wrong.
- A basic working knowledge of the ways in which health care and social services are provided. There is a great and increasing variation around the country as to how this is done; whenever possible, some local knowledge should be passed on, as a foundation to be built on as experience accumulates.
- Necessary practical skills, such as safe lifting and handling techniques and how to help with medicines.
- How to keep useful records, while respecting the residents' right to read whatever is written about them, and also their right to privacy.

- Communication skills, to help wardens listen effectively and pass clear information to other professionals, to residents and to their relatives.

You might like to discuss your training needs with your organisation's Training Officer or with your line manager. You could also write to the Principal Education Officer at the Institute of Housing for information about the National Wardens' Certificate Course, or to the Centre for Sheltered Housing Studies for details of the various courses on offer.

Change and housing management

The role of housing manager will also have to change in parallel with that of the warden. It is very important for managers to keep in touch with what is happening in their schemes; changes, however unwelcome, must be recognised or they cannot possibly be dealt with appropriately. Managers themselves may require training; further information is available from the sources suggested above. As wardens will need to call on managers for support and advice in the care aspects of their work, their supervisors will need care management skills as well as the ability to manage housing.

A Code of Practice for wardens and other workers in sheltered housing has recently been drawn up, and has been endorsed by a number of organisations. Copies are available from the Centre for Sheltered Housing Studies.

Explaining to residents what the warden does

Residents and their families often do not know what duties the warden can and cannot undertake. This should be explained when they are considering the move, and they should be given the same information in written form so that they can refer to it afterwards. It is a good idea to make a later opportunity to discuss what residents and their relatives think of the information they have acquired and to find out whether they have got an accurate impression; this can often prevent a great deal of later misunderstanding.

Many sheltered housing providers produce information booklets describing the warden's role in large print and clear language. Some have separate editions for residents and for their relatives, while others issue a single all-purpose manual. Printed materials of this sort must be kept up to date; when change is rapid or where there is a lot of variation between one of an organisation's schemes and another, a loose-leaf format may be sensible. As well as outlining the warden's role, these booklets should reassure residents that their right to privacy will be respected. One states that the warden is strictly forbidden from entering residents' homes using his or her master key except in an emergency or when urgent repairs are necessary. The call system is also explained: the warden cannot listen into conversation in the flat unless the resident has pressed down the switch on the speaker. This means that the resident has complete control over what can and cannot be overheard.

Planning for the future – respecting residents' wishes

It may be possible to extend the scope of these discussions with residents and their relatives. One sensitive topic that is rarely touched on is how residents would like to be cared for if at some time they became unable to decide this for themselves or to express their wishes – perhaps because of a dementing illness or a severe stroke. This is an extension of the idea of the 'living will', when someone still in good health gives instructions as to how they should be treated were they to become severely ill in the future. The will sets out what resuscitation or life support measures they would want taken, and explains what sort of disability would prove so unbearable that they would prefer not to be kept alive to endure it.

This sort of advance planning has obvious snags. One is that people change their minds. Many older people get a lot out of life despite disabilities that their younger selves might have thought incompatible with any sort of pleasurable existence; others reach a point when, despite being neither ill nor depressed, they feel it is time to die. Another is the complexity and vagueness of the information required. 'Do you want to be resuscitated if you suffer a heart attack?' is easy to answer compared with 'How much do you want me to do and decide for you if you become confused?' However, one objection to these discussions that probably has been over-rated is the fear of upsetting the old person. Obviously this sort of information has to be gathered with sensitivity, and certainly no one should be pressed to continue against their will if they are becoming distressed. On the whole, though, older people are not fragile blossoms but sound, mature fruit: they are probably less likely to be upset than to be pleased to be treated as responsible adults with control over their lives.

During the time the residents spend in the scheme, the warden can add to what she or he already knows about their personalities or opinions. Though no one can ever really know how another thinks, the information gained may help the warden to act in the residents' best interests should they become unable to state their views for themselves.

TALKING ABOUT HEALTH WITH RESIDENTS

This section covers the issues of what questions to ask and how to keep the information secret.

Confidentiality

Health and illness are private matters, and people have a perfect right to keep these intimate details of their lives to themselves. It may be that, in order to get advice and help, they have to share this important information with someone else, such as a doctor or nurse. When they do this, the shared information still remains the private property of the patients concerned. Doctors and nurses get into serious trouble – and rightly so – if they fail to keep their patients' affairs strictly confidential.

As health care has become complex, more people need to know a patient's medical history. For instance, an elderly woman resident who goes into hospital to have her broken hip pinned will meet radiographers, physiotherapists, occupational therapists, a medical social worker and possibly a dietician, as well as an assortment of doctors and nurses. As residents become frailer and the warden's role changes, wardens are likely to hear more medical secrets. They will of course be expected to keep this information strictly confidential.

Some breaches of confidence are obvious and easily avoided: no sensible or competent warden would blurt out, 'You'll never guess what's wrong with Mrs Smith next door!' However, it is dangerously easy to break a confidence by accident, for instance by:

- Forgetting to shut the door when making a private phone call concerning a resident.

- Leaving a memo on a pad where it can be read by a casual eye.

- Omitting to make sure that medical articles such as parcels of incontinence pads are given to their recipients in private.

- Discussing a resident's medical problems with a colleague in a public place, such as a bar or restaurant.

Necessary knowledge only

How much do wardens need to know about their residents' health problems? Less than is sometimes thought. If a new resident is suddenly taken ill, the warden who hardly knows them will still be able to take emergency action: the most important component of this is to call for the doctor or ambulance. Until qualified help arrives, the warden can still do what appears to be necessary – for instance, to clear the airway or attempt to staunch bleeding (see p 117). Furthermore, reference to a number of unsorted facts might have harmful results. Out-of-date information might unwittingly be handed on: for instance, a warden might compile a list of medication from office records and send it to hospital with an acutely ill resident, unaware of the changes that had been made during a recent visit to the surgery or out-patient department. In blissful ignorance, hospital staff might accept the list as a true record and act accordingly – with disastrous results. There is also the risk of hiding important points in a mass of irrelevant detail: a list of all the illnesses and operations someone has suffered in 80 years of life makes daunting reading, and ancient history can distract attention from current problems.

All the same, a small amount of current and relevant information can sometimes be crucial to a resident's welfare: a warden who knows that a resident with diabetes is prone to 'hypo' attacks (see p 124) can give sugar quickly and prevent the risk of serious complications if precious time is lost. One way to gather a few important health facts is to say to the new resident, 'Is there anything I ought to know about your health so I can help you if you are taken ill? Anything you tell me stays strictly confidential, of course.' The same question can be asked of the relatives, and the answers noted. Records should be compiled in consultation with the resident, who should know that they can see their file and read the contents at any time. If you do not have a secure, locking drawer or cabinet to store confidential papers, you should ask your employers for one.

Experience suggests that most residents in sheltered housing are more than willing to discuss their health problems, and feel safer because the warden knows about them. A few feel differently, and wardens should remember that residents who so choose have a right to be reticent. In the unlikely event that they suffer harm as a result of this decision, the risk was one they were entitled to take; no one should blame themselves for allowing an older person freedom of choice.

RESIDENTS WHO GO THEIR OWN WAY

Respecting choices

Some residents behave in ways that worry wardens. Caring for people often involves striking a precarious balance. On the one hand, people have a right to run their lives as they wish within certain limits, and to take risks if by doing so they will improve their quality of life. On the other hand, people who are unable to make sensible decisions for themselves have a right to be protected from the results of their ill-judged actions. A further problem is that no one lives in isolation. For instance, in the close quarters of a sheltered housing scheme, one resident's musical interest is another resident's headache. More seriously, whilst residents may choose to take risks on their own account, they cannot be allowed to endanger other people. In this area of a warden's work there are no set rules or easy answers, but it can help to explore the difficulties and discuss possible approaches to them. Risk taking is discussed further in the section on mental frailty (see p 170).

Age alone does not destroy judgement skills. Older people who are mentally intact have a right to be wrong and to take the consequences of their unwise decisions just as other adults do. For instance, a warden does not and should not have the power to stop residents from drinking more than is good for them; older people should not have to suffer interference from other people who think they know best just because they are younger.

When to intervene

However, illness may cloud thought and judgement. When a woman with dementia wants to go out into a freezing winter night wearing only her nightdress to meet imaginary children from school, it would obviously be foolish to do nothing about it. This does not mean that mentally frail people have no rights over their own lives. Many are capable of expressing preferences as to where and how they live. Every effort should be made to find out what they want and to respect their wishes as far as possible.

Use of advocacy

When residents, especially mentally frail ones, find it difficult to make their choices clear and to speak up for themselves, they may need someone to do this for them. The warden who knows the resident well may be able to do this, but sometimes will be too close to the situation to think clearly. (Doctors are discouraged from treating their close families for the same reason.) A disinterested person may be most helpful here, and it is worth finding out from the Citizens Advice Bureau or local branch of Age Concern whether an advocacy scheme operates locally.

It can be very difficult to decide at what point concerned help becomes interference. Wardens worry especially about this when a resident who appears to be unwell refuses to see the doctor. This often seems to happen at night, when wardens have little but their own judgement to depend on.

Finding the reason for refusal

It is often useful to try to find out why the resident is refusing medical help. Some such people do not like doctors or the medicine they practise, and prefer to rely on their own resources, whatever the consequences; this is obviously a choice they are entitled to make. Others have not had adequate explanations of their illnesses and treatment in the past. Some are depressed, and because of their illness feel unworthy to receive any sort of treatment, whilst some have a physical illness causing mental confusion that will disappear once the illness is treated. Others fear that if they admit to a need for any sort of help, their lives will be taken over by well-meaning bullies who will force them to do things they do not want to 'for their own good'.

A warden who is trusted enough to act on the resident's behalf can be very useful, often in places or at times when no other sort of advocacy is available. For instance, the warden can politely persist in asking questions of doctors until the resident has enough information to make a decision, and can support the resident in resisting undue pressure to accept a service or a move into a residential home.

Too sick to decide?

Deciding what to do when the resident who is refusing help seems confused or mentally ill is especially worrying. It can be difficult for an experienced specialist in old age psychiatry to diagnose depression or to discover the cause of a confusional state, so it is obviously unreasonable to expect a warden to do this without the benefit of training or the backup of hospital facilities. Also, a warden whose sick or confused resident got worse and died without seeing a doctor would be likely to find the failure to summon help difficult to defend. The best – or perhaps the least bad – course is to call the doctor so as to get an expert opinion on the resident's mental state. Once this is done, the warden can still act as resident's advocate when decisions have to be made as to what happens next.

As wardens find their role developing and extending, it becomes even more important that they remember that they are there primarily to provide assistance rather than interference. Residents' views should be heard and their wishes respected whenever this is possible, and their independence should be encouraged at all times.

1 Good Health in Old Age

The positive side of growing older is presented in this chapter, with the emphasis on enjoying retirement years by maintaining healthy habits. Sexual activity can and should continue into later life; this sensitive topic is discussed as well as the sensible use of alcohol and how to give up smoking.

The care of eyes, teeth and feet is also covered, as is the wise use of health checks.

This chapter aims to give wardens the information they need to advise residents sensibly if asked to do so.

MAKING THE MOST OF RETIREMENT

Many recently retired people find that their worth to the community and to themselves seems suddenly to diminish when they are no longer going out to work. The older people who manage to counteract this feeling of worthlessness and who seem happiest are often those who keep busy, perhaps by making an occupation out of an established hobby – for instance, an ex-civil servant who always enjoyed pottering in the garden may build himself a greenhouse, propagate cuttings and grow his own vegetables; a retired teacher who has always been active with her needle may make herself a new wardrobe or find self-expression in embroidery.

Others explore the possibilities of painting or some craft or hobby that they have not tried before, and sometimes unexpected talent is discovered. Grandma Moses started painting after retirement age and then continued until after her hundredth birthday.

GOING BACK TO SCHOOL

Some older people find a stimulating new interest by extending their education during retirement. Local authority classes in many subjects and skills are available; the cost of these varies from place to place. Many are held in the daytime rather than the evening, when people are often reluctant to go out. Most courses start with the academic year, in September.

Other sources of adult education are the Workers Educational Association, correspondence courses advertised in newspapers and magazines and of course the Open University, though persisting with these last two can require a good deal of commitment. Most public libraries have a list of local authority courses as well as details of clubs and societies offering discussion groups and lectures. Age Concern England produce a Factsheet about leisure education. You may want to display this, with local information, on your scheme notice board.

REMEMBERING THE PAST

Older people often enjoy reminiscing and may channel an interest in the past into enthusiasm for local history. In some parts of the country there are oral history projects where the memories of older residents of a neighbourhood are recorded and sometimes published and illustrated with old photos. One particularly successful project takes older people into schools to talk to pupils about their memories of their own school days – an enlightening experience for both generations.

You may like to test whether there is any historical interest among the residents of your scheme by the use of reminiscence material at a coffee morning. The use of the 'Recall' pack, obtainable from Help the Aged or sometimes available on loan from the social services, can make for an enjoyable session. Each part of the pack covers a decade or so within the lifespan of an elderly resident, and includes a set of slides of everyday sights, a tape of contemporary music or other sounds and a booklet suggesting topics for discussion. Other professionally prepared reminiscence material is produced by Winslow: you could write for a catalogue. Age Exchange is another source, and this organisation also runs courses on conducting reminiscence sessions.

Alternatively, an anniversary may provide an occasion for hunting out mementoes and collecting memories of 'Where I was on VE Day', for instance. Postcards showing local landmarks as they used to be may stimulate recollections, and reveal unexpected points of contact between residents who have lived near each other or shared a work experience.

GIVING TIME TO THE COMMUNITY

Many people who are now elderly have led busy lives, often caring for others, and do not suddenly become passive objects of charity because they have entered the retirement age group. The need to give does not disappear with age, and the recently retired are an underused source of community action. The image of a voluntary worker as a Lady Bountiful in a flowered hat dispensing charity to the poor is now out of date: most voluntary work is a matter of enabling others to help themselves rather than distributing handouts. A would-be volunteer usually has little difficulty in finding a niche. Likely organisations such as Age Concern may be approached directly, or there may be a local volunteer bureau.

KEEPING PHYSICALLY FIT

Although older people are sometimes said to become more rigid in their ideas, it may be their middle-aged relatives who are hidebound in their attitudes as to what activities are suitable for their elders to undertake. 'Really, Mum, at your age!' is unkind and usually inappropriate as a damper to burgeoning elderly spirits. Physical activity is often thought to be increasingly unwise as the years pass, but, provided health is good and the level of exertion sensible, this is not the case.

Exercise in later life can improve stamina and circulation, strengthen bones and muscles and make joints more supple. All this improves wellbeing and independence, helps prevent falls and increases stamina, fitting the older body to face the challenge of extra activity or sudden illness.

Those who have heart, chest or joint problems, who smoke heavily or who are severely overweight should, however, consult their doctor before undertaking a programme of vigorous exercise.

Classes are an excellent way to keep fit together with others. Your local public library will have details of these in your area, or you could get in touch with EXTEND or the Keep Fit Association. Though some highly motivated people may exercise at home alone, perhaps to music and with the help of a book, it is easier to persevere in the company of friends. Even the laziest and least agile are well advised to put each joint through its complete range of movements daily, perhaps first thing in the morning, just as a waking cat stretches itself.

Many sports stay within the capabilities of the older enthusiast. Swimming is excellent for suppleness, and retired people are often able to enjoy the use of the local pool at times when it is almost empty. They may also rediscover the joy of cycling, though in London and other large cities it may be wise to think hard about traffic dangers. Walking is perhaps the ideal exercise: it costs nothing, and the means are always to hand. The older walker should aim to build up gradually to covering a mile in 20 minutes, once or twice a day.

Everyone who is in good health should try to get out of the house at least once a day; the mental stimulation of a change of scene is just as important as the toning-up of heart and circulation. You might try suggesting to residents that they should not have their daily newspaper delivered but should go to the shop and fetch it, perhaps doing the same errand for a housebound friend. More leisurely activities such as ballroom dancing promote suppleness and rhythm in social surroundings, and may be useful for the less athletic. Those who can no longer participate in their favourite sport can still enjoy club life: cricket umpires and scorers are always needed.

WITH AN EYE TO SAFETY

Active residents should be encouraged to continue with sensible road safety habits such as using pedestrian crossings; when going out at night they should wear light colours or even a Dayglo band to reduce the risk of accidents. When the weather is wet or icy, it is especially important that shoe soles do not slip and that rubber ferrules on walking sticks are not worn down.

If residents avoid going out because they are worried about street crime, you could contact the Crime Prevention Officer (CPO) at the local police station for advice. CPOs are often willing to come and talk to residents about the local situation. People who venture out at night should keep their door keys in a pocket separate from their address. It is wise to leave large sums of money or precious keepsakes at home. Obviously, if residents are attacked, they should not resist.

EATING WELL IN LATER LIFE

A good diet is necessary for both health and wellbeing. Unfortunately, many older people eat poorly, often for a combination of reasons. Eating habits may have been laid down in harder times when diet was considered to be good enough if your stomach was full, and when bread and jam was all there ever was for tea. Many retired men have never learned to cook, partly because the roles of the sexes were more rigidly defined when they were younger, but also because working hours were then so long that men had little time to help in the house.

What is eaten and how food is prepared varies a great deal from one culture to another. If you are trying to advise or help a resident whose cultural background differs from your own you may need guidance. You could ask advice from the appropriate community or religious leader about forbidden foods or habits associated with eating, such as the need to wash beforehand or to cut up food into bite-sized pieces if chopsticks are to be used. It is as well to remember that people from the same group may still vary a good deal in their personal preferences, as well as in how strictly they follow dietary laws and customs.

CHANGING WRONG HABITS

Social isolation is one of the saddest features of old age, and it undermines good eating habits. Few of us would cook well-balanced and varied meals just for ourselves. Attending a luncheon club may improve both nutrition and social life, and, if an older person is not housebound, is often preferable to receiving Meals on Wheels. In some sheltered schemes residents occasionally make arrangements to share the cooking and eat together – we all make more effort for company and all weary housekeepers know that a meal you have not shopped for and cooked yourself tastes twice as good. The occasional meal eaten with relatives or friends away from the scheme is another way to lessen a person's isolation. This could be suggested to relatives who are too busy or too frail themselves to do more; Sunday lunch is a popular choice.

Help with shopping or food preparation from a relative or home care assistant can improve poor eating habits. An occupational therapist can suggest appropriate cooking aids for a disabled person. Large-handled knives may be easier for arthritic hands to hold, and other gadgets are available for those with a single good hand or who are hampered by poor sight. Contact your local Disabled Living Centre for details: the Disabled Living Foundation in London keeps a list of these.

People with dementia are particularly likely to eat poorly, often living on biscuits, tea and other foods that need little preparation. Depressed people show a similar pattern of behaviour, and poor nutrition will worsen their general state of health. In these cases things cannot be put right unless the underlying illness or disability is recognised.

Poverty is an obvious cause of poor diet, especially in the winter months, when a pensioner may have to choose between paying for heating or for food. Any older person may find it difficult to cope with the changing value of money: a three shilling (15p) orange may seem ruinously expensive and a bad bargain. Try to make sure that residents in your scheme know about all the welfare benefits to which they are entitled and encourage them to see these as theirs by right. Age Concern's publication *Your Rights* is a useful source of information about money benefits for older people.

A poor appetite is common in convalescents, especially if they live alone and have no one to prepare tempting dainties for them. Alcohol abuse may also lead to poor nutrition; there are heavy drinkers of all ages, and a tendency to indulgence may be worsened by the loneliness that some people experience as they get older.

There are also elderly people who continue scrupulously to follow a diet prescribed by a doctor many years ago but which is now outmoded. If you have a resident like this, you could suggest that they find out from the doctor whether the diet is still necessary.

Finally, older people may eat an adequate diet but have intestinal problems that make it difficult for them to absorb food properly. This 'malabsorption syndrome' causes weight loss, usually with diarrhoea, and this requires medical attention.

GETTING A BALANCED DIET

Malnutrition in elderly people is almost always preventable. The first step in dealing with it is to identify those at risk – depressed or lonely people, those who have recently suffered a bereavement, residents who are housebound because of a disability and men or women with little kitchen experience. Residents like these may welcome a kindly interest in their welfare, be glad of your knowledge of what is available and be open to your suggestions of sources of help. You should not interfere, however; it is very difficult indeed to change people's cooking and eating habits, and constant nagging on small points is likely to be counter-productive.

It is wise, though, to know a little about nutrition so that you can give sensible advice if asked. This will also be important if you help with a luncheon club in your scheme. Here is a summary of essential dietary requirements to pass on to your residents.

Proteins

These are contained in red meat, chicken, fish, milk, cheese and eggs, and also in the vegetable pulses such as peas, beans and lentils, as in dahl. Proteins are needed for growth, maintenance and repair of the body, and each day's diet should include two portions. Sometimes extra protein is required – for example, after an operation or long illness or when protein has seeped away in the fluid oozing from a sore or wound. This will also be necessary when someone has not eaten proteins because of difficulty in chewing meat or because of the high price of some items.

Carbohydrates

Unrefined carbohydrates found in wholemeal bread, wholegrain cereals, brown rice and pasta and jacket potatoes are needed for energy and warmth and as a source of fibre to prevent constipation. These foods also contain vegetable protein, and should form the basis of the daily diet, being eaten at every meal.

Refined carbohydrates in sugar and white flour should be eaten very sparingly and regarded as an occasional treat, because these foods contain only 'empty' calories and have no other food value. Over-indulgence in refined carbohydrate foods makes weight control extra difficult. However, glucose drinks are sometimes a useful energy source in illness or during convalescence.

Fats

The richest sources of these are oily fish, butter, margarine and cheese. They are needed as sources of the fat-soluble vitamins D, A and K and to make other foods taste better. However, they are rich in calories, and people with a tendency to put on weight are wise to eat all fats sparingly. While many of us would benefit from cutting down on fats, a few would not – for instance, frail old people with small appetites who need a lot of calories in a small volume of food if they are to be properly nourished. 'Saturated' fats of animal origin may be linked with heart disease. However, this connection becomes weaker with the passing years, as the most vulnerable people do not survive middle age. It may be sensible for younger, newly retired people to reduce total fat intake and replace animal fats by 'polyunsaturates' such as sunflower oil products. Older people over 75 seem unlikely to benefit much from this.

Vitamins

These are widely found in food and, though essential, only very small amounts are required. Healthy people eating a balanced, varied diet do not require supplements, though some sick people may do so. Excess vitamins in tablets or unusual diets may be harmful.

Vitamin A

Vitamin A is contained in liver, carrots, other vegetables and dairy produce. Extra is needed by people with some stomach and bowel diseases, but it should not be taken without medical advice, as this can be dangerous.

Vitamin B group

B group vitamins are contained in most foods. Extra vitamin B_1 (thiamine) is needed by people who abuse alcohol and by those living mostly on highly refined, easily prepared processed foods. Vitamin B_{12} deficiency causes pernicious anaemia. Affected people usually cannot absorb B_{12} taken by mouth and need injections of it instead. People on strict vegetarian diets (vegans) need B_{12} supplements. Vitamin B_6 (pyridoxine) causes nerve damage if taken in large quantities. It can also interfere with the action of levodopa used to treat Parkinson's disease.

Vitamin C

Vitamin C cannot be stored in the body, so it is best to take it every day, in fresh fruit and vegetables or a rosehip or blackcurrant drink. People suffering from iron-deficiency anaemia need vitamin C because it helps the body to absorb iron. Lack of vitamin C causes scurvy, and milder deficiency is quite common in older people taking poor diets. Whenever possible, fruit and fruit juice should be added, with tablets as a last resort. Larger than normal amounts of vitamin C may help healing in people who are recovering from injuries or operations. Very large doses (megadoses) do not seem beneficial to health, and they may cause toxic effects such as diarrhoea and kidney stones.

Vitamin D

Vitamin D is found in oily fish such as sardines and pilchards, fortified margarine, eggs and liver. It is also manufactured in human skin when exposed to sunlight. Together with dietary calcium, vitamin D helps to prevent ageing bones from becoming brittle and breaking easily, but overdosage from self-medication can cause kidney damage. Vitamin D supplements may be prescribed for housebound people, for those who absorb it poorly or for people who are taking some drugs for epilepsy. Older people from the Indian sub-continent are especially likely to lack vitamin D. This results from a combination of genetic factors, lack of sunlight and a diet low in sources of vitamin D and high in chapatti flour, which interferes with vitamin D absorption. Advice can put things right only if dietary customs are respected: seek help from an Asian community leader if necessary.

Vitamin K

Vitamin K is widely distributed in food and helps in normal blood clotting. Extra may be needed by people with some stomach or bowel diseases or who have been taking some anticoagulant drugs, especially before surgery.

Minerals

Iron

Iron is found in meat, especially offal, eggs and dairy foods. It is needed by the red blood cells to keep the blood healthy. Elderly people may develop iron-deficiency anaemia if they are losing blood from the gullet, stomach or bowel, and dietary deficiency may make this worse.

Calcium

Calcium helps to prevent the bones from becoming brittle. It is mainly found in dairy produce, and half a pint of milk a day and half a pound of cheese a week is needed. Semi-skimmed or skimmed milk and low-fat cheeses contain as much calcium as full-fat varieties. People who cannot take dairy products may be prescribed calcium tablets by the doctor. As too much calcium can damage the kidneys, it is unwise for people to buy their own supplements and take them without medical advice.

EMPHASISING THE ESSENTIALS

When advising your residents about the constituents of a healthy diet, you should emphasise the importance of fruit and vegetables, fluids and fibre: easily remembered as the three Fs.

Fruit and vegetables

These are an important source of vitamin C and fibre, especially when eaten raw. However, some elderly people find uncooked vegetables difficult to chew and digest.

Cooking vegetables requires care, as vitamin C is easily destroyed by the strong heat of boiling or frying. To preserve vitamin C, vegetables should be prepared and washed just before use, cooked in about an inch of fast-boiling salted water (no bicarbonate of soda, which destroys vitamin C), with the lid on the pan so that the vegetables are steamed rather than boiled. They should be served immediately, as keeping them hot will destroy more vitamin C. Ideally, gravy should be made from the cooking water.

Citrus fruits are excellent because their vitamin C comes wrapped in fibre, but some people find oranges difficult to peel. If residents complain that citrus fruits sting the mouth, sweeter rosehip and blackcurrant syrups may be more acceptable.

Fluids

These are very important for older people, who should drink at least 3 pints (1.7 litres) daily and more if possible. In hot weather when water loss as perspiration is increased, 5 pints (3 litres) may be nearer the mark. It may help for the resident to measure this amount into cups and glasses to make the quantity obvious. The best simple guide as to whether a person is drinking enough is the colour of urine. Except for first thing in the morning, urine should be pale; perhaps the best way to explain this is 'more like a glass of ready-to-drink lime juice than a glass of orangeade'.

Frail or convalescent residents may become dehydrated because fetching a drink involves too much effort. It helps to make sure that such people

have drinks at hand in a jug or vacuum flask; depending on circumstances, a relative, a home care assistant, a fitter resident or you yourself
may see that this is done.

Fibre

This helps to prevent constipation. There is also some evidence that a
fibre-rich diet can prevent 'western world' diseases. These include diverticular disease and bowel cancer, and perhaps others such as appendicitis,
gallstones, diabetes, piles and varicose veins. When vegetable protein
replaces fatty animal protein, the incidence of heart and blood vessel diseases may be reduced. Also, the increased bulk of the high-fibre diet produces a feeling of fullness, and makes it easier to avoid over-eating and
becoming overweight.

Fibre-rich foods are cheap, and are readily available in supermarkets and
other food shops. Baked jacket potatoes are rich in fibre, warming and
nourishing. If dressed with flavoured yogurt or cottage cheese, they contain few calories for the amount of food value they give. People fortunate
in having no weight problem can get their daily vitamin D ration by
adding butter or margarine. Wholemeal bread and flour, wholegrain
cereals, beans and lentils are also rich in fibre.

Dried beans and lentils can be cooked quickly in a pressure cooker, or
bought ready-cooked in tins. Baked beans on wholemeal toast are a dietician's delight, and they could hardly be easier to prepare. For further suggestions about eating and health, see Further Reading on pages 225–228.

PRINCIPLES OF FOOD HYGIENE

If you have a luncheon club in your scheme, you will need to conform to
the requirements of the Food Safety Act; your employers will be able to
advise you about this. Reminders about food hygiene are also important
for residents who have little kitchen experience or who have suffered
from food poisoning in the past. The important points are listed below.

- Before preparing food, wash hands thoroughly – especially after using the
  lavatory.

- Cool hot food quickly, and store it in the cold. Remember that low temperatures prevent bacteria from multiplying, as all organisms, whether human or bacterial, are more likely to reproduce when comfortably warm.

- Buy food that will be eaten cold, such as pork pie or cooked ham, from a reliable shop where food is properly stored.

- Keep raw food that may contain salmonella germs (eg raw meat and poultry) separately from cooked food, to prevent contamination. Put raw meat on the lowest shelf of the refrigerator, so it cannot drip on other food.

- Cook food such as poultry well, as this kills salmonella germs. Large turkeys must be thoroughly cooked, and frozen ones must thaw completely before cooking.

- Store leftovers in the cold, and reheat them rapidly to boiling temperature to kill any germs – just 'warming up' will multiply bacteria.

- Do not eat food that is past its best because you want to save money, and keep to 'sell by' and 'use by' dates on food packaging. Food that makes a person ill is a waste of money.

CHANGING SLEEP PATTERNS

The pattern of normal sleep changes with increasing age. Though probably none of us sleeps continuously through the night, with advancing years sleep certainly becomes more restless. Older people may wake several times during the night, perhaps fully enough to remember afterwards that they have done so, and may wrongly believe that they never closed their eyes all night. At all ages there is a great variation in the amount of sleep that people require; it is a mistake to think that eight hours are necessary for health or that mild sleep loss is in any way harmful.

The changed sleep pattern in later life includes a tendency to sleep more in the daytime. Many fit older people cope with this by taking an after-lunch siesta; together with night naps, this often adds up to a respectable sleep quota over each 24-hour period.

Some causes of insomnia

Sometimes physical problems such as pain from arthritic joints, breathlessness from heart failure, indigestion or leg cramps keep older people awake, and treatment of these conditions will enable them to sleep well again. Elderly confused people may be unable to describe what is making them uncomfortable and restless. Likely causes of their distress could be a full bladder or constipation. A cold bedroom may also keep people awake, and the cold air they breathe in will aggravate any tendency to cough.

Mental factors may also interfere with sleep. The early morning waking of depression may not be recognised for what it is, and if sedatives are prescribed without proper investigation, the patient's mental state may be made worse. Anxiety commonly prevents people from falling asleep. Counselling and suggesting some relaxation techniques or a change of routine can be more helpful than prescribed drugs in helping people to deal with anxiety; a community psychiatric nurse may be able to help with this.

Self-help for poor sleepers

Older people can help themselves to sleep better. A first step is to establish a regular bed time. Sufficient day time activity is also important, especially exercise in the fresh air to produce a feeling of healthy tiredness by evening. Before retiring to bed, it helps to let the wheels run down for half an hour or so by enjoying some pleasant pastime such as knitting, reading an undemanding book or watching television, though the late news will probably not have the desired effect.

If these measures fail, it is a mistake to lie rigidly in bed willing oneself to fall asleep. It makes much better sense to put the light on and, if necessary, get up and potter about for a while. Very often activities such as reading or writing a letter have the desired sedative effect.

A milky drink taken at bed time does seem to make sleep less restless, but coffee and tea should be avoided because caffeine keeps people awake. Some older people like an alcoholic nightcap, and *small* amounts are not harmful, though they may not work very well. Though alcohol decreases restlessness early in the night, wakefulness will usually follow later on. Larger amounts can have more dangerous unwanted effects than small doses of a suitable sleeping medicine. It is a mistake to regard alcohol as safe because it is familiar. For more information about sensible drinking, see p 40.

Avoiding sleeping tablets

Sleeping pills are certainly not the answer in all cases of insomnia, and doctors differ in their attitudes to prescribing them. It is unkind never to give a sedative to an older person, but it should be regarded as something exceptional to tide someone over a difficult patch and help re-establish a normal sleep pattern.

Many people are first prescribed a sedative in hospital, when anxiety, discomfort and noise may interfere with normal sleep. If after recovery they are given a supply of the tablets to take home, they may wrongly conclude that these form part of their treatment and should not be omitted. In fact the comfort of familiar home surroundings often restores the normal sleep pattern, and people should in these circumstances try to manage without drugs.

Whatever the circumstances of the original prescription, it is obviously sensible for only a small quantity of a sedative to be dispensed. After finishing the tablets, the patient should then see the prescribing doctor again, and the prescription should certainly not be renewed indefinitely. Taking someone off sleeping pills is usually done gradually. A period of wakefulness and sometimes a little agitation is common during the withdrawal period, but this soon passes.

The Over-75s check is a good occasion for discussing sleeping patterns and the need for sleeping tablets (see pp 46 and 100).

SEX IN LATER LIFE

Sex seems to be the least discussed and accepted activity of older people, sometimes by themselves and often by those who help to care for them. Because of their upbringing, many older people are reticent about the subject and may give the false impression of a lack of interest in sex.

In fact, research studies have shown that over half of all married couples over 60 years old still have sexual intercourse, at a frequency varying from once a month to a three times a week. Seven out of ten men 68 years old are sexually active, though this falls to only one in four of those aged 78. This drop is probably associated with the decline in health that commonly afflicts people over 75, and it may be that as improved health care and social conditions produce healthier very old people, they too will persist with sexual activity. Older men most commonly give up sex because they cannot get an erection (impotence); in women, love-making usually ends because of the loss of a sexually active partner.

Why, then, is it so difficult to accept older people as sexual beings? It may partly stem from the childlike difficulty we all have in accepting the sexuality of our parents and their friends. In addition, there is the wrong image fostered by advertising, television and films that physical love is dependent on youth and beauty. Some of us with sexual difficulties ourselves find it difficult to accept that older people, or people with a disability, are more successful than we are in their sex lives. Reluctance to accept the sexuality of an elderly parent is sometimes due to relatives' unwillingness to permit a 'replacement' for a dead father or mother. They may also fear the loss of their inheritance if a parent remarries.

Sexual performance over 60

The effect of ageing on sexual function is, in fact, much less than is generally supposed. In men there is some decline in erectile capacity, but generally erections remain sufficiently firm for intercourse to be satisfactory for both parties. There may also be some delay in ejaculation, and orgasm may occur without ejaculation taking place at all. When a man expresses concern that this represents the beginning of the end for his prowess, he should be reassured that this is not so. Impotence (the inability to achieve an erection) is abnormal and may be treatable, especially if the cause is the unwanted effect of a medicine.

In women, sexual problems may develop with the menopause. As the levels of female hormones fall, lubrication of the vagina and adjacent areas becomes less efficient and takes longer to achieve, while the lining membrane becomes thinner and less elastic. Sometimes the problem is solved by the use of a simple lubricant such as KY jelly or baby oil (not baby lotion, which can cause soreness). It is occasionally necessary to use replacement oestrogens (female hormones), either locally or as tablets. These hormones make the vaginal lining thicker, softer and more elastic, as it was during the childbearing years. In some areas there are menopause clinics run by the gynaecological departments of local hospitals. These are particularly skilled in the management of hormone replacement therapy and the GP can be asked to refer the woman to one of these clinics.

When sexual performance declines, the loss of a source of pleasure and expression of love in a relationship of many years' standing adds yet another bereavement to those that commonly pile up as the years pass. More importantly, the sexual aspects of a relationship always affect its general quality. If a woman rejects her husband's sexual advances because sex has become painful for her since the menopause, he will feel rejected as a person, particularly if difficulties in communication prevent her from explaining the situation fully. The whole relationship is then liable to deteriorate, and it may be sadly difficult for the affected partners to find help.

How wardens can help

Firstly, you can help to ensure that older people do not accept a decline in their sexual performance as a consequence of old age. You could, for instance, give your residents the opportunity to become better informed by adding books on relationships and sexuality to the scheme library (see Further Reading on pages 225–228). If asked about a sexual problem, encourage your residents to seek help, from the GP in the first instance or by getting in touch with their local branch of Relate (formerly the Marriage Guidance Council) or with the Association to Aid the Sexual and Personal Relationships of Disabled People (SPOD). People with disabilities or who have stomas or wear a catheter may wonder how this will affect their sex lives. Sensitive advice and literature can be obtained from SPOD.

Try not to be over-protective in dealings with your residents, as this diminishes them as individuals. When it may seem that an older man is 'making a fool of himself over a woman who is just after what she can get', remember that older people, like the rest of us, are entitled to decide on their own fate. For an older man to enliven his declining years with apparently unsuitable women may be undignified, but it is no one's business but his own.

Do not separate elderly lovers when the association seems unwise, even when asked to do so by relatives: this is not your concern. Also, resist the temptation to do a little matchmaking; clumsiness may blight a potentially life-enhancing relationship.

Do not presume that a resident's sexual preference is for a partner of the opposite sex; at least one in 20 of the population, and possibly considerably more, is exclusively homosexual. To such a person, sexual activity with a person of the opposite sex seems as unnatural, repellent and 'queer' as homosexual relationships may seem to some heterosexual people.

Older people are less likely to 'come out' and admit their gayness than younger ones, and it is not necessary to delve into the sexual intimacies of a relationship or to force confidences. A long-standing homosexual relationship should be accepted as corresponding to a marriage, and you should be able to provide appropriate sympathy and support in severe illness or following a partner's death; the Gay Bereavement Project may be able to provide further help.

It is essential to remember that sexual activity between people is psychological as well as physical. Older people, like the rest of us, fall in love, court each other, kiss and cuddle, and suffer the agonies of sexual jealousy. Regarding sex purely as a matter of anatomy and physiology and its difficulties as 'plumbing faults' is a mistake.

When sex becomes a problem

Mentally frail people may expose themselves or masturbate publicly. This happens because learned patterns of acceptable behaviour have been forgotten, because of brain damage from the dementing illness. Such behaviour is very distressing to the family and sometimes to carers. It is important to be sure that a sexual incident is, in fact, taking place: for instance, a stroke patient may be thought to be exposing himself when he is merely seeking help in doing up his fly buttons.

The GP, geriatrician or psychogeriatrician may be able to help by making sure that the resident's mental state is as good as possible and by getting rid of medical conditions that attract undue attention to the genital area: an itchy thrush infection is an example. When the resident is as well as possible, the community psychiatric nurse or clinical psychologist may be able to give useful advice on coping with remaining behaviour problems. Interesting occupations and privacy for sexual activity will help. The aim is to ensure the best possible quality of life for the mentally frail resident and for those around them; achieving this is often difficult and involves painful decisions. Sedation is not the answer: it may be dangerous and is usually ineffective, and, though it is possible to use drugs to castrate chemically, the decision to use these poses ethical problems.

A move to other accommodation may sometimes seem to be the best option, especially for residents who are becoming less able to look after themselves and are willing to move. People in sheltered housing who are distressing others by their behaviour are likely to be in breach of their tenancy agreement, but managers are understandably reluctant to start legal proceedings in this sort of case. There are no easy solutions, and all professionals concerned can only work for the best outcome that can be achieved in the circumstances.

SMOKING AND DRINK PROBLEMS

There is no good word to be said for smoking tobacco – the habit kills perhaps as many as 100,000 people every year in Britain, smokers dying on average ten years before their time. Smoking causes lung cancer, chronic bronchitis and emphysema, coronary artery disease and the disease of the limb arteries that makes amputation necessary. It worsens other illnesses such as peptic ulcers, and makes it more difficult and dangerous for an anaesthetic to be given for any surgical procedure. What is more, smokers hurt others besides themselves; they injure both the passive smokers who are forced to inhale the fumes they produce and children who learn to take up the habit.

These risks are reduced as soon as smoking is stopped, and continue to fall thereafter.

Though cigarettes are the most dangerous, cigars and pipes also carry their own hazards. Changing the way tobacco is smoked is not an alternative to giving up the habit altogether.

Giving up smoking

It is never too late to stop smoking; there are benefits to health even in extreme old age. People who attempt to give up will be more likely to succeed with appropriate help and advice; there may be a clinic or support group at the doctor's surgery or health centre, for instance. The organisation ASH (Action on Smoking and Health) produces good literature, including an excellent free 'Give up' pack. ASH can also supply any 'No Smoking' notices you need for the public rooms in your scheme.

Nicotine-containing chewing gum helps some people kick the habit by reducing physical withdrawal symptoms. Other nicotine preparations, such as patches and mouth sprays, are also available. Both gum and patches can be bought over the counter in chemists' shops, with a stronger form available from the doctor on a private prescription; this has to be paid for. People who have peptic ulcers or suffer from angina may want to check with the doctor before using these preparations.

People trying to stop smoking can be reassured that the worst of the withdrawal period is usually over within a month; they should be encouraged to think instead of ways to spend the money saved on something less dangerous. A weight gain of about half a stone (3kg) is quite common after smoking is stopped but does not always happen. It can usually be lost without too much difficulty, and, even if retained, it poses much less of a danger to health than continued smoking.

Alcohol – use and abuse

Older people are more vulnerable

Drinking alcohol differs from smoking in that light and occasional drinking seem to do little harm. Nevertheless, there has been a great increase in problems of excessive alcohol consumption since the 1960s, and older people have followed this trend. Unfortunately, even habitual drinkers become more vulnerable to the effects of excessive alcohol as they get older, because of the bodily changes of ageing. This effect is worsened in people who have other ailments or who are taking medication.

Older people who abuse alcohol often fall and may bang their heads, causing brain damage. Malnutrition is common, and any tendency to incontinence or mental confusion is worsened. Heavy drinkers who smoke in bed or drive cars put themselves and sometimes other people at risk of injury. Residents who behave unpleasantly when drunk are often ostracised; they then drink more to relieve their loneliness and thus aggravate the problem.

Older men may have drunk heavily all their lives, and do not trouble to hide the fact. Older women may conceal their drinking, as alcohol was not considered a respectable indulgence for 'ladies' in their young days. Some of these 'take to drink' in later life, having previously drunk little or no alcohol. This often seems to be a response to bereavement, loneliness, poor health or other stress and distresses. Unlike lifelong drinkers, this group may respond well to kind and competent help with their problems, and become able to enjoy life without abusing alcohol.

Sensible drinking

The risks from drinking alcohol become greater as the intake rises. Men can drink more alcohol safely than women can because of their different body composition. A safe upper limit for a retired person is: 3–4 units two or three times a week for an older man (6–12 units per week) and 2–3 units two or three times a week for an older woman (4–9 units per week).

A unit of alcohol is the amount of alcohol found in:

half a pint of beer, *or*

one pub single of spirits, *or*

one glass of wine, *or*

one small glass of sherry, vermouth or port.

Strong beers, large glasses and unmeasured drinks poured at home contain extra units. People with balance problems may find it wise to space their intake well, and it is sensible to remember that some medicines do not mix with alcohol at all.

The warden and residents who abuse alcohol

Most wardens seem to have heavy drinkers among their residents. Some of these are quite open about their habits, or become so obviously drunk that there is no question of secrecy. In other cases the warden may have uneasy suspicions. These may have been kindled by a smell on the breath noticed early in the day, taken together with medical problems; for instance, the warden may have been called to help up a resident who often falls down.

Old people have a right to choose their own living habits; wardens are not supposed to be informers or health police, and most have no desire to interfere in their residents' lives. Nevertheless, being 'on the spot' in more senses than one, wardens can worry that alcohol abusers are ruining their health and putting themselves and others at risk. They may also fear criticism from managers and relatives if something goes wrong. What is more, other residents may be distressed by the drinker's noisy or unruly behaviour and demand that 'something must be done'. There are no easy answers to problems like these, but a few guidelines on how to act are set out below.

In the first place, try to take an objective view: how bad are things, and how much worry is appropriate? This depends on how much the resident is drinking, whether there are any complicating factors such as poor health or incompatible medicines, and whether the resident is behaving in a dangerous or seriously disruptive way.

Next, try to weigh up how capable the resident is of making a free choice. Lifelong heavy drinkers without mental health problems can be presumed to be able to make their own decisions and to take the consequences. However, some of the people who start drinking late in life may be clinically depressed or developing a dementing illness. Such people are unable to look after themselves, and have a right to the protection and care of others.

Lastly, think about confidentiality. In some cases the problem is out in the open, but in others the resident is trying to hide it. You should not then broach the subject with relatives or even the doctor without careful thought.

Let us consider some examples of the sort of situations commonly met in sheltered housing. When residents drink heavily but are mentally intact and have no obvious health problems, the warden need do nothing unless asked for advice. If consulted, the warden should be able to talk sensibly about safe drinking and to provide the addresses of agencies that help with drinking problems, such as Alcohol Concern, Alcoholics Anonymous and DAWN.

If a resident's drinking seems to be affecting their health, you should discuss the situation with them and ask if they would like you to call the doctor on their behalf. If you are seriously concerned about their physical or mental health, you should say so, and try to persuade them to agree to medical help. You may sometimes need to speak to the doctor even without their consent. This breach of confidence may be a lesser evil in some circumstances than allowing a resident to suffer harm when too ill to make sensible decisions for themselves. If you do speak to the doctor, you should explain the grounds for your suspicions, the reasons for your serious concern and the resident's wish for secrecy.

Suppose one of your residents is in real danger – perhaps through starting fires by dropping off to sleep when smoking while fuddled. Things are usually out in the open by the time this stage is reached. In any case, the risks may be grave enough to outweigh your duty of confidentiality: you should inform your managers in writing of what is going on, and discuss the situation with any concerned relatives.

Some people who seek help for an alcohol problem aim for controlled drinking. Others are advised to abstain from all alcohol permanently. However, an alcohol-dependent person may become acutely confused when drink is suddenly withdrawn. Medical treatment can prevent this, and hospital care may be necessary. Some specialists believe that older alcohol abusers are easier to treat and do better than younger ones – as a group of 'survivors', they may have tougher personalities and bodies than the average person.

After all this, it is important to remember that most people enjoy alcohol sensibly; the older man who spends a sociable hour nursing a half pint in the local every day and the older woman who enjoys a glass of sherry occasionally are deriving good rather than harm from their little indulgence.

ESSENTIAL BODY MAINTENANCE

Just as a car requires regular servicing, people's eyes, teeth and feet need regular maintenance, no matter how old they are.

Saving sight

All old people should have a regular eye examination every two years. They should do this even if they have no eye problems, and should go more often if they have difficulties. Some eye symptoms require immediate attention, and these are listed on pages 125–127.

An eye test is free for older people who:

- have glaucoma or are closely related to a glaucoma sufferer;
- have diabetes;
- are on low incomes (see Social Security leaflet G11, from the Benefits Agency office or Post Office);
- are registered blind or partially sighted;
- need certain sorts of complex lenses.

Older people outside these groups may be charged a fee, though not all opticians do this.

The eye examination will detect treatable conditions such as glaucoma that may threaten sight without causing obvious symptoms. It is also a chance for spectacle lenses to be checked, to ensure that vision is as good as possible.

You may be able to help your residents to look after their spectacles properly. To be useful they must be kept clean, and may need a gentle wash in mild detergent, with careful drying of metal parts. They should be stored lenses downwards in the case provided, so as not to scratch the lenses or distort the frame. Attaching a chain or cord to be worn around the neck may prevent loss. Even though they are an expensive item, it is a false economy for residents to wear a pair of glasses originally prescribed for a friend or relative, or to make do with a pair of their own that are no longer satisfactory. You could remind them that cheaper spectacles are available to people on low incomes (leaflet G11, as above).

Suitable lighting is very important in making the most of whatever sight a person has, and also for safety in the home. Adjustable angled lights are very useful for close work and should be directed over the shoulder directly onto a book or handwork. Prevent glare by proper shading. People with cataract may find over-bright light makes vision difficult; tinted spectacle lenses also help with this. Occasionally, using a more powerful light bulb may be enough to solve someone's visual problems. If you advise this, you should make sure that the recommended wattage for the lampshade is not exceeded, or the excess heat may start a fire.

Avoiding dental problems

The major dental problem of middle and old age is the build-up of plaque, sometimes called tartar, on and between the teeth. The bacteria in plaque produce substances that cause gum inflammation and disease, an early sign of which is bleeding. If the gum disease is not treated, the teeth may become loose and eventually fall out. Plaque can be removed from teeth by regular brushing and by the conscientious use of dental floss every other day to reach the spaces between teeth. Frequent visits to the dentist are important both for thorough cleaning and for advice about care. Even people who have full dentures should go at least once a year to ensure that the dentures remain well fitting and that the mouth is healthy. Age Concern England's Factsheet 5 *Dental Care in Retirement* includes advice on finding a dentist and how to arrange treatment. It also explains how the charging system operates and how to get help with these costs.

Dental problems can have more far-reaching effects on health than might at first be expected. For instance, many older people avoid fibre-rich foods and take only a soft diet because they have problems with their teeth, and it is not uncommon to meet people who take out their dentures at meal times because they do not fit properly. Speech usually becomes indistinct when someone has no teeth, and most people prefer to avoid the 'ageist' image of gummy senility given by a toothless old person. It is usually wise to remove dentures only for cleaning and at night, unless advised otherwise by the dentist.

Healthy, comfortable feet

Contrary to their popular image as 'plates of meat', the feet are beautifully engineered and precision built. Just as buildings deteriorate when subjected to excessive loads and stresses, our feet often complain under the pressure of increased weight after middle age. Losing weight can often help not only a person's feet but also the weight-bearing joints above them.

Foot problems are also often caused by ill-fitting shoes. Even those of us who shop carefully, putting fit before fashion, may have difficulty in finding satisfactory shoes. Unusual fittings are available, albeit at a cost in both time and money, but it is worth the trouble and expense to have your shoes properly fitted. A chiropodist or the Disabled Living Foundation should be able to suggest where to buy shoes for people with problems.

Try to encourage residents to wear shoes rather than bedroom slippers around the scheme, as shoes are more stable, help to prevent feet from swelling and preserve morale and self-respect. For comfort and hygiene, everyone should wash their feet every day in warm water, using a nail brush to clean the toenails. Careful drying is important and hand cream or body lotion should be applied if the skin has a tendency to be dry. The easiest time to cut toenails is when they are soft, after bathing or washing. Special nail clippers may be easier and safer to use than scissors.

Residents who have difficulty reaching their feet, are shaky or have poor sight will find it difficult to attend to their own foot care. Chiropodists or foot-care assistants are not always available to cut toenails as often as is necessary, and this may present a difficulty. In some cases a relative may help; in others, a resident who also receives bathing help at home or at a day centre may be able to have their feet attended to at the same time. To find out about nail-cutting services in your area, you could suggest that the resident gets in touch with social services or with the NHS chiropody service.

It is unwise for elderly people to attempt to deal with corns and callouses themselves; instead they should consult a chiropodist. Only state registered chiropodists, who can use the letters 'SRCh' after their names, may work in the NHS. Non-registered chiropodists have various forms of qualifications and training. Chiropody is vital for diabetics, because lack of sensation, poor healing abilities and a tendency to acquire infections may mean that serious septic foot wounds can develop unnoticed.

Older people are entitled to free chiropody under the NHS, but in some parts of the country the service is sparse. This can result in long delays before being seen in the first place, and in some areas a long wait between appointments thereafter. Because of this, many older people resort to private treatment; the local NHS chiropody service may keep a list of registered chiropodists who do private practice.

Information about NHS costs and of benefits to help with them can be found in the current edition of *Your Rights* (see p 231).

SENSIBLE USE OF HEALTH CHECKS

The Over-75 examination

Under the new NHS contract, GPs have to offer every patient over 75 years old on their lists an annual consultation, either at the surgery or at home. This is designed to identify unreported or unnoticed illness, and also to make it easier for older people to get any help they need. The check may be performed by the doctor, or by a practice nurse, health visitor or another staff member, who can then refer the older person to the doctor if this seems necessary.

The examination takes special note of the older person's daily living abilities. It also checks on sight and hearing and on general physical and mental health. Medicines can be reviewed and altered if necessary, and appropriate equipment and help arranged if the older person wants and needs it.

People over 75 do of course have the right to refuse this examination if they so wish. Some people who refuse it are very fit and active, have no current social problems or health needs and feel perfectly able to ask for help if and when they need it. Others fear they are failing in health, but are frightened of what may be found if they see the doctor. If you have a resident in this second group, you might want to suggest that they reconsider their decision and have the examination. They have nothing to lose from having their problems identified, and may be pleasantly surprised that the diagnosis is less serious and the outlook more hopeful than they had supposed. If, after the position is clear, they are unwilling to have treatment, they can always refuse it.

The Over-75 check has been operating for only a short time, and it is too early to know whether or not it is generally useful. The other tests your residents are most likely to encounter are the cervical smear, mammography and measurement of blood pressure; the first two of these of course apply to women only.

Medical examination of people who have no obvious signs of disease is called 'screening'. It is useful only when it detects a potentially serious condition at a stage when the sufferer would not otherwise know it was there. There is no point in finding out about an illness unless it can be treated, and no value in an early diagnosis unless it gives a better result than waiting until the condition becomes obvious. The benefits of screening have to be set against the drawbacks – the financial costs, the discomfort or inconvenience of the test procedure, and the needless anxiety over the 'false positive' result that turns out to have been wrong. It is still not certain whether, or to what extent, the tests described below are useful, and experts differ strongly in their views about them.

The cervical smear

This detects changes in the cells of the cervix that could later progress to cancer. The cells are scraped off the cervix during the internal, vaginal examination. This tends to be more uncomfortable in older women than in younger ones, and bleeding is more likely to follow. On the other hand, more than 40 per cent of deaths from cancer of the cervix in England occur in women over 65, so older women are still at risk of the disease.

Balancing factors for and against, the most sensible course for a woman over 65 who has been or still is sexually active is to have a cervical smear if she has never had one before. Older people who have had smears in the past should ask for advice from the doctor or clinic they usually attend. Many women whose smears have been normal up to the age of 65 are at very low risk from then onwards, so further smears may not be necessary.

These details are included to explain why different older women may be given apparently opposite advice about whether smears are still necessary in later life. You should not, of course, attempt to advise your residents on complex medical matters, but suggest that anyone who is puzzled should discuss the situation with her doctor. The Women's National Cancer Control Campaign is another good source of advice about this aspect of women's health.

Mammography

This is a special form of X-ray which can detect breast cancer while the lump is still too small to feel with an examining hand. Mammography may cause discomfort, though this soon passes off. As with other sorts of screening, its benefits are still unclear. It is offered free to women between the ages of 50 and 64, and older women may be able to get it on request. Women with a family history of breast cancer are the most likely to want to do this, and they may also want to persevere with breast self-examination. Again, useful information is available from the Women's National Cancer Control Campaign.

Blood pressure (BP)

People with higher than normal blood pressure have a higher than usual risk of suffering a stroke or a heart attack than those whose BP is within normal limits. Adults up to 75 years old should have their BP taken at least every five years; people over 75 will have this done at their annual check. The benefits of lowering the BP have to be balanced against the drawbacks of the unwanted effects of medicines, which can be disabling in some older people. An individual decision about what is best to do must be made in each case.

Old age need not necessarily be spoiled by poor health; the measures outlined in this section are designed to achieve the goal of 'dying young as late as possible'.

2 Common Illnesses in Later Life

Many of the disabilities that older people – and their carers – put up with because they wrongly attribute them to 'ageing' are, in fact, due to medical conditions that can be treated. By reading about these, you will be better able to help your residents get appropriate medical attention or other help when they need it.

The illnesses described in this chapter are grouped according to the body system they affect, except for cancers which are explained together.

HEART AND BLOOD VESSELS

The heart is a muscular pump which circulates the blood round the body through the blood vessels (arteries and veins). Its powers of endurance are amazing – what other piece of equipment would work up to seventy times a minute, day after day, without a break or a service for seventy or more years? Because the heart works so hard, it needs a good blood supply to give it oxygen.

Common problems

Angina

The chest pain of angina occurs when the blood supply to the heart muscle is insufficient because the coronary arteries are partially blocked. Angina is often brought on by exercise, such as hurrying up a hill, or by emotion that makes the heart beat faster. It is relieved by rest, when the heart needs less oxygen.

Heart attack or coronary

This happens when part of the heart muscle dies because the coronary blood supply is too poor to keep it alive. In young people a coronary is accompanied by very severe, crushing chest pain, often radiating up into the neck and down the arms, with breathlessness and distress. Sometimes the patient collapses, becomes unconscious, and may die. An older person may not experience pain, but instead may faint, fall, vomit or become confused or breathless.

The doctor will arrange for treatment at home or in hospital. One new treatment involves the injection of a substance that dissolves the clot blocking the coronary artery and thus restores the blood supply to the heart muscle. This has to be given soon after the block has formed if it is to work properly. Some people who have suffered a heart attack, as well as those with severe angina, may be offered coronary artery bypass surgery. This aims to re-route blood around an arterial blockage by grafting in a piece of blood vessel from elsewhere. Alternatively, a narrowed artery can be stretched during the procedure of angioplasty. Medicines called beta-blockers seem to reduce the chances of suffering a further heart attack, and a small dose of aspirin may be prescribed for the same purpose.

A heart attack is not a trivial event, but should not lead the sufferer to despair. In general, normal activity can be resumed afterwards unless the doctor advises lifestyle changes.

General guidelines include a firm commitment to stop smoking if further attacks are not to follow. However, a little alcohol is harmless and may even be beneficial, so long as it does not lead to weight problems. People who have had a coronary should avoid becoming overweight. Cholesterol-lowering diets are rarely suggested to elderly people, as they do not seem to be very helpful. Moderate exercise is excellent, and in some areas of the country there are special exercise programmes for people who have had heart attacks. The local Community Health Council will know whether these are available. However, violent and sudden exertion such as moving heavy furniture or shovelling snow should be avoided.

Both angina and heart attacks are twice as common in people from the Indian sub-continent as in native Britons. However, they are only half as common in Afro-Caribbeans.

Heart failure

This happens when the heart cannot provide adequate blood circulation because the muscle has been weakened by a heart attack, or strained by high blood pressure. After a chest infection, someone whose heart failure was well controlled before it may become breathless, develop a bluish colour around the lips, and their ankles may swell. Urgent treatment with appropriate drugs is needed.

Disturbances of heart rhythm (cardiac arrhythmias)

These can cause a number of symptoms such as palpitations, an uncomfortable awareness of the heart beat, breathlessness, falls and attacks of unconsciousness. Severe problems can be fatal. Treatment may involve the use of drugs or the implantation of a pacemaker.

A pacemaker is a simple electrical device consisting of a battery with a wire to conduct an electrical impulse to the heart and thus stimulate it to beat. Pacemakers are not only life saving but can also improve the quality of life even in very elderly people. Problems with pacemakers are rare, but if they do occur the person should be sent immediately by ambulance to the hospital unit that supplied the device. Someone with a pacemaker should check with the clinic about whether it is affected by equipment such as a microwave oven or electronic security checks at airports.

Ankle swelling

This condition on its own, without breathlessness or other signs of illness, is common in older people. It is not serious, and is often due to sitting too much. Diuretic tablets with their occasional ill-effects are therefore not needed. To help reduce the swelling, patients should prop their feet up above the level of the bottom when seated. Moderate exercise such as walking also helps to disperse the fluid.

Elastic stockings or support hose are helpful. They should be kept on the bedside table overnight and put on in the morning before putting a foot to the floor.

High blood pressure (hypertension)

Because blood pressure (BP) depends on the strength of the heart beat and the condition of the blood vessels, it can vary considerably in the same person under different conditions. It has, however, been shown that a higher than average resting blood pressure can go with an increased tendency to suffer from heart attacks, stroke or kidney failure. High blood pressure is thus a risk factor for these conditions. Afro-Caribbeans, who are especially likely to suffer from high blood pressure, are also more likely to have strokes.

People up to and including those in their late 70s benefit from taking medicines to lower high blood pressure, but for someone past the age of 80 the situation becomes less clear. Though octogenarians and nonagenarians with high blood pressure still appear more likely to have a stroke or heart attack than someone of the same age whose blood pressure is normal, unwanted effects from BP-lowering medicines seem to be more likely to occur than in younger people, and cause more disability when they do happen. Confusion, incontinence and a tendency to fall brought on by the medicines may be too high a price to pay for reducing the risks of future illness. Until more research is available, an individual decision needs to be made in each case, balancing the benefits and drawbacks of treatment.

Arterial disease

This is more common in smokers and in people with diabetes, and the leg arteries are the ones usually affected. They become narrowed, and therefore supply insufficient blood to the muscles and other tissues. The affected person's symptoms depend on how bad the disease is. In the mildest form there is pain only during exercise, when most blood is needed, and this gets better with rest. In more severe cases the muscles get painfully short of blood even at rest. In the worst situation there is not enough blood to keep the tissues alive, so ulcers and gangrene result.

Treatment aims to improve the blood supply. This is done by curing heart failure, anaemia or dehydration, and progressing to surgery if necessary. This may involve operations to relax arteries, to remove blockages or to bypass them with grafts. A few patients require amputation to rid them of a dangerous infection or a painful and useless limb.

People with arterial disease can help themselves by giving up smoking, by taking exercise within the limits of their pain and by taking great care of the fragile skin of their feet and legs. Regular chiropody is essential.

Varicose veins and ulcers

A vein that becomes varicose is wider and longer than a normal one. It looks unsightly and it works poorly, because the valves that normally prevent blood from flowing backward cannot work properly when they are stretched. Aching and swelling of the leg follow, and in the worst cases the swollen tissues break down to form an ulcer, often just above the ankle on the inner side of the leg. Other complications include itchy varicose eczema and phlebitis, which is infection of a vein. Bleeding may be severe if a varicose vein is injured (see pp 117–118).

Elastic stockings help varicose veins to empty, and reduce backward flow and swelling. They should be put on in bed before the person stands up and the veins distend with blood. Walking helps blood flow, but sufferers should not stand still for long, as the blood pools in the veins. The feet should be raised when sitting down (see 'Ankle swelling', p 51).

Varicose ulcers are usually treated with pressure bandaging applied by the community nurse. Occasionally the sufferer needs to be admitted to hospital for bed rest to heal the ulcer, and sometimes a skin graft is applied.

If you or your residents would like to know more about heart and blood vessel disease, you might like to write to the British Heart Foundation for one or more of its free leaflets.

LUNGS AND AIRWAYS

These are responsible for getting oxygen into the body, where it is needed to burn up food for heat and energy. As the chest expands when breathing in, air rushes down the airways into the lungs. Here oxygen from it crosses a thin membrane to reach the blood and the red blood cells which carry it around the body. At the same time the waste product, carbon dioxide, passes back from the blood into the lungs, and, as the chest returns to its resting state, is breathed out.

Common problems

Chest infections

Many older people, especially men, have chest trouble (bronchitis or emphysema) which gets worse in the winter months. Some may have a hereditary tendency, but this is worsened by smoking and air pollution. How common chest infections are in ethnic minority groups largely depends on smoking habits; for instance, they are less often seen in Asians and Afro-Caribbeans, who rarely smoke, than in native Britons. People of Irish extraction, who tend to smoke heavily, are very prone to chest infections. A 'chesty' person who has a cold may cough up mucus that changes from its usual clear or whitish appearance to yellow, showing that the cold has developed into bronchitis. In acute attacks the person may become severely short of breath, and when really ill may become drowsy or confused. In these cases medical help is needed urgently. However, all people with chest infections should be seen by a doctor so that an antibiotic may, if necessary, be prescribed.

Colds

People with a cold may take a paracetamol or aspirin preparation as necessary for discomfort. Aspirin should never be taken on an empty stomach; paracetamol is better for someone with peptic ulcers or dyspepsia. Sufferers should also drink plenty of fluids, keep warm and take whatever comforting hot lemon drinks they prefer.

The doctor should be called if the cold develops into a chest infection or heart failure, or if the person does not recover as rapidly as would be expected.

'Flu

True influenza is a viral illness which occurs in epidemics. In the early stages the temperature is higher than with a simple cold; headache and muscle aches may be severe and the sufferer may become very unwell. After recovery, a period of depression is quite common.

Because colds and 'flu are caused by viruses rather than by bacteria, antibiotics are not helpful in combating the original infection. They may, however, be useful if secondary infections attack the person who has already been weakened by the virus.

Older people with heart or chest disease or diabetes may like to ask the doctor for a 'flu injection; this is usually available in the autumn for protection in the coming winter.

Pneumonia

Whereas cold viruses attack the upper respiratory tract and bronchitis affects the airways just below, pneumonia is an inflammation of the lungs themselves. It may happen because an upper respiratory tract infection has spread downwards, it can occur on its own, or it may develop as a complication of another illness.

When pneumonia occurs in someone who has previously been unwell and 'chesty', it is usually quite easy for the doctor to diagnose by listening to the patient's chest. However, pneumonia in an older person can cause other symptoms such as mental confusion or a tendency to fall. If this happens in someone with few signs of chest illness, their mental state may be wrongly attributed to 'senility' and the pneumonia missed. This mistake can be avoided if the warden is on hand to tell the doctor that the resident's confusion is of recent onset and apparently related to the physical illness.

DIGESTIVE SYSTEM

This consists of a long tube running from the mouth to the opening of the back passage, together with various glands that open into the tube. It processes food into a form that can be absorbed into the blood and used in the body for energy, maintenance and growth. Undigested food, bacteria, bile and intestinal juices are passed out as stools (faeces).

Common problems

Diverticular disease

This is a very common condition, especially in people who over a long period have not taken in enough fibre in their diet, so the bowel muscle does not have a residue of undigested food to squeeze against. The pressure inside the bowel then becomes high, and pockets of the lining tend to be forced outwards, rather like portions of an inner tube ballooning through weak places in a bicycle tyre. These soft pouches are called 'diverticula'.

Many people with diverticular disease have no symptoms at all. Others have pain on the left side of the abdomen and suffer from constipation or diarrhoea. A few develop complications such as infection, abscesses, peritonitis or bowel blockage. These complications make the person seriously ill, with abdominal pain and sickness, and urgent medical help will be required.

However, such problems are rare, and people with diverticular disease should be reassured that it is a nuisance rather than a danger and is not likely to shorten their lives. A high-fibre diet will help, and the doctor will be able to prescribe medicines to relieve bowel muscle spasm if this proves necessary.

Peptic ulcers

These occur when acid gastric juice attacks and starts to digest an unprotected part of the stomach or duodenal lining. The commonest complaint of ulcer sufferers is of abdominal pain, which usually occurs before meals or during the night when the stomach and duodenum are empty of food. The ulcer may go on giving trouble in this way for a few days or even weeks before it gets better, and the person then may be well for some time before symptoms recur. People with uncomplicated ulcers do not usually vomit or lose weight.

The GP will usually refer a person with a suspected ulcer to the hospital for diagnostic tests. Common ones include gastroscopy, when the stomach lining is inspected through a slim telescope passed down the gullet. An alternative is the barium meal, when the ulcer is made visible on an X-ray when it is coated with a thin liquid drunk by the patient. The resident should follow the hospital's instructions as to how to prepare for the tests. Once a diagnosis has been made, the ulcer can usually be healed by a course of tablets or medicine. Most patients are able to eat a normal diet and drink a little alcohol, but smoking slows ulcer healing. Surgical treatment is now rarely necessary to treat uncomplicated peptic ulcers, but may be needed occasionally to stop bleeding or to close a perforation, if the ulcer eats right through the gut wall. These complications are serious, but uncommon.

Hernias

A hernia happens when a part of the gut slips into the wrong position. Two sorts of hernia are especially common in older people: inguinal hernia and hiatus hernia.

Inguinal hernia

Commonly called a rupture, this happens when a piece of bowel pushes out of the abdominal cavity into the groin or into the scrotum in men or the labium in women. The swelling enlarges when the person strains or coughs and may become uncomfortable by the end of the day. By lying down, the sufferer may be able to push the swelling back into the abdomen and thereby 'reduce' the hernia.

A neglected hernia may sometimes become stuck (irreducible), and the bowel loop which cannot return to the abdominal cavity is at risk from losing its blood supply. This is a serious condition ('strangulated hernia'), causing abdominal pain and vomiting, and it requires urgent treatment.

The best treatment for an inguinal hernia is surgery. The usual operation reduces the hernia and repairs the tunnel, so that the exit route of the bowel loop is blocked.

Sometimes a truss is supplied instead when a person is unwilling to have an operation or is unfit to undergo surgery. This is put on before getting out of bed, so that the pressure pad blocks the exit tunnel and keeps the bowel loop from emerging. The truss should be kept on until bed time. Not all hernias are suitable for control by a truss.

Hiatus hernia

This happens entirely out of sight within the body when a part of the stomach slips upwards through the diaphragm. Several symptoms can follow: the person may have pain because stomach acid irritates the gullet, food may stick at the bottom of the gullet, and an ulcerated or compressed area may bleed. However, someone with a hiatus hernia may have none of these symptoms.

Hiatus hernia sufferers may be advised by the doctor to sleep with the head of the bed raised, to lose weight and to avoid bending which pushes stomach acid into the gullet. Alternatively, the amount of acid in the stomach may be reduced by tablets or the sore area coated by a protective liquid taken after meals.

Stomas

A colostomy is an opening made in the abdominal wall through which the bowel empties into a stoma bag. An ileostomy is an opening made higher up the bowel, and a urostomy drains urine to the outside via a bowel loop. A colostomy is the likeliest sort of stoma for an elderly resident to have.

Stomas are formed for several reasons. Sometimes they are temporary, but a permanent one is inevitably an upset to the individual. However, normal life is still possible with a stoma, and equipment and know-how are improving all the time. A stoma nurse is the expert on stoma care. A new stoma patient will also be helped by contact with someone who has already learned to cope with a stoma, and with the appropriate self-help organisation, such as the British Colostomy Association (see p 221 for the address).

Haemorrhoids (commonly called 'piles')

In this condition, part of the lining of the back passage slips down, swells and bleeds. The blood is usually bright red, comes just after a stool is passed and stains the lavatory paper. In between times, piles hurt and cause itching round the back passage opening.

Most bleeding from the back passage is caused by piles. However, there is a small chance that the blood is coming from a bowel cancer, and therefore anyone who notices this sort of bleeding should see the doctor for an examination to rule out the possibility of a cancer. The doctor can also help the symptoms of piles by prescribing creams or suppositories; surgical treatment is occasionally needed.

Gall bladder disease

The gall bladder concentrates the bile ('gall') produced by the liver; bile helps to digest fat in food. Bile may solidify, to cause gallstones; these cause severe pain, vomiting and jaundice if they block the bile passages. The gall bladder may sometimes become infected – the condition of 'cholecystitis'. However, many people with gallstones have no trouble from them.

Because neglected gallstones sometimes cause complications, people with gallstones producing symptoms are usually advised to have treatment for them – usually removal of the gall bladder, called 'cholecystectomy'. People waiting for this are more comfortable if they take a high-fibre, low-fat diet. Occasionally, gallstones can be dissolved by bile acids taken by mouth, and new techniques for breaking them up inside the body are being tried.

Malabsorption

Some old people become malnourished because they cannot absorb the nutrients from their food; this is called malabsorption. One common cause of this is coeliac disease, when any food containing wheat flour causes bowel inflammation. Malabsorption also follows when digestive juices are not produced properly by a diseased liver or pancreas, and when the bowel has been damaged by injury, operation or poor blood supply.

People with malabsorption often lose weight and usually show signs of nutrient lack, such as anaemia or bone disease from vitamin D deficiency. They may have fatty diarrhoea, and if this is severe they may become incontinent of stools.

The treatment is to correct the cause whenever possible; people with coeliac disease need to avoid wheat flour in their diet. When the cause cannot be completely removed, affected people may need extra nutrients.

NERVOUS SYSTEM

The brain, the spinal cord running down from it within the backbone and the network of nerves carrying information through the body make up the nervous system. It is responsible for communications within the body, and also processes information reaching it from the outside world via the senses. This it compares with information stored in the memory and then organises the body's response.

Common problems

Stroke

A stroke (called a cerebrovascular accident by doctors) happens when a brain blood vessel blocks or bursts. Strokes are especially common in Afro-Caribbeans because of a tendency to high blood pressure. In a major or completed stroke, the section of the brain normally supplied by the damaged vessel loses its blood supply and dies, while the surrounding sections swell and work less well than before. The part of the body controlled by the dead area of brain loses its function. The person may become gradually or suddenly unconscious, or in a milder case may be confused and may vomit. When examined by the doctor, evidence of damage to the brain may be found.

The most common pattern is one of paralysis of movement and loss of sensation down one side of the body. Speech may be interfered with – either the ability to understand or to speak, or both. Vision may also be disturbed, and the person may also become incontinent. In a completed stroke the symptoms last longer than 24 hours.

In a transient ischaemic attack (TIA) the symptoms and signs disappear within 24 hours. They may include confusion, a fall, weakness of one limb or half of the body, drooping of the eyelid or one half of the face, or speech disturbance. Symptoms of TIA should always be reported to the doctor, as treatment at this stage may prevent a later stroke.

The recovery of a person who has suffered a stroke depends on the severity of the damage to the brain and on the quality of rehabilitation received from professionals and from family and friends. Someone who is paralysed may be rehabilitated in hospital, or may attend a day hospital. Here physiotherapists, occupational therapists, speech therapists and others help the stroke sufferer to strengthen muscles and make the best use of remaining abilities. In some parts of the country, rehabilitation may be carried out in the person's home.

Residents who have had a stroke may need aids and equipment to help them to live as independently as possible. These can be obtained through the occupational therapist in the social services department, but there are sometimes long delays. You could suggest that the resident or relatives ask at a Disabled Living Centre for information about aids for stroke victims. The Stroke Association is another useful resource, and in some areas sponsors Stroke Clubs. These are useful for social contact, particularly for people with speech difficulties. A local club may also provide support for relatives caring for stroke victims; the Stroke Association national office has information about where these clubs are. Carers may also want to get in touch with the Carers National Association.

Parkinson's disease

This is a disorder of the ability to move, often associated with tremor, and was originally called 'the shaking palsy'. It may start with difficulty in using one arm or with performing complex movements such as climbing out of a car. Because the facial muscles are stiffened, people with Parkinson's disease lack expression and may drool saliva. Despite this appearance, they may be mentally normal and merely imprisoned in an unco-operative body, though mental decline may be noticeable in the later stages of the disease. Walking may be difficult, and they will shuffle their feet and adopt a hunched posture.

Correctly prescribed and used medication can make a great difference to the independence and comfort of the sufferer from Parkinson's disease. Your resident may benefit from reassessment of their condition by a neurologist. They can arrange this through the GP.

People with Parkinson's disease should be encouraged to remain as active as possible. They may be helped considerably by physiotherapy, speech therapy and by the provision of aids to help with eating, dressing and other daily activities. Depression should be treated appropriately if it arises in the course of the illness. Both patients and their relatives and carers may benefit from contact with the Parkinson's Disease Society.

Depression

This is an illness that is common in elderly people, though very often it is not properly identified, especially in people who do not speak English. Depressed people may be obviously sad, though some keep up a front of apparent cheerfulness. They usually have a disturbed sleep rhythm, waking in the small hours of the morning when they feel worst. Some sufferers become mentally and physically slow, with loss of interest in life, concentration and memory. They may be wrongly thought to be suffering from dementia. Other people become agitated, demanding of attention and fearful of being left alone. Depressed older people may complain of physical symptoms that have no obvious cause; this pattern is especially common in those from ethnic minority communities. If they have a genuine physical illness, they may seem to lose the will to recover, and chronic problems may seem to be 'getting on top of them' more than usual.

Depression poisons the lives of sufferers and those around them. It can be fatal: sufferers can neglect themselves so much that they become dangerously ill, or they can kill themselves. If a resident threatens suicide, you should notify the doctor without delay (see p 113).

Two sorts of treatment are available for depression. These are the various sorts of psychotherapy, and medical treatment with medicines or electro-convulsive therapy (ECT). Most people have both sorts of treatment. In general, less severely ill people benefit most from psychotherapy, whilst sicker ones may need to respond a little to medical treatment before they can usefully have psychotherapy. General measures help too: it is easier to overcome depression with good physical health, satisfactory social circumstances, adequate money, control over one's own life and things to look forward to.

An excellent booklet about depression can be obtained from the Royal College of Psychiatrists.

Shingles

This is a localised form of chickenpox (herpes zoster). After the original attack, the virus lies dormant in the spinal cord until it is reactivated, when it causes shingles. The commonest area to be affected is one side of the trunk, but an especially unpleasant form affects the forehead and eye (ophthalmic herpes).

Shingles starts with pain and soreness, after which the affected skin becomes red and blisters appear. The shingles patient is infectious until the blisters dry to form scabs. Someone giving personal care to a resident with shingles could catch chickenpox; pregnant women can develop a serious form and have a miscarriage.

Most people with shingles can be treated at home (see p 102). Those with ophthalmic herpes or severe disease elsewhere may need to go into hospital. A few people who have had shingles develop persistent, unpleasant pain called post-herpetic neuralgia.

THE EYES

The eyeball has a transparent window, the cornea, at the front for light to enter. The light is then focused by the cornea, the lens and the fluids within the eye onto the retina which lines the back of the eye. Visual information is carried from the retina along nerve pathways to the brain, where it is interpreted and stored.

In middle age, people need to hold books and objects away from their eyes in order to see clearly. This is due to ageing changes in the lens and is usually corrected by reading glasses. However, no other change in sight should be accepted as normal, but should be reported to the optician or doctor. For information about conditions needing urgent attention, see 'Eye emergencies' (p 125).

Common problems

Cataract

This happens because of irreversible changes in the protein that makes up the lens of the eye, so that it becomes opaque and light can no longer pass through it. The person notices a gradual clouding of sight, and the doctor or optician can see the opacity with an ophthalmoscope. Cataracts are six times as common in older Asian people as in native Britons. This happens because diabetes is common in this group, and sometimes because of excess exposure to ultraviolet light in early life in the Indian sub-continent.

Treatment for cataract

The lens has to be removed surgically so that light can reach the retina again. This operation is usually done when the person's sight has deteriorated to the point where reading or daily life become difficult. Although cataracts often affect both eyes, usually one eye is affected more seriously than the other, and the worse one will be operated on first.

After surgery a new lens has to be put in the line of vision to replace the cloudy one. Best results follow when an artificial lens is implanted in the eyeball where the old one used to be, but this is not always technically possible. Instead, cataract spectacles may be provided; the wearer needs to become accustomed to these gradually. Contact lenses are rarely suitable for older cataract patients. Suggestions for further reading about cataract and other eye conditions can be found on pages 226–227.

Macular degeneration (age-related maculopathy)

This affects the macula, the central part of the visual field. Affected people first notice distortion of their vision, straight lines appearing curved. They have difficulty in matching colours and in adjusting to changes in light intensity, as when going out from a well-lit house into a dimly lit street. Later it becomes difficult to read small, faint print, to thread needles and to do similar fine work.

One form of macular degeneration, the 'wet' form, can be treated by laser therapy. Unfortunately, 85–90 per cent of older people have the 'dry' form, which cannot be helped in this way.

People with macular degeneration do not go completely blind, as the periphery of the visual field is not affected. Because of this, sufferers remain fairly independent, especially if they make the most of their remaining sight (see p 155).

Glaucoma

This happens because the pressure of the fluid inside the eye rises, causing damage to the light-sensitive retina, which is unable to repair itself. Someone with acute glaucoma feels nauseated and ill. The affected eye is red and painful, with little vision. Anyone with these symptoms should seek medical help urgently. The more common, chronic cases produce a gradual loss of sight, which may not be noticed by the sufferer until considerable damage has occurred. Seeing coloured haloes around lights suggests that pressure is rising, and this should be reported to the doctor promptly.

Medical treatment involves the use of drugs, as eyedrops, as tablets or both. If this is insufficient, surgery may become necessary. This is now much less disturbing because of the development of lasers. People with glaucoma must use their drops regularly, and if they are not able to cope with this themselves, the doctor should arrange for the drops to be inserted by someone else. With adequate treatment and good follow-up, sight should not deteriorate, though retinal damage that has already occurred will not get better.

Glaucoma seems to run in families, so it is wise for close relatives of glaucoma patients to have the pressure within their eyes measured regularly. This is done with a tonometer, and the procedure is neither painful nor time consuming.

Diabetic retinopathy

In some people with diabetes, new blood vessels grow in the retina of the eye. These can endanger sight, gradually by replacing nervous tissue or suddenly by bleeding into the eye. This sometimes causes retinal detachment. The changes of diabetic retinopathy can be seen when the eye is examined through an ophthalmoscope.

It is now possible to coagulate the new blood vessels as they develop with a laser beam and thus prevent them impairing sight. Detecting the proliferation process early is therefore important, so people with diabetes should have regular eye examinations to detect such abnormalities.

Retinal detachment

This may happen because of a blow on the head, but it also occurs in people with diabetes. The first signs are new 'floaters' in the field of vision; these consist of blood or bits of pigment from the torn retina. As traction in the retina increases, the person sees flashing lights in the affected eye. Eventually the retina is pulled away from the back of the eye and crumples up; as this happens, part of the visual field goes blank and is lost.

A detached retina can produce partial or complete blindness, but urgent repair using a laser beam prevents further tearing and preserves sight. Anyone who suffers a sudden loss of vision should go at once to the GP or the emergency department of the nearest eye hospital.

Giant cell arteritis (GCA)

In this condition the arteries supplying the face, scalp and eyes become inflamed and partially blocked by the big cells that give the disease its name. The sufferer feels generally unwell and complains of pain in the side of the head; it hurts to chew food, and the face is often tender to touch. If sight deteriorates, this shows that the retina is at risk of damage because its blood supply is threatened. This can lead to permanent blindness if untreated.

Steroids are an effective treatment; if sight loss seems imminent, steroids are started before the diagnosis is clinched by tests. In less urgent cases, blood tests are performed and a biopsy of the temporal artery is taken. This can be looked at under the microscope to see if tell-tale giant cells are present. Once the condition is under control, the dose of steroids can be reduced, and they can often be stopped altogether after a year or so.

People with giant cell arteritis have an above-average risk of developing polymyalgia rheumatica (see p 72).

Conjunctivitis

This is an infection of the outermost membrane covering the eye, which becomes red because of the dilatation of tiny blood vessels: hence the name 'pink eye'. Pus may stick the eyelids together when the person is sleeping, and it also collects during the day in the corner of the eye, which feels gritty and uncomfortable. Conjunctivitis usually gets better quickly if treated with antibiotic ointment; the patient should see the doctor so that this can be prescribed, and also to make sure that the symptoms are due to conjunctivitis and not to more serious causes of a painful red eye.

THE EARS

The outer ear canal funnels sound waves inward to the eardrum, which in turn transmits them through the tiny linked bones of the middle ear. The sound waves then reach the inner ear, which is concerned with balance as well as hearing. The hearing organ in the inner ear transforms sound vibrations into impulses that are carried by the auditory nerve to the brain, where they are interpreted and compared with past experiences.

Common problems

Most older people lose some hearing for high-pitched sounds, but this does not cause inconvenience or affect social life. Anyone who finds it difficult to join in group conversation, who cannot hear the doorbell or telephone ring when still in the house or who needs the television or radio turned up abnormally loud has hearing loss (deafness) and should be encouraged to seek help. Deafness is medically described as being either conductive or perceptive (sensorineural).

Conductive deafness

This is due to an impairment of the transmission of sound waves from outside the body to the boundary between the middle and inner ear. It is easier to treat than perceptive deafness.

Wax in the outer ear canal is a common and easily remedied cause of conductive deafness. Because of the fragile skin lining the canal and the risk of damage to the eardrum, objects should never be poked into the ear in an attempt to remove wax – even cotton wool sticks can push it further into the ear and tamp it down into a solid mass. People who suspect that accumulated wax may be affecting their hearing should go to the doctor's surgery to get it removed.

Damage to the eardrum also causes conductive deafness. This may happen because of an injury, either directly or through blast, or because of an infection and subsequent perforation of the eardrum. It is sometimes possible to restore hearing by repairing the damaged eardrum.

Otosclerosis, another form of conductive deafness which may start in middle age or before, happens when one of the tiny bones in the middle ear becomes fixed in place and can no longer conduct sound waves. Otosclerosis is treated by a delicate surgical operation which restores hearing.

Perceptive (sensorineural) deafness

This is due to disease or damage of the inner ear or of the auditory nerve connecting it to the brain. Because nerve tissue is unable to heal, this sort of deafness cannot usually be cured, but good care and help can make life more enjoyable for the deaf person (see p 159).

Presbyacusis is the nerve deafness common in elderly people. It produces hearing loss, especially for high-pitched sounds such as t's and s's, so that speech is distorted. 'Loudness recruitment' means that a slight increase in the loudness of a sound is heard painfully loudly. Hearing abilities may vary from day to day, and deafness may be accompanied by tinnitus (see below). Because hearing aids only make sound louder, they are not always very helpful in this type of deafness.

Menière's disease, another cause of perceptive deafness, usually occurs in middle age, with attacks of giddiness, sickness and deafness. Gradually the attacks cease, but the deafness persists into old age. Nerve damage to the ear can also result from drug treatment, a head injury, a blast or loud noise during working life or war service.

Tinnitus

This condition, which means 'noises heard in the ear', can be particularly bothersome at night. The noises are usually due to the malfunctioning of the inner ear, and are very rarely a sign of illness. Occasionally they are the result of aspirin taken in large quantities, and they will clear up if this is stopped.

It often helps people with tinnitus to be examined by an ENT (ear, nose and throat) specialist and be reassured that there is no underlying serious illness. Once they are no longer listening apprehensively for the noises, they may be able to ignore them, as they would the continued presence of a ticking clock. In other cases where the noises continue to be a nuisance, a tinnitus masker can be helpful. It fits behind the ear like a conventional hearing aid and produces a noise that conceals that of the tinnitus. The equipment needs to be fitted by an expert, and is unfortunately not nationally available under the NHS. The British Tinnitus Association provides information, funds research and runs self-help groups for sufferers.

THE BLOOD

This is the body's transport system. It carries oxygen and nutrients to wherever they are needed and takes waste products to the kidneys for excretion in the urine. Chemicals such as hormones produced within the body or drugs introduced from outside also travel in the blood, and it also distributes heat.

Common problems

Anaemia

In this condition the blood contains less than normal of its red pigment, haemoglobin, which carries oxygen around the body. Anaemia is common among elderly people and the cause may be difficult to identify. Anaemic elderly people are often confused or apathetic; they may neglect themselves and their homes and be subject to frequent falls. They may also be dizzy, tired and breathless, and sometimes develop heart failure. They are usually pale, but skin colour can be deceptive, as many people with reddish hair in younger life may have very fair skin but normal blood. A sore mouth and tongue is also common in anaemia.

Anaemia is diagnosed from a blood test. Further testing can identify the sort of anaemia that is present, for there are many different causes. Some people, unknown to themselves, may be losing blood from the gut. The leakage may be from some comparatively harmless condition such as piles, or from a hiatus hernia, diverticular disease or a peptic ulcer, but anaemia can also be the first sign of cancer of the bowel. Bleeding from the gut may also follow the use of some drugs in the treatment of arthritis. Again there is the so-called 'toast and tea' anaemia caused by a diet low in iron and other nutrients, but diet is probably less important as a cause of anaemia than has sometimes been thought. Once the cause of the anaemia has been found, treatment can be started.

Pernicious anaemia

This is due to difficulty in absorbing vitamin B_{12} from food, and is serious if left untreated. The usual symptoms of anaemia may be present, and mental and nervous symptoms may be quite severe. Vitamin B_{12} deficiency is, in fact, one of the reversible causes of mental confusion in elderly people. This sort of anaemia is treated by replacement of the deficient vitamin B_{12}; this has to be done by injection as these people cannot absorb it by mouth. Once pernicious anaemia has been diagnosed, the individuals must continue with injections every few weeks for the rest of their lives to prevent illness.

BONES AND JOINTS

The bones consist of a protein scaffolding stiffened by calcium salts, in the same way as fabric is starched. Bones meet and move on each other at the joints, where the bone ends are covered in shiny cartilage, enclosed in a capsule and lubricated by synovial fluid to reduce friction. Bone mass tends to decrease with age, especially in women after the menopause, and this osteoporosis may result in an increased tendency for bones to break.

Common problems

Arthritis

The commonest form of this condition is osteoarthritis, called OA for short. OA is especially severe in people with injured joints or who are overweight. Women seem particularly likely to get OA in their hands, which become knobbly or gnarled, and acquire a 'squared-off' shape if the joint at the base of the thumb is affected. This impairs the ability to grip tightly, as when undoing screw tops. Other areas of the body commonly affected are the hips, the knees and the spine.

People with arthritis have dull and aching pain which often worsens in bouts and then improves. It tends to be affected by changes in the weather. Stiffness especially in the morning is also a problem. These symptoms may interfere with daily activities.

A good deal can be done to make life more pleasant for the arthritis sufferer. Someone with arthritis is helped both physically and mentally by keeping as active as their pain will allow.

Pain killers help, and the individual and doctor should work together to ensure that the effect of these medicines 'peak' at the time the pain is most troublesome. In addition, painful joints should not be overworked – for instance, someone with arthritic knees should avoid climbing a lot of stairs, and someone whose hips or knees are affected should sit down to do household chores wherever possible. A calorie-controlled diet is useful to reduce excess weight on painful joints.

Stiffness is often helped by warmth, and a thermostatically controlled heating pad is a useful household appliance to have available. Paraffin wax baths may be medically prescribed for arthritic hands, and a hot bath taken first thing in the morning is a useful way of limbering up the whole body for the day.

Some osteoarthritis sufferers also benefit from physiotherapy to strengthen muscles and encourage joint movement. The physiotherapist may suggest the use of a walking stick to help the person remain as mobile as possible. It should be carried in the hand opposite the side of the painful hip or knee, and the arthritic leg and the stick should strike the ground at the same time. Daily activities are often made easier by the use of equipment provided by the occupational therapist.

Some people with OA eventually need to have an arthritic joint replaced by an artificial one made of metal and plastic. The hip is the joint most often operated on, but the knee, shoulder, elbow and smaller joints can also be replaced. The usual reason for the operation is to relieve pain that cannot be helped by medicines or other forms of treatment. Most older patients do well, becoming pain-free and more independent. A few develop complications such as infection, blood clots or loosening of the artificial joint.

Osteoporosis

Bone thinning with age may be severe enough for the bones to break more easily than usual. Softened vertebrae may squash under the weight they carry, becoming wedge-shaped; this produces severe back pain and a stooped posture ('dowager's hump'). Osteoporosis happens in both sexes but proceeds more quickly in women than in men; this means that in general an older woman has thinner, weaker bones than a man of the same age, and is therefore more likely to suffer a fracture.

Hormone replacement therapy (HRT) starting at the menopause reduces bone loss. Other treatments are being developed for women who cannot take HRT. People of either sex can help to keep their bones strong by exercising, taking adequate dietary calcium and vitamin D and refraining from smoking and drinking excess alcohol: both of these last two worsen osteoporosis.

Paget's disease

In this condition, bones become abnormal. This happens patchily in the body, most commonly in the pelvis, spine, skull and bones of the legs. No one knows the cause.

Some people with Paget's have no symptoms at all, and the condition is found by chance on an X-ray taken for some other reason. Others suffer pain, and their bodies can change in shape – in particular, the head gets bigger, the legs become bowed and the spine stooped. The abnormal bone can press on nerves, and it breaks more easily than healthy bone does. In a few cases, bone cancer develops. These complications are rare, however; in most people the disease causes little trouble, pain is easily controlled and other helpful treatment is available if necessary.

Gout

Crystals of sodium urate form in the cavity of a gouty joint, inflaming it and causing bouts of very severe pain and tenderness. The commonest joint to be affected is the one at the base of the big toe, but gout can occur elsewhere in the body. Sodium urate crystals sometimes form lumps called 'tophi' on ear flaps, fingers and toes.

The doctor's diagnosis of suspected gout can be confirmed by laboratory tests done on the patient's blood and on fluid from the affected joint. Treatment is by tablets. Sometimes the person with gout will be advised to alter unwise eating or drinking habits, but this is not always necessary; gout can and does occur in people with a healthy lifestyle.

Polymyalgia rheumatica (PMR)

This seems to go together with giant cell arteritis (GCA) (see p 65). Both conditions may be due to faults in the immune system. PMR causes aching pain and stiffness in the muscles around the shoulders and hips, worse in the mornings and after rest. Affected people feel generally unwell, with a low fever and weight loss.

A blood test will help establish the diagnosis, and GCA may be looked for at the same time. Treatment is with steroids, which quickly make the patient feel better. PMR tends to go away within about two years of the diagnosis being made, and when this happens, steroid therapy can be stopped.

THE GLANDS

Within the body are a number of glands that produce hormones. These have widespread effects on various organs and tissues and help to control many body processes, such as the metabolism of food, growth and reproduction. If the glands secrete too much or too little of their hormones, or if the balance between them is disturbed, illness results and affects several body systems.

Common problems

Diabetes

This is very common in older people. Older people from the Indian subcontinent are five times as likely to suffer from it as native Britons, and Afro-Caribbeans also seem to be at increased risk. In older people, diabetes is not usually due to lack of the hormone insulin as it is in young diabetics who have 'type 1' diabetes.

Instead, diabetes (type 2) occurs because the ageing body tissues become less sensitive to insulin. When insulin is lacking or does not work and glucose cannot enter the cells, the extra glucose remains in the blood, and some then passes out of the body in the urine. Water is needed to dissolve it, so the person passes a great deal of urine. In an older person, the onset of diabetes can precipitate incontinence of urine because of this. The water loss causes dehydration, which in severe cases can be dangerous.

Though young diabetics often become acutely ill and are usually thin, older diabetics tend to be overweight and develop complications of the disease gradually. The eye problems have already been described on page 65. Diabetics are also especially liable to develop blood vessel disease. This impairs the blood supply to the limbs, meaning that diabetic skin and flesh may be slow to heal. It also makes those with diabetes more prone to heart attacks and strokes than are people without diabetes.

Some people with diabetes also lose the sense of pain and touch in their feet and legs, and may have other signs of nerve impairment, such as diarrhoea, disorder of bladder function or impotence. Because of the combination of poor sensation, poor healing and increased liability to infection, diabetics may develop septic foot wounds which go unnoticed and may even become gangrenous. It is therefore very important for older diabetics to have regular professional chiropody.

Some newly diagnosed diabetics are ill enough to need to go into hospital for their disease to be stabilised, whilst others can be managed as outpatients. All diabetics need a special diet which they must follow. Some must also take tablets to control the sugar level, and a few may need insulin injections.

The complications of diabetes seem less common in people whose diabetes is well controlled, so it is worthwhile to follow treatment instructions carefully. More information is available from the British Diabetic Association.

Thyroid disease

The thyroid is a U-shaped gland at the base of the neck, and its secretions control energy output in most body processes. Under-activity leads to sluggishness, weight gain, mental dullness and apathy. It also predisposes to hypothermia. Treatment is by replacement of the missing hormone, called thyroxine.

Over-activity of the thyroid gland in older people causes heart failure, weight loss and poor general health. It can be treated in one or more of three ways, depending on the patient's needs. Radioactive iodine may be given to switch off the thyroid cells; this has to be done in hospital. Drug treatment can also be used, and surgery is occasionally required when the enlarged gland is causing symptoms by pressing on another part of the body.

A swelling of the thyroid gland is called a goitre. In older people these are usually nodular – that is, they consist of hardened nodules or lumps of thyroid tissue. A thyroid scan can show whether these are 'hot' nodules composed of functioning tissue, or 'cold' nodules, which do not secrete hormone. About one in twenty cold nodules is cancerous, and a biopsy (see p 75) can be performed if this is suspected; cancer almost never develops in hot nodules. The treatment of thyroid nodules depends on whether or not they are malignant, whether they are causing pressure symptoms and whether the gland as a whole is over- or under-active.

CANCER

What it is

Normally, body cells work together for the health of the whole person, but when a cell becomes cancerous or, in medical jargon, malignant, it starts to grow and divide without regard to the needs of the rest of the body. In the worst sorts of cases bits may break off from the 'primary' growth and spread directly or by the blood stream and lymph channels. These spreading cells form 'secondary deposits', sometimes called metastases, in other organs such as the lungs, bones or the brain. Growth of the primary or of the secondaries may produce symptoms by pressing on or otherwise impairing the function of vital organs. Gradually, normal body processes may fail; the sick person will become debilitated and vulnerable to infection and other complications, and will eventually die.

Cancer is less common in people from the Indian sub-continent than in native Britons. Afro-Caribbeans are especially likely to develop prostatic cancer, but otherwise get less cancer than native Britons do.

There are many different sorts of cancer, some of which are curable, some containable and a few for which little curative treatment is yet possible. Older people in particular are likely to regard a diagnosis of cancer as a death sentence, and one that will be carried out in a short time with great suffering.

The truth is rather different, for many cancers in elderly people do not shorten life and may cause little disability. Even when no more can be done in the way of a cure, good care can ensure that life continues tolerably and even enjoyably before death follows peacefully and without distress.

Tests for cancer

When cancer is suspected, the individual will usually have various investigations, including blood tests, X-rays and scans. Whenever possible a bit of the abnormal tissue will be sampled so that it can be examined under the microscope; this is called a biopsy. These investigations aim to answer three questions: Does the person have cancer? If so, what sort? How far has it spread? Treatment is then planned according to the answers.

Treatment for cancer

The three basic sorts of treatment used for cancer are surgery, radio-therapy and cytotoxic (cell-poisoning) drugs. The idea of surgery is to remove the primary growth before it can cause severe local symptoms, and theoretically before it has a chance to spread.

Radiotherapy and cytotoxic drugs both act in the same way; they kill cells, and the more rapidly a cell is dividing into new cells, the more likely it is to be killed. The usefulness of this sort of treatment depends on the fact that cancer cells divide more quickly than normal cells, and are thus killed first.

In addition, some cancers respond to hormone treatment. The principle of this is to interfere with the action of any hormone causing tumour growth, or to oppose its effects.

Coming to terms with a diagnosis of cancer

Sick people differ in how much they want to know about their illness, and doctors vary in how much information they volunteer and how good they are at imparting it. Often, people have to take in bad news a little at a time; if offered information too early or too much at a time, they may be unable to absorb it. Sometimes the message is confused with the messenger; if the news is bad, even the most sensitive breaking of it may be perceived as brutal. Someone's account of what they have been told about the illness may be much coloured by their feelings about it, and it is wise to bear this in mind.

If a resident with cancer seems to want to know more about their illness, you should suggest that they ask someone who is properly informed. Suitable people include the doctor, Macmillan nurses and members of a hospice outreach team, depending on who is available. Other good sources of information and support are organisations such as BACUP and Cancerlink, and where appropriate specialist groups such as the Breast Care and Mastectomy Association.

General health and spiritual wellbeing are especially important in serious illness, and neither should be neglected. Of course people have a right to opt for whatever forms of help and treatment they prefer, but it is wise to be wary of any unorthodox treatment that seems to offer a cure. None of these has been shown to work, some are actively harmful and they may delay or interfere with more effective measures. In any case, it is best if people following 'alternative' therapies tell their doctors about them, as it is impossible to look after a patient properly without all the relevant information.

Some common types of cancer

Lung

This is usually diagnosed after a person with respiratory symptoms such as coughing up blood, shortness of breath or chest pain goes to the GP and has a chest X-ray. Surgery to remove the tumour is occasionally possible, but is uncommon in elderly people. Radiotherapy may be used to shrink primary or secondary tumours that cause pressure symptoms, pain or bleeding. Cytotoxic drugs are rarely used.

Breast

This is one of the commonest cancers in women, and usually comes to light when someone finds a lump or other abnormality in her breast. In older women, tumour growth is usually held back by drugs that block the response to female hormones. Research is under way to try to establish what treatment is best for breast cancer, and different combinations of surgery, radiotherapy and drug treatment are being tried. Surgery now is much less drastic than it was. Patients who have had a breast removed (mastectomy) may benefit from contact with the Breast Care and Mastectomy Association.

Bowel

The patient usually consults the doctor, complaining that bowel habits have changed or that blood has appeared in stools. The presence of a cancer may be confirmed by X-ray studies, usually involving the injection of barium up the back passage (a barium enema). Alternatively, a modified telescope may be used to inspect the diseased area and to take a sample for laboratory analysis. This is called sigmoidoscopy or colonoscopy, depending on the area examined.

If surgery is used to remove the cancer, it may be possible to join up the two ends of the bowel so that the stools may still be passed in the normal way. Sometimes this cannot be done, and the person will have a colostomy. Some of these are temporary, and are closed later at a second operation, whilst others are permanent.

Womb (including cervix)

This can occur either in the body of the womb or in its neck or cervix, where it can be detected by a cervical smear. Abnormal bleeding is the main symptom of this condition, either between periods in younger women or recurring after the menopause in women whose periods have stopped. Any woman who has abnormal bleeding should report it to the doctor at once so that it can be investigated further. When cancer is present, treatment is usually surgical, sometimes using a laser. This may be followed by radiotherapy using radium, which is implanted in the body for a short period during a hospital stay and is then removed.

Bladder

The usual symptom is blood in the urine, and investigation is by cystoscopy – that is, the passing of a thin telescope up through the urethra. This is done under anaesthesia, and the bladder lining can be inspected through the cystoscope and samples taken for laboratory analysis. Smaller cancers can be removed either through the cystoscope or during an open operation. Occasionally the bladder is removed entirely and the ureters are transplanted into a loop of bowel which drains externally into a bag; this is called a urostomy.

People who have been treated for bladder tumours are usually recalled for regular cystoscopies so that any recurrence can be detected and treated early. Many bladder tumours are comparatively harmless, and people who have them commonly lead a normal, healthy life, eventually dying of an unrelated condition.

Prostate

Cancer of the prostate produces the same symptoms as benign enlargement of the gland (see p 148). The clinical diagnosis is based on the patient's account of his symptoms, and the results of physical examination can be confirmed by blood tests, a needle biopsy, X-rays and scans. Afro-Caribbean men are especially prone to this form of cancer.

Treatment depends on the circumstances of the case. Many prostate cancers grow and spread very slowly, so it is sometimes best simply to keep the sufferer under careful observation and relieve his symptoms as appropriate. If and when further treatment becomes necessary, this may involve surgery, radiotherapy or medicines. As prostate cancer depends on the male hormone testosterone to help it grow, hormone treatment opposing its action is often effective (see p 106).

Skin

Skin cancers appear as lumps, warty masses or ulcers that grow slowly. Any ulcer or lump not clearing up after three weeks should be examined by a doctor. The commonest skin cancer is the rodent ulcer, almost always on the face. The 'malignant melanoma' is much less common and is more serious. It looks like a mole, and may bleed or enlarge noticeably. Skin cancers are treated by surgical removal and sometimes also by radiotherapy, and treatment usually produces a complete cure. Most skin growths are benign, but where there is any doubt, medical advice should be sought. If the growth is harmless, the person can be reassured; if not, the earlier a growth is removed, the less noticeable the remaining scar will be.

Leukaemia

This is a blood disease in which very many abnormal white blood cells are made at the expense of red cell and platelet production. Some people have no symptoms, whilst others become anaemic and very vulnerable to infections. They also tend to bleed excessively because their blood clots poorly.

The diagnosis is made by examining specimens of the affected person's blood or bone marrow under the microscope. Other tests may be needed if the liver, spleen or lymph nodes are thought to be affected.

Treatment depends on the type of leukaemia and how it is affecting the sufferer; cytotoxic drugs are often used (see p 106). The outlook is very variable and depends on individual circumstances; some types of leukaemia in older people progress very slowly.

HIV AND AIDS

The human immunodeficiency virus (HIV) causes the Acquired Immunodeficiency Syndrome, commonly known as AIDS. The virus is present in the body fluids of an infected person, and can be passed on to someone else by blood, semen or breast milk.

How HIV is spread

People can be infected:

- By sexual intercourse, whether heterosexual or homosexual. 'Safe sex' techniques, such as using a condom, reduce the risk.

- By contaminated blood or blood products, such as Factor VIII used to treat haemophilia. In the UK, testing and processing of blood for transfusion and treatment mean that transmission in this way is very unlikely to occur.

- By contaminated injection needles, scalpel blades or similar apparatus. This can happen when health workers suffer 'needle-stick' injuries, when intravenous drug users share needles and syringes or when reusable equipment is not properly cleaned and sterilised.

- By organ or tissue donation; people who are HIV positive should not donate blood, tissue or organs, or carry donor cards.

- By the passage of virus from mother to child before or during birth, or afterwards via breast milk.

HIV cannot be spread by coughs and sneezes, by using the same lavatory as an infected person, by sharing crockery or cutlery or by normal social contacts.

AIDS testing

Blood testing (the HIV test) will show that the person has been infected by HIV about two months after the virus has entered the body, though 'seroconversion', as it is called, can take longer. About one in sixteen (6–7 per cent) of people infected with HIV will develop signs of AIDS each year. We do not know for certain whether or not everyone who is infected with HIV will eventually develop AIDS.

What AIDS illness is like

AIDS can take several different forms. Some happen because people with AIDS have a diminished ability to fight infection. They may develop unusual illnesses such as pneumocystis carinii pneumonia (PCP). Alternatively, they may become much more severely ill than would be expected if they are exposed to shingles, tuberculosis or candida (the fungus that causes thrush). People with AIDS also develop unusual forms of cancer, such as the skin tumours of Kaposi's sarcoma and various types of lymphoma. AIDS can also appear as persistent fever, diarrhoea and weight loss; this is especially common in parts of Africa, where it is called 'slim disease'. Nervous system disorders such as dementia can also be part of the AIDS complex of illness.

Treatment for AIDS

Various forms of treatment are used. The drug zidovudine seems to be helpful in some cases, but its unwanted effects can be severe: they include nausea, vomiting and interference with blood cell production by the bone marrow. Appropriate antibiotics are given to fight infections, and radiotherapy can shrink the nodules of Kaposi's sarcoma.

HIV-positive residents

An HIV-positive resident of a sheltered housing scheme poses no risk to other residents in normal social circumstances. His or her sexual partners could catch the virus, and blood or equipment contaminated with it could infect others. If a resident who was HIV positive or with AIDS also had diabetes requiring insulin injections, disposal of injection needles would require special care, as would checks on blood sugar level by doctors and nurses. However, research shows that the risk to health workers in such situations is very small. Carers such as wardens are at even less risk, but it is advisable to take sensible precautions. If you need to mop up spilt blood or other body fluids, you should wear disposable gloves which can be discarded and use household bleach for cleaning, diluted in the proportion of one part of bleach to ten parts of water. You should get into the habit of doing this for every such incident, not just when you know the resident to be HIV positive. Blood-stained clothes and bedding should also be handled with gloves and machine washed at a high temperature.

In case you encounter such a task in the course of your working day, you should cover any cuts or grazes you suffer with a water-proof dressing until they seal themselves with a scab. If you do get blood or body fluids on your skin you should wash them off with soap and water, not bleach.

Sharp objects such as injection needles should always be handled carefully, and should be disposed of safely in a specially designed 'sharps box'. Saliva, sweat, tears and urine produced by an HIV-positive person have not been shown to be infectious. No special treatment is necessary for cutlery or crockery used by an HIV-positive resident: they can be washed in hot water and detergent in the usual way.

Combating ignorance and keeping confidences

Many people are not well informed about HIV and AIDS, and this ignorance has often reinforced prejudice; residents may be ostracised or treated unkindly because they or a relative have AIDS, or because of their lifestyle. AIDS is not a 'gay plague': in large parts of the world heterosexual intercourse is the commonest route of transmission of the HIV virus. Sensational publicity about HIV and AIDS often seems to have led to victimisation of gay men, whether infected or not; it hardly needs saying that there is no justification for this.

People with AIDS or who are HIV positive are often understandably reticent about their health. If a resident confides in you that he or she is HIV positive or has AIDS, or if you find out in some other way, you must of course be especially careful to keep the information confidential. Should the news become known in the scheme, you will need to know the facts about HIV and AIDS so as to be able to reassure the other residents that they are quite safe and at no risk of acquiring the infection. They will be watching you and noting your attitude and behaviour, so it will be important that your actions are as sensible and kindly as your words. If you or the residents need further information, you might like to get in touch with the Terence Higgins Trust and read some of their excellent publications.

Although this chapter has concentrated on illness, remember that health is the normal state for older people. Age alone produces no illness or disability – you are ill because you are ill, not because you are old.

3 Residents and their Medicines

WARDENS AND RESIDENTS' MEDICINES

Effects of increased frailty

As residents become frailer, they become more likely to ask wardens to help them with their medicines. The effects of community care legislation and the tendency towards earlier discharge from hospital have also meant that more residents need help of this sort. Wardens have found themselves giving advice, setting out a day's tablets in egg cups or 'memory boxes' and sometimes actually administering medicines. This may involve complicated tasks such as supervising reducing doses of steroids or adjusting the dose of anticoagulants, as well as giving out tablets, putting in eyedrops and applying skin lotions or creams.

A difficult situation

Not surprisingly, many wardens have found this new part of their work worrying. They fear that what they are doing may be unsafe, as they often receive little or no training or instruction in how to deal with medicines. They worry about the legal position: could they be held liable if anything went wrong because of the medicines they had given? Though unlikely, this could happen, and it is also possible that a bereaved family in its natural anger could fix on a warden to 'blame'. Such accusations are very distressing even when they turn out to be groundless.

This issue is of special concern to wardens whose employers have forbidden them to get involved with residents' medicines. Many such wardens would dearly like to follow such instructions, but find it very difficult to do so. Residents, especially mentally frail ones, need medicines and cannot be relied upon to take them without reminders or help. Relatives may be absent, otherwise occupied or elderly and frail themselves, and help from NHS and social services staff is dwindling. If wardens do not take charge, no one else will, and then residents will suffer. Wardens may feel anxious and uncomfortable, but can see no alternative to doing their best to help.

This situation is obviously most unsatisfactory, especially if employers refuse to recognise that a problem exists. Unfortunately, a few managers seem to be out of touch with what is actually going on at scheme level. They hang on to the comforting fiction that 'Our wardens are not concerned with residents' medicines' and appear to be deaf to any suggestion that this is no longer true.

Evolving a sensible medicines policy

Difficulties of this sort cannot be made to disappear as if by magic, but here are some suggestions that may help to improve matters.

Firstly, if your employer's declared policy on medicines seems inappropriate and unworkable in present circumstances, you should tell them so in writing. Make sure that you have facts to support your opinion – the number of residents who are too confused to cope with their medicines unaided, the number who have recently been discharged from hospital needing help with eyedrops, how often the district nurse or other helpers are able to call, and so on. A timely report called 'Medication in Sheltered Housing', available from Anchor Housing Trust, brings the problem into the open and recommends courses of action. It would probably be useful for both you and your managers to read this report and to discuss its implications.

The next thing to do is to consider whether the policy should be revised. Some wardens and managers who have done this have concluded that in their particular circumstances no change is necessary. If this decision is reached, employers must then support those wardens who refuse to give medicines when pressed to by residents, their relatives or doctors. A warden who will not undertake duties of this sort risks being seen as lazy and uncaring; it is much easier to refer enquiries to an official who can take the blame without endangering a long-term day-to-day relationship.

In many cases it will be obvious that the original medicines policy has outlived its usefulness. A new one is needed, and it is most useful if clear guidelines are worked out and written down. Employers can then make sure that any warden acting within these guidelines is covered by liability insurance. Legal cover of this sort is likely to be much less costly than any sort of legal dispute.

Helping with medicines – do's and don'ts

If you help with medicines, you should resist the temptation to 'take over'; instead, you should ensure that as far as possible your residents keep control over this aspect of their lives. Residents with disabilities may need treatment or equipment; confusion may improve or disappear if underlying illness is treated; someone with a visual handicap may become more independent if their medicines are labelled in large, bold print or in Braille.

'Memory boxes' filled at intervals by relatives or nurses may reduce your involvement to prompting rather than actual administration, and devices that make eyedrops easier to put in may help residents to manage on their own. Monitored dosage systems such as Surgichem's NOMAD and Boots' MDS are a new development. These are free to the user, who is supplied with medicines in a device filled by the pharmacist, with compartments labelled for different times of day. This makes it easy for the resident to know which medicines are due, and for the warden or other carer to check whether or not tablets have been taken. Further information can be obtained from the companies concerned.

It is not the warden's job to make sure that residents take medication if they are unwilling to do so, and of course it is quite wrong ever to deceive them into taking medicines against their will. If you are concerned that a resident may become ill through refusing to take medicines, you should let the doctor know. The doctor will then be able to decide whether or not this is a decision the resident is mentally competent to make, and can take appropriate action.

If you take on more responsibility for your residents' medicines, you will need to discuss your working pattern further with your employers. One important consideration is the way in which your workload is likely to increase: if you help one resident, all other residents are likely to expect similar care if in a similar situation. Another practical point is off-duty cover: who will supervise the residents' medicines when you are not there? More and more wardens switch scheme alarm systems over to a control centre during off-duty periods; a Central Control Operator cannot give out medicines or supervise their use by remote control. Alternative solutions may need to be explored depending on local circumstances; wardens and employers who are changing their own working practices have a right to expect a similar degree of flexibility from others. Problems with medicines and their administration come about because sheltered housing is changing; we will all need to work well together if vulnerable older people are to get the care they deserve.

The information in this chapter should make it easier to help residents to use their medicines properly. It is also useful to know why medicines are given and what are the more common unwanted effects.

DIFFERENT NAMES FOR MEDICINES

Every medicine has a 'generic' name, which is usually an abbreviated form of its chemical one. When a doctor writes a generic name on the prescription form, the dispensing pharmacist will usually supply the cheapest form of that preparation in stock. In some circumstances, however, doctors might prefer to use a particular drug company's preparation because they know it to be of consistent and reliable quality, quicker acting or better absorbed. They would then specify the drug by its 'trade' name. A drug that is marketed by several different companies will have several different trade names. Because proprietary drugs (prescribed by trade names) usually cost more than the generic preparation, doctors are encouraged by the Government to prescribe generic drugs except where the branded goods are definitely superior.

Sometimes a resident may become upset because the doctor seems to have changed the usual tablets or the pharmacist to have dispensed the wrong ones. Confusion may result because a generic preparation has been dispensed instead of the accustomed proprietary one, or vice versa – for instance, a person may be disturbed to be given temazepam (generic name) having become used to seeing Normison (trade name) on the bottle. In fact, the person can be reassured that the two are, in fact, the same substance.

UNWANTED EFFECTS OF MEDICINES

People tend to become confused about the 'side effects' of drugs. These are better described as 'unwanted effects' because most drugs have more than one effect, and which of them are wanted and which are unwanted can vary from one occasion to another. There is no such thing as a good or bad drug, only one that is used well or badly by the doctor and/or the patient.

Unwanted effects of over-the-counter preparations (obtainable from the chemist without a prescription) will depend on the constituents of the medicine. They are unlikely to arise if the person asks to see a qualified pharmacist, explains the symptoms carefully and specifies what prescribed medicines are already being taken.

Using a medicine is no different from using a knife; either can cause damage if used carelessly or by someone with poor sight, or if used for suicide or murder – misuse is not the fault of the knife or the medicine but of the person using it.

Older people are especially prone to the unwanted effects of medicines for a number of reasons. Because of ageing changes in the body, medicines are metabolised and removed from the body more slowly than in younger people. This means that normal adult doses may accumulate and produce toxic effects, and therefore elderly people often require smaller doses of medicine than younger adults with similar illnesses.

In addition, some doctors seem insufficiently well informed about the needs of older people, and may prescribe with insufficient thought and care. People sometimes reinforce this by being reluctant to leave the surgery without a prescription as a 'talisman', even when the doctor has suggested that this is unnecessary. Repeat prescriptions sent through the post are convenient, but often lead to drugs being given when the need for them has passed. A prescription should not be repeated over more than a six-month period without the doctor seeing the person to re-evaluate the need for the drug. Many surgery computer systems will now alert the doctor that the time to review the prescription has arrived.

Even if the need for the drug has been carefully considered and the correct dose meticulously dispensed, the effort involved will be wasted if the older person does not take the medicine correctly as prescribed. This may be difficult if health problems interfere with memory, with reading small print or with extracting tablets from their packaging. As a warden you can make taking medicines much easier for your residents by following some of the suggestions in this chapter.

USING MEDICINES CORRECTLY

To avoid confusion about medication, all drug containers should be labelled with two kinds of information: firstly, the medical name of the drug and its dosage (to help any deputising doctor who is unfamiliar with the person's case); and, secondly, the details that the resident and their helpers can understand – for example, 'Heart pill, take every morning' or 'Two for pain when necessary'.

It is particularly important that the resident knows which tablets need to be taken every day regardless of circumstances, and which are only necessary to relieve a particularly bothersome symptom, such as pain or breathlessness, and can be left out when these symptoms are absent. When a container is too small to be labelled in sufficiently large letters, you could suggest that the resident ties on a luggage label and uses a thick felt pen to identify the medicine. For people with poor sight, labels in large print and written in Braille can be obtained from the Royal National Institute for the Blind. When a resident is unsure what the medication is for and how it should be taken, you or the resident could ask the GP, the practice nurse or the pharmacist for advice and help.

When a resident has a number of different drugs to take each day, you could suggest that a memory device is used, such as a specially designed box; the district nurse or pharmacist will know about these. The resident may also want to consider a monitored dosage system (see above).

A forgetful resident may be unsure whether a tablet has been taken or not and you may have no way of checking. You should not take on yourself the responsibility of deciding whether to risk omitting the dose or, conversely, doubling it; instead the resident should ask the doctor or pharmacist for advice, with your help if necessary.

Many older people, especially those with arthritic hands or poor sight, find child-resistant containers or bubble packs difficult to deal with; they should ask for their medicines to be dispensed in screw-top bottles. Butterfly lids with prominent flanges are also useful. Pharmacists use their discretion in deciding what container should be supplied, and suitable bottles should be available on request.

If a tablet or capsule is difficult to swallow, it sometimes helps to put the tablet in the mouth at the point when a mouthful of chewed food is ready to be swallowed, so that the two can go down together. Not all medicines can be taken in this way, so the resident should check with the pharmacist before trying this method. Alternatively, the doctor can be asked to prescribe the same substance in a liquid form.

HELP FROM THE PHARMACIST AND OTHERS

Regular contact with the GP can be very helpful in preventing problems with drugs – for instance, a doctor may be unaware of the person's memory difficulties, so cannot prescribe sensibly unless properly informed. The simpler the pattern of drug taking, the more likely it is to be followed accurately. Morning and evening doses are the easiest to remember, and, provided the doctor is aware of the memory problem, it is often possible to simplify the treatment plan to this pattern. When supervision is required, you should explain just how much you are able and willing to do in this respect, so that other arrangements can be made if necessary.

You can also help to encourage a regular review of therapy and the reduction of tablets to a minimum. It is very useful to help the resident to collect all tablets and medicine bottles for the doctor to inspect and review; the collection can be taken to the hospital ward or out-patient department if necessary.

It is worth trying to find a pharmacist near to the scheme who knows the needs of older people and is prepared to take trouble in dealing with them. Pharmacists are a useful source of general advice about prescribed and over-the-counter drugs, but should not be expected to provide a diagnostic service.

The practice or district nurse may be able to assist by teaching a resident how to take medicines, and may also help with labelling or with the filling of 'memory boxes' when relatives or friends are not available to do this.

An increasing number of hospital wards now make a point of training patients to cope with their medication themselves before discharge. If this is not the case in your area, you may be able to suggest that this policy should be adopted.

Older people from ethnic minorities and their medicines

Some sorts of British medicines and ways of taking them are unacceptable to older people from certain ethnic groups. Here are some points to remember:

- Muslims who fast during Ramadan may need their usual medicines altered so that they can be taken twice a day or less often.

- Devout Muslims, Hindus, Sikhs or Buddhists may be reluctant to use preparations containing alcohol, whether they are to be swallowed or applied to the skin. The pharmacist will be able to find out the ingredients of a particular preparation, and can if necessary help the doctor choose a suitable alternative.

- Gelatin capsules are made from animal bones and hides, including those of cows and pigs. Medicines in such capsules will not be acceptable to religious Hindus, Sikhs and Muslims, to many Jews or to vegetarians or vegans of any faith or none. Again, it will usually be possible to find an alternative.

SOME COMMONLY PRESCRIBED MEDICINES

This section describes some of the medicines that older people take most often. Unwanted effects of medicines should always be reported to the doctor. Whenever possible, residents should do this themselves; only when they are too confused or unwell to look after themselves should you act on their behalf.

For heart disease

Digoxin

This is used to stimulate the heart and/or to regulate its rhythm. It should be taken regularly every morning to maintain a constant level in the blood.

Unwanted effects include slowing of the pulse, mental confusion, nausea, vomiting and yellow vision. These are usually a sign that the dose is too large, so such symptoms should be reported to the doctor as soon as possible.

Vasodilators

These expand (dilate) blood vessels – that is, they cause vasodilation. Examples include nitrates such as glyceryl trinitrate and isosorbide dinitrate, and calcium channel blockers such as nifedipine and diltiazem.

Glyceryl trinitrate (GTN) and other nitrate preparations are used to treat angina. Tablets should be put under the tongue at the onset of pain or, better still, before embarking on the sort of activity that provokes pain (eg walking uphill, sexual intercourse). 'Sustained-release' preparations of isosorbide dinitrate give long-lasting protection and these should be taken as directed, usually regularly. Nitrates are also available in aerosols and in forms absorbed through the skin.

Unwanted effects of nitrates include throbbing headache, flushing, faintness and fast heart beat. People should take GTN tablets while sitting down, and should spit out the remains of the tablet once the pain is relieved to reduce unwanted effects.

People with frequent angina attacks may do better with treatment designed to prevent them from occurring. Beta-blockers are sometimes used for this (see below). Another alternative is a calcium channel blocker; these medicines reduce the heart's activity as well as dilating blood vessels. They also lower the blood pressure, so can be used to treat high blood pressure.

Unwanted effects of calcium channel blockers vary, depending on which preparation is used. If the heart's action is depressed too much, the patient may develop heart failure or heart rhythm disturbances. Faintness, flushing, headache and swollen ankles may also occur.

Vasodilators have been tried in the hope of improving the blood supply to the legs of people with arterial disease or the brains of people with multi-infarct dementia. Unfortunately, they do not seem to work.

Beta-blockers

These include propranolol, oxprenolol, atenolol and timolol, used to prevent angina, to treat thyroid over-activity and to lower high blood pressure. They can also prevent the recurrence of a heart attack. Beta-blockers should be taken as prescribed for the special circumstances of the person and the illness.

Unwanted effects include worsening of asthma or heart failure, cold hands and feet, sleep disturbances and tiredness. They may also mask the effects of hypoglycaemia (low blood sugar) in people with diabetes.

Diuretics

Examples include bendrofluazide, frusemide, amiloride and triamterene. Often called water pills, these are used to remove water from the body as urine in heart failure and oedema (watery swelling). They are also used to treat high blood pressure.

Diuretics are usually taken first thing in the morning so that the need to pass water does not lead to a disturbed night. Potassium (chemical symbol K) is lost in the urine and may need to be replaced in people taking diuretics. Some tablets with 'K' in their names contain both substances.

Unwanted effects include muscle weakness, confusion and unsteadiness due to potassium loss, and incontinence because extra urine needs to be passed. Some diuretics make gout and diabetes worse.

For infections

Antibacterial drugs, commonly called 'antibiotics', kill bacteria but not viruses such as those that cause colds or 'flu. The choice of antibiotic depends on the likely cause of the illness, so the doctor will sometimes take a specimen of the patient's blood, urine, spit, etc to find out which germ is responsible.

Antifungal agents are used to treat infections such as thrush. These can be very serious in people with low resistance, such as those with AIDS.

Antiviral agents are occasionally used against herpes viruses (see 'Shingles', p 62).

Antibiotics must be taken at intervals throughout the day. The course of tablets must be finished even if the patient feels better before the bottle is empty, in order to make sure that the infection is thoroughly cured. If the resident does not improve after taking the tablets for 48 hours, they should let the doctor know.

Unwanted effects include nausea, diarrhoea, skin rashes and thrush (sore mouth with white patches, or severe itching of vagina, vulva or penis). Some people are allergic to antibiotics, especially penicillin. It is wise to tell the doctor at once if this seems to be happening, and to make sure the doctor knows and has a record if an antibiotic has caused upset in the past.

For chest diseases

Bronchodilators

These relax the bronchial tubes so that air can pass in and out of the lungs more freely. They may be given as tablets or by inhalation as an aerosol spray. Some drugs given by aerosols need to be taken regularly to prevent illnesses, rather than to relieve symptoms. Steroid therapy for chest disease is sometimes given this way.

94

Inhalers are very effective if used properly, so technique is most important. If a resident does not seem to be benefiting from an aerosol spray, you should suggest that they consult the doctor, nurse or pharmacist, who will demonstrate how to use it properly. It is unwise to use inhalers more often than prescribed, as this may be dangerous.

Unwanted effects of bronchodilators include hand tremors, nervousness, headache and, occasionally, fast heart beat. Slow-release preparations taken by mouth to control wheezing overnight sometimes interfere with sleep.

For coughs

Suppressants

These are used to suppress a dry cough. Simple linctus is mild and harmless but comparatively ineffective. Codeine and pholcodine are strong, effective drugs and should be taken strictly as prescribed. Unwanted effects include constipation and retention of mucus. They should not be used for a wet cough, as phlegm may then accumulate and clog the lungs.

Expectorants

These are used to help bring up thick mucus, and are usually taken in hot water on waking in the morning. They have little if any unwanted effects, but probably do little if any good.

Steam inhalations

These are cheap, readily available and useful for liquefying thick mucus; however, there is a risk of scalds. It is not necessary to add anything to the water, but a scenting agent such as Friar's Balsam can be used if liked.

For indigestion

Antacids

These are an effective treatment for discomfort due to unwise eating or anxiety. Liquid preparations are more effective than tablets, though less portable. Two over-the-counter preparations are magnesium trisilicate, which also has a slight laxative effect, and aluminium hydroxide, which tends to constipate. One to three teaspoonsful should be taken up to three times a day between meals and at bed time.

Unwanted effects include interference with absorption of other drugs. Some types of antacids may worsen heart failure. The resident should check with the pharmacist or doctor if in doubt about this.

For peptic ulcer

Reducing acid

The commonest preparations are ranitidine and cimetidine, which are usually given in four- to six-week courses until the ulcer is healed. A small 'maintenance' dose is also sometimes prescribed.

Unwanted effects are rare with ranitidine. Cimetidine may occasionally cause diarrhoea, dizziness, rashes, confusion and impotence, but this seldom happens.

Protecting the stomach and duodenal lining

Bismuth preparations such as De-Nol coat the ulcer and help it to heal. They should not be taken within two hours before a meal and half an hour after it, as the medicine will stick to the food rather than to the ulcer. Tablets may be more acceptable than the liquid form.

Unwanted effects are only serious in people with poor kidney function. Mild effects include the darkening of stools and a tendency to constipation.

Sucralfate acts in a similar way and can also cause constipation.

Liquorice preparations such as carbenoxolone protect the lining of the stomach and duodenum, reinforcing it against acid attack.

Unwanted effects happen because the drug retains salt and water in the body. This worsens high blood pressure and heart failure, and means that the drug is not usually suitable for older people.

Manufacturers have produced a liquorice preparation called Caved-S which does not cause fluid retention, but unfortunately it has little healing effect either.

For hiatus hernia

The pain or heartburn happen because stomach acid runs back into the gullet and irritates it (reflux oesophagitis). Reflux preventers such as alginic acid with an antacid (eg Gaviscon, Gastrocote) form a thick jelly layer on top of the acid in the stomach. This makes it less likely to run back into the gullet, and coats the sore area protectively if it does.

Antacids or ranitidine reduce acid damage. Preparations such as metoclopramide are used to help the muscle encircling the gullet base to stop stomach acid from running back. Unwanted effects such as muscle spasms and movement disorders can be serious.

For diarrhoea

In acute cases medicines are much less important than ensuring that the person drinks enough to replace the lost fluids. Drugs are occasionally used when diarrhoea is very inconvenient or has lasted for more than 24 hours.

Absorbent chalk mixtures and kaolin preparations are popular and harmless. Methylcellulose is useful for people with colostomies. Drugs that reduce gut activity include codeine, morphine or opium compounds, diphenoxylate and loperamide. Unwanted effects include faecal impaction, sedation and the risk of dependence. In addition, these drugs may slow the rate at which the body gets rid of toxins, and, by masking symptoms, suggest that the illness is less severe than it is. Elderly people should not take these drugs except on medical advice.

For constipation

Laxatives

These should be avoided as far as possible, as they impair normal bowel-emptying patterns. When necessary, a doctor or nurse may advise a suitable preparation, but sometimes a resident may wish to take their own. Elderly people are often very attached to the laxative they have always taken, and occasional use is probably not very harmful.

For occasional use:

- Lactulose is a syrupy preparation which produces soft, easily passed stools; it is harmless, but rather expensive.

- Methylcellulose granules are harmless and cheap but unpalatable to take, and not always effective in severe cases.

- Senokot is supplied as tablets or granules; the effective dose varies from person to person. Unwanted effects include abdominal pains and dangerous loss of salts and water.

- Bisacodyl is similar to Senokot and can be taken as a suppository.

- Glycerol suppositories lubricate the actual passage of stools and stimulate the bowel. They may cure mild cases, or be useful when taken with another drug for more severe constipation.

To be avoided:

- Senna teas or 'brews' vary in strength and overdosage is common. Unwanted effects include abdominal pain, diarrhoea, faecal incontinence and disturbances of body chemistry.

- Liquid paraffin has as its unwanted effects leakage at the anus and faecal soiling, impaired absorption of fat-soluble vitamins A and D, and the production of tumours.

- Epsom and other 'health' salts can result in excessive loss of fluid and salts, and faecal incontinence because the stools are difficult to control.

A high-fibre diet often renders laxatives unnecessary. Large amounts of unprocessed bran should not be taken because it interferes with absorption of nutrients and, rarely, can cause bowel blockage. A spoonful added to soups or cereal is harmless and helpful, however.

For gallstones

Only a small minority of patients have the sort of gallstones that can be dissolved by bile acids.

Unwanted effects of bile acids include diarrhoea, skin rashes and liver disorders. There is also a risk of the stones forming again if treatment is stopped.

For diabetes

Oral hypoglycaemics

These are used together with a prescribed diet to lower the sugar level in the blood. They must be taken strictly at the times and in the dosage prescribed, as changes of dose or timing of the tablets or missing a meal may cause dangerous hypoglycaemia.

Unwanted effects include flushing of face on drinking alcohol, loss of appetite, sickness, vomiting and symptoms of hypoglycaemia ('hypo') such as drowsiness, irritability and mental confusion. As this condition impairs thinking abilities, you will have to act on behalf of a hypoglycaemic resident; call for help at once and take emergency action (see pp 124–125).

Insulin injections

These are used for people with diabetes whose condition cannot be controlled by diet or tablets. They must be given exactly as prescribed in both dose and timing. Older diabetics with poor sight may have difficulty with this, and will need help from a visiting nurse.

Few older diabetics need insulin injections all the time, but people usually treated with diet and tablets may need insulin for a short while during an acute illness or to tide them over a surgical operation.

Unwanted effects include hypoglycaemia, infections and other skin complications at the injection site.

For thyroid disease

Under-activity

This is treated by replacing the missing hormone, thyroxine. Once started, treatment continues for life, and it is important that someone taking thyroxine never runs out of supplies.

Unwanted effects include irregularities of the heart beat, angina, headache, restlessness, weight loss, flushing and diarrhoea. Thyroxine has to be used carefully in people who also have heart disease.

Over-activity

This is treated with medicines such as carbimazole or propylthiouracil, which reduce production of thyroid hormones. These may be used alone, or together with radio-iodine or surgery.

The commonest unwanted effect is an itchy rash. A rare but more serious complication is suppression of white blood cell production. This may cause a sore throat, so people taking carbimazole are told to report such symptoms to the doctor.

For anaemia

Iron tablets

These are used to treat anaemia due to iron deficiency. They should be taken as prescribed, usually with food.

Unwanted effects include nausea, diarrhoea or constipation. These should be reported to the doctor, as a change of preparation may enable iron treatment to continue without complications.

Vitamin B$_{12}$

This is used for the treatment of pernicious anaemia and is given by injection into muscle. Once pernicious anaemia has been diagnosed, B$_{12}$ injections will be needed for life, at approximately two- to three-monthly intervals. B$_{12}$ has no known unwanted effects.

For abnormal clotting

Anticoagulants

These are used to prevent a blood clot from forming, or, if it is already there, to prevent it from spreading further. Treatment needs to be taken strictly as prescribed, and dosage is adjusted according to results of frequent blood tests. The resident should always carry a card with details of tests and treatment to show to a new doctor. This is necessary both because of possible complications of anticoagulant therapy and because new medicines can interfere with previous stable anticoagulant therapy.

Unwanted effects include bleeding, especially into urine or the gut. Fainting and collapse may occur due to hidden, internal blood loss; this needs urgent medical treatment.

For sleep

Hypnotics

These sleeping tablets or sedatives should be used for short periods only. When difficulty in sleeping is a long-term problem, other strategies should be tried (see pp 33–34). Hypnotics should be taken after retiring to bed.

Unwanted effects include confusion, decline in mental functioning, falling and incontinence. These should be reported to the doctor as they are indications that the drugs should be stopped, usually gradually. A normal sleeping pattern is then slowly regained.

For mental illness

Antidepressants

These are usually taken in a single dose in the evening, and rarely need to be split into separate doses through the day. Their antidepressant effect may not be felt until two to three weeks after starting treatment, but sleep and appetite improve sooner. Treatment is continued for weeks or months.

Unwanted effects may be troublesome. Minor ones, which usually disappear within a few days, include dry mouth, giddiness on getting up quickly and drowsiness. More serious effects such as painful red eyes with blurred vision (a sign of glaucoma), difficulty in passing water or mental confusion should be reported to the doctor at once. You may need to do this on behalf of a resident who is too unwell to act unaided.

Antipsychotics

These neuroleptics or major tranquillisers are usually given for an established psychiatric condition such as schizophrenia, often as a regular monthly injection. They are used with great caution, if at all, in people over 70. A resident who has been on these drugs for a number of years will need careful reassessment by a psychiatrist. A community psychiatric nurse (CPN) may be very helpful in day-to-day care.

Serious unwanted effects include the production of abnormal movements and of a condition like Parkinson's disease. They may also lead to falls and to impaired temperature regulation, so residents taking them are vulnerable to hypothermia in cold weather. Because of their underlying illness, people on these medicines may be unable to take proper care of themselves. If this is happening, you should notify the doctor or CPN.

Anxiolytics

These minor tranquillisers such as Valium or Librium are rarely necessary in elderly people, and unwanted effects are especially troublesome. These include confusion, falling, incontinence and worsening of depression.

For Parkinson's disease

Levodopa

This is usually given as Sinemet or Madopar to relieve difficulty in starting to move. It must be taken strictly as prescribed, as the dose is tailored to each person's requirements. Changing meal times or taking extra vitamin B_6 (pyridoxine) can interfere with levodopa therapy.

Unwanted effects include nausea, vomiting and movement disorders; these should be reported to the doctor. Fluctuations in effect can sometimes be smoothed out by adding the newer drugs bromocriptine or selegiline.

Anticholinergics

These are used when the main problem is tremor or dribbling of saliva. Examples are benzhexol, procyclidine and orphenadrine.

Unwanted effects include dry mouth, confusion, drowsiness, constipation, retention of urine, blurred vision and glaucoma in predisposed people. These should be reported to the doctor.

NOTE   Drugs given for Parkinson's disease should never be stopped suddenly. The doctor should be informed if the person is unable to take the tablets because of illness, or if he or she 'seizes up' and finds movement difficult; someone with moderate to severe Parkinson's disease is likely to need assistance in obtaining medical help.

For epileptic fits

Phenytoin

This needs to be taken very regularly, in a dosage tailored to the person's requirements. It should **not** be stopped suddenly.

Unwanted effects include impaired absorption of folate and vitamin D from food. These substances need to be replaced in people on long-term phenytoin. Phenobarbitone is rarely used in elderly people because it causes severe drowsiness and confusion.

For shingles

Antiviral agents such as acyclovir and vidarabine are occasionally given to people in severe pain or with reduced resistance to infection.

Unwanted effects include skin rashes, digestive upset, liver and blood disturbances, headache and tiredness.

Idoxuridine painted on to affected skin may shorten the period of pain, but will work only if it is started as soon as the rash appears and is applied regularly thereafter. It stings the skin and may damage it.

People with shingles often need pain killers. Some doctors think that steroids help to shorten the time during which pain is felt. Shingles affecting the eye (ophthalmic herpes) needs special treatment prescribed by an eye specialist.

For pain

Mild analgesics (pain killers)

Mild household remedies such as paracetamol and aspirin are often bought over the counter to treat ailments such as headaches and muscular pain. Expensive compound preparations have little advantage over cheaper forms, and compound tablets containing constipating agents such as codeine are best avoided.

These mild analgesics can be taken 'as required' up to the limit stated on the packaging. If the painful condition does not get better quickly, it is wise to consult the doctor.

Paracetamol has few unwanted effects in normal dosage, but is very dangerous in overdose. Seek help at once for anyone who seems to have taken excess paracetamol, as treatment is effective only in the early stages.

Aspirin can irritate the stomach lining and cause bleeding. This is less likely if it is taken after food or in a soluble, 'buffered' or enteric-coated form. On balance, paracetamol is probably more suitable than aspirin as a mild pain killer for an older person.

Strong analgesics

Strong pain killers, mostly related to morphine, are used for short-term relief of acute pain, such as that of a heart attack, and to control pain in people who are dying. When used for terminal care, these pain killers are given according to a specially designed plan, so that pain is not allowed to develop.

Unwanted effects include nausea and constipation, which may need further medicines to put them right. Cough is suppressed and breathing becomes shallower.

The use of these drugs is strictly controlled by law. Dependence is of no practical importance in terminally ill people; they should not be denied effective pain relief because of a false fear of 'addiction'.

For arthritis

Pain killers such as paracetamol taken regularly may be sufficient to give relief in mild cases.

Non-Steroidal Anti-Inflammatory agents (NSAIs) are used in more severe cases to relieve pain and inflammation. Examples are benorylate, ibuprofen and diclofenac.

The main unwanted effect of NSAIs is digestive upset, ranging from mild indigestion through pain, nausea, vomiting and diarrhoea to severe bleeding. These medicines are not usually given to people with active peptic ulcers. Some people with a healed peptic ulcer who really need an NSAI take it with an acid-reducing drug such as ranitidine. This makes the ulcer less likely to flare up again. NSAIs should always be taken with food or milk. Anyone who has digestive symptoms while taking an NSAI should stop taking the medicine at once and should consult the doctor.

It is sometimes difficult to decide whether the genuine help many arthritis sufferers receive from their NSAIs is outweighed by the risk of unwanted effects. Residents who have arthritis may want to discuss this with their doctors.

For Paget's disease

Simple pain killers are all that some people need. Further treatment may be necessary for uncontrolled pain, or when overgrown bone is causing pressure symptoms or deformity.

Calcitonin is a hormone that relieves these symptoms. It is given by injection as a course of treatment. Unwanted effects are usually mild; they include nausea, vomiting and flushes. An alternative is Didronel (disodium etidronate), which can be given by mouth on an empty stomach. Unwanted effects include nausea, diarrhoea and a metallic taste in the mouth. It can make the bones thin and fragile if taken for too long.

For gout

Acute attacks are treated with NSAIs. Some people with persisting high levels of urate in their blood need continuing treatment to lower it. Allopurinol slows the formation of urate, whilst probenecid and sulphinpyrazone help the body to dispose of it, helped by plenty of fluids to flush out the kidneys.

Unwanted effects are rare, though allopurinol may cause skin rashes. An acute attack of gout may be caused if allopurinol is started without 'cover' from an NSAI.

For vitamin deficiency

Vitamins should be given only when a normal balanced diet cannot be taken, when extra vitamins are required because of illness or when they cannot be absorbed properly from the diet. Vitamins should not be used as a tonic; very large doses, as in megavitamin therapy, can produce serious toxic effects.

- Vitamin A may be needed by people who cannot absorb dietary fat.

- B group vitamins are used to correct malnourishment, and can be taken as tablets or by injection. Unwanted effects are few in the prescribed dosage. Thiamine (vitamin B_1) is needed by alcohol abusers.

- Vitamin C is used to prevent scurvy and to promote healing, and can be given as tablets or in vitamin-rich fruit or fruit juice. Unwanted effects include diarrhoea and dyspepsia. Large doses may cause kidney stones.

- Vitamin D is used to prevent osteomalacia, the painful weakness of bones caused by dietary deficiency and lack of sunlight. It can be given as tablets, often with calcium, or by periodic injections. The dose should not be exceeded, nor should vitamin D be taken by healthy people unnecessarily, when it can be dangerous. There are no unwanted effects if the recommended dosage is taken.

- Vitamin K may be needed by people who cannot absorb it from food. It is important in blood clotting.

Steroid therapy

Steroids are used in the treatment of many conditions, including giant cell arteritis, polymyalgia rheumatica, asthma and rheumatoid arthritis. They may be taken as tablets, as inhalations or as skin creams. Therapy is tailored to the person's needs; it should be taken strictly as prescribed and **never** stopped suddenly. Unwanted effects include acute confusion, raised blood pressure, heart failure and diabetes when steroids are given in high doses. Someone taking steroids for a long time may suffer from thinning of bones, back pain from spinal fractures, peptic ulcers and fungal infections. Steroid creams or ointments may cause thinning of skin, which becomes fragile, bleeds easily and is slow to heal.

NOTE   People taking steroids should carry a card with details of their treatment and dosage. They should be careful never to run out of their medicines. The doctor should be notified if someone taking steroids becomes ill, as the dosage may need to be altered. The resident is likely to be too unwell to do this, so you may need to call for help on his or her behalf.

For cancer

Two sorts of medicines can be used to halt the growth of cancerous cells in primary and secondary tumours; these are cytotoxic drugs and hormone therapy.

Cytotoxic drugs

These poison cancer cells by interfering with their growth or metabolism. They are most effective against leukaemia and lymphoma (tumours of lymph gland tissue), and tend to be less useful for solid tumours.

Unwanted effects come about because normal body cells are partially poisoned too. Common complaints are of sickness and vomiting, lowered resistance to infection because of a lack of white blood cells, and loss of hair. Treatment with cytotoxics is usually supervised by a medical oncologist with special knowledge and experience of their use.

Hormone treatment

This may be used to treat tumours of the reproductive organs such as the prostate and breast. Treatment involves either blocking the action of a hormone that causes growth or using one with the opposite effect.

Breast cancer may be treated by tamoxifen, which opposes the action of the female hormone oestrogen. Unwanted effects are uncommon, but people whose cancer has spread to their bones may find their pain becomes worse for a short while, after which the bone deposits shrink and the pain gets better.

Prostate cancer is helped to grow by the male hormone testosterone, so treatment aims to prevent this effect. One way of doing this is to remove both testicles surgically, but medicines can give the same result. They include goserelin, buserelin and diethylstilboestrol (DES). The main unwanted effects are impotence, shrinkage of the genitals and enlargement of the breasts. These may get better if and when treatment is stopped.

OVER-THE-COUNTER MEDICINES

In general, it is sensible to discourage the use of these, as it is unwise for an older person to attempt self-diagnosis, and money spent on these remedies might be better used elsewhere. Most minor ailments get better spontaneously within a few days; if a resident has symptoms that persist for longer than this, you should suggest that they see the doctor.

Do encourage your residents to be honest with the doctor about the medicines they are taking. For example, they should say if they have stopped taking a prescribed medicine they found unhelpful, or if they have started using an over-the-counter drug or complementary therapy. Failure to do this could lead to unwanted effects from treatments that do not mix.

COMPLEMENTARY OR ALTERNATIVE MEDICINE

Sheltered housing residents of course have every right to decide what sort of medicines they want to take, and when or whether to use complementary, alternative or traditional treatments as well as or instead of orthodox scientific Western medicine. Beliefs about health and illness vary a great deal, especially in people from different cultural backgrounds. Elderly people from ethnic minority groups commonly use several types of medical care; one common pattern would be to use traditional remedies for chronic, vague disorders and orthodox Western medicine for acute illness or injuries.

Practitioners of complementary medicine are skilled at listening to patients and finding out about their background. They are able to spend time doing this because of their working circumstances; doctors practising scientific medicine often wish that the NHS gave them the opportunity to do the same.

As a general rule, those complementary therapies that can be shown to have useful effects may also be harmful in some circumstances. Other types of treatment which seem to do little good probably also do little harm; they may, however, delay the use of effective treatment.

Herbal remedies

Many of the drugs now available in a conventional form were originally derived from plants. For example, digitalis (digoxin) came from foxgloves, aspirin from willow bark and colchicine from the autumn crocus.

Western herbal medicines may be obtained from a herbalist or over the counter in health food shops. Herbal remedies are especially popular with the Chinese community, where they are believed to act by restoring the 'energy balance' in the body. They may help in some cases of eczema, but some preparations have been found to contain steroids as well as herbs: this makes the effectiveness of the herbs difficult to assess.

Unwanted effects from herbal treatments are quite common, and they may be serious or even fatal. They include kidney and liver damage, with reports of liver cancer, blood disorders and skin rashes. Herbal preparations may also interact with orthodox Western medicines in someone who uses both.

Homoeopathic preparations

The practice of homoeopathy is based on several principles. One is that 'like cures like': giving a medicine that reproduces or supports the symptoms will encourage the body to throw off the disease. Another theory is that the minimum dose has the greatest effect: homoeopathic preparations contain only very diluted solutions of their active ingredients. They are therefore unlikely either to relieve symptoms or cause unwanted effects. Their use might, however, delay effective treatment, and they are best prescribed by a qualified doctor specialising in homoeopathy.

Osteopathy and chiropractic

These varieties of 'manipulative medicine' seem to have good effects in some cases of back pain and of joint diseases. They are among the most popular of the complementary therapies, and many orthodox doctors find them both acceptable and useful.

Osteopathic and chiropractic manipulations can cause damage to bones, joints and nearby structures such as nervous tissue in the spinal cord or peripheral nerves. It is important that the medical diagnosis is known before manipulation is attempted, and good practitioners usually make sure that this is done.

Acupuncture and Shiatsu

Acupuncture is a Chinese therapy which involves the insertion of fine needles at points on the body corresponding to the condition or organ under treatment. In Shiatsu, finger pressure is applied to acupuncture points. Both are said to work by releasing the body's natural pain killers, called endorphins. Studies suggest that the techniques may be helpful in a small proportion of cases, but the effects are not consistent.

An important unwanted effect is the spread of hepatitis B or the HIV virus if contaminated needles are not properly sterilised before reuse.

Traditional Asian medicines

Muslims may consult a hakim or traditional healer and take the medicines he provides. These may contain metal compounds: toxic amounts of arsenic and mercury from these sources have caused serious disability from nerve damage, and even some deaths.

Faith healing

Reputable faith healers offer spiritual support in addition to orthodox medicine, rather than attempting to replace it. The healer will suggest that the sick person consults a doctor for diagnosis, and he or she will not countermand the doctor's advice.

Someone who stops orthodox treatment, such as tablets for epilepsy, after a healing in the wrong belief that they are no longer necessary can suffer serious harm. In addition, some people who are not cured develop a crippling sense of guilt: they come to believe that, lacking sufficient faith for a healing, their illness is all their own fault.

It can often be very difficult to tell how effective a treatment is, whether it is orthodox or complementary. Many people have long-standing, recurring conditions (eg arthritis, eczema, migraine) whose symptoms wax and wane mysteriously. They may be affected by the person's psychological state, their diet and workload, chemicals they are in contact with, changes in the weather and other even less well-understood factors. When someone gets better, it is easy to attribute the improvement to whatever orthodox or complementary treatment was in use at the time, and to disregard other possible influences. There is also the 'placebo effect': in about a third of cases, something the person believes to be effective will produce an improvement in symptoms, whether or not the 'treatment' contains active ingredients. Placebos have their drawbacks, however: the improvement does not always happen and when it does, it does not last for long. Also, once a symptom has responded to the placebo 'medicine', the patient finds it difficult to accept a psychological element in the cause of the trouble; this can then interfere with effective psychological treatment. In any case, many doctors prefer to work in partnership with their patients, and think it is paternalistic and insulting to deceive a patient with a placebo.

As orthodox medicines are powerful for both good and harm, good scientific testing is needed to ensure that they are used well. Many people think complementary therapies should be tested in the same way: then they could be used if effective, or if useless, discarded.

Modern medicines, used properly, can be of great benefit to older people, but doctors and patients need to work together to achieve this. Good doctors like well-informed patients who take responsibility for their own health and treatment; you may like to suggest that your residents increase their confidence and competence with medicines by referring to the section on Medicines in *Keeping Well* (see Further Reading).

4 What to do in an Emergency

Forewarned is forearmed

This chapter summarises the action you should take when residents are taken ill or have accidents. However well prepared you may be in your own mind for something going wrong, you may be surprised by the strength of your feelings of alarm and distress when emergencies happen. A little knowledge will make you more effective and comfortable when working under this sort of stress.

Preparing yourself

A few simple preparations will help things run more smoothly in a crisis.

If you are a resident warden, make sure that your list of emergency telephone numbers and register of residents' personal details are readily accessible and up to date. Check that your deputy or relief is also able to use the information system quickly and efficiently when under pressure. Secondly, check on the contents of your first aid kit; ready-made ones may be incomplete, or may contain equipment that is too small to be of much practical use. Yours should include:

- Sharp scissors for trimming dressings, strong enough to cut through clothing if necessary.
- Packets of non-adherent sterile gauze wound dressings, 10cm (4in) square (eg Melolin).
- Cleanser such as surgical spirit or cetrimide.
- Clean gauze and cotton wool, for extra absorbency around sterile dressings or for padding.

- Sterile cotton wool in small packets for cleaning wounds.
- Sticking plaster and Micropore tape for securing dressings.
- Adhesive plaster dressing strip (plaster with attached lintstrip); this may be cut to size to dress small wounds.
- Incontinence pads; the need for at least one of these may arise unexpectedly, as when a patient suffers a stroke. They are also useful in a variety of messy situations, and may be placed beneath the head of someone who is vomiting or under a bleeding wound.
- Crepe bandages about 10 cm (4 in) wide – at least two. These are used for support bandaging of sprains and strains, for securing dressings and steadying injured limbs until help arrives.
- Tweezers or forceps for removing splinters.
- Safety pins.

If you are a mobile warden, as well as the worrying situation you will perhaps have the added strain of not knowing well the person or area you are visiting. Make sure that someone else knows your exact whereabouts; this is especially important when visiting people who may be confused and aggressive and when working in inner city areas.

Learning to recognise and treat illnesses and injuries takes doctors many years of study and experience; wardens who have their own jobs to do are not expected to display high-powered medical skills as well as all their other talents. When a decision about an accident or illness needs to be made, it is wise to get qualified help whenever you feel unsure of what to do. As well as reading this chapter, it would also be wise for you to attend a recognised first aid course, as first aid techniques cannot be learned from books.

Taking charge

When you are forced to take charge in a medical emergency, try to appear calm and reassuring, however you are feeling inside. Calmness does tend to seep inwards, until you actually feel as self-controlled as you appear. The sick or injured resident will then feel less anxious, and bystanders will be more likely to behave sensibly and helpfully and not get in the way. Stop for a moment, take stock and plan ahead. In the case of an accident, your first priority is to make sure that no one else –

including yourself – is in danger. For instance, if a resident is knocked down by a car outside the scheme, prevent a second accident by making sure that traffic and would-be helpers are kept apart.

Next, review your sources of help: residents with nursing experience may be able to help you care for the casualty, while others could be asked to watch out for the ambulance and to prevent other residents from 'happening' on the scene of the accident.

Getting professional help

In the case of severe illness or accident, a resident warden should call the affected person's doctor and/or the ambulance as soon as the patient's most urgent needs have been attended to – that is, you have made sure that the breathing is not obstructed, that bleeding is controlled and that broken bones have been immobilised.

When phoning the GP, say who you are, the telephone number you are ringing from and give a full address. This is essential; though residents may know the scheme as 'Churchill Court, Cedar Street, New Town', the doctor may have '286 Cedar Street' on the medical records. Vital time is wasted when emergency services have to search for an inadequately described or poorly signposted housing scheme. Give the name of the resident, with the flat or bungalow number and a brief account of what is wrong – for instance, 'We found Mrs Jones on the floor unconscious and she's breathing very noisily'.

Difficulties may arise outside normal working hours, when the doctor's calls may be referred to another doctor or to an answering service. If you have to leave a message about an emergency with a deputy, find out how long it will take to reach the doctor.

Though the best policy in an emergency is to call the person's GP first, you should call the ambulance if:

- the person is very ill and there is no time to lose;
- hospital attention will obviously be needed eventually – eg when a broken bone is suspected;
- if the doctor or a deputy suggests this should be done, perhaps because he or she cannot reach you quickly.

Do not call an ambulance without careful thought. To be jolted around, examined by strangers in an emergency department and then jolted home again, often after a considerable delay, is not a pleasant experience for an older person.

When dialling 999, there may be a delay at busy times before the head-quarters answers. You will first be asked which service you require and will be put through to ambulance control. The controller will ask at once for your telephone number, so that if you are cut off by mistake, you can be reached again. As when telephoning the doctor, you must give the name of the injured or ill person, an exact address and an explanation of what has happened. If you suspect a heart attack, say so, as an ambulance with special equipment may be available. Do not put the phone down until the person taking the emergency call has all the information needed.

Pitfalls to be avoided

It is easy to make mistakes when under the stress of an emergency, so here are some reminders:

- Check that the sick or injured person's airway is open; unconscious people are safest in the recovery position (p 137).

- Don't try to give a drink to someone who is unconscious, as it may drown them, or to someone who may need an anaesthetic shortly. A person with a broken arm who has been given a cup of tea may have to wait in pain for several hours while their stomach empties before the arm can be set.

- Don't use a tourniquet above a wound, as it may worsen the bleeding and endanger the healthy parts of the limb.

- Don't attempt cardiac massage unless you are sure the heart has stopped.

- Don't attempt to move someone who is too badly hurt or unwell to get up alone, except to maintain the airway: serious damage may be done if the person's neck, back or limb bones are broken. If he or she must be moved away from further immediate danger, get another helper to steady the head and back during the transfer, and try to immobilise injured limbs as well as possible. You will be taught techniques for this at a first aid course.

- Don't use hot water bottles to try to warm up someone who is unconscious or who is suffering from shock; this may cause burns and will also draw the blood supply away from vital organs to the skin.

- Don't put yourself at risk, for instance, by entering a smoke-filled room, touching an electrocuted person without turning off the current or by attempting heavy lifting without adequate help.

Being prepared in a control centre

Some mobile wardens also take emergency calls for some of the time. You can prepare yourself for this by gathering your papers in order beforehand and making sure everything you are likely to need is nearby. When a call comes in, expect to feel tense. These feelings can show in your voice and be transmitted to the caller. Anxiety makes most of us sound like a tape recorder playing a little too fast; you can avoid this by speaking a little slower than usual, and consciously lowering the pitch of your voice.

Having reassured the caller, do not be panicked into unwise action. There is always time to stop and think, and you may find it useful to take a few deep breaths while you consider what to do next. If you are calling out an emergency service or doctor, get the reason for the call clear in your mind: a clear description of what is going on will help the people on the other end of the phone to make their own preparations, such as packing the right equipment. Make sure that you give adequate information: who the patient is and exactly where they are. Finding a patient at night is easier if someone at home can switch on the lights at the front of the building.

AN ABC OF EMERGENCIES

This section summarises the action you should take in the emergencies you are most likely to come across in a sheltered housing setting. The conditions are arranged in alphabetical order.

Abdominal pain

See also 'Diarrhoea and vomiting', page 125.

This is a common complaint in older people. Mild constipation or indigestion can be the cause, but sometimes the situation is more serious. Even quite mild attacks of diarrhoea and vomiting can lead to salt and water depletion and to illness and disability in frail people. Constipation that can cause abdominal pain merits advice on how it can be treated and prevented.

Remember also that, as with many other conditions in older people, symptoms of severe abdominal illness tend to be less acute than in younger people. This can sometimes produce a false sense of security. You should therefore make sure the doctor is called to a person complaining of abdominal pain unless:

- the pain is mild and passes off within half an hour or so;
- the person has previously been investigated and treated for abdominal pain, and is having one of the usual attacks.

In the early stages of abdominal illness, it is often difficult for the doctor to tell exactly what is wrong. A return visit may be necessary to reassess the resident and find out how the condition has developed. During the gap between visits you should notify the doctor if the resident gets worse; it may be useful to ask the doctor whether there are any special signs you should look for.

SUMMARY
Call the doctor to anyone with abdominal pain, except when the episode is trivial and short lived.

Bites

Animal bites that break the skin carry germs that may cause infection. The resident will need to see a doctor for the wound to be cleaned properly and to make sure that tetanus protection is up to date. While waiting for the doctor, clean the wound with soap and water, and control bleeding by applying direct pressure and raising the part that is bleeding above the level of the heart. If the wound is extensive or the resident's condition is otherwise worrying, call an ambulance without further delay. Human bites that break the skin should be treated in the same way.

SUMMARY
Skilled cleaning, wound closure and tetanus protection may be needed.

Call for help; clean the wound and control bleeding till help arrives.

Bleeding

See also 'Cuts, grazes and puncture wounds', page 123.

Nose bleeds

The person with a nose bleed should sit in a chair and bend forward over a bowl to catch the blood dripping from the nose. Tell them to pinch the nostril on the affected side, to breathe through the mouth and to maintain the pressure for at least ten minutes. If the patient gets tired, a helper should take over 'pinching duty'. Any blood in the mouth should be spat out, as it may cause vomiting if it is swallowed. After ten minutes the pressure can be released, but if bleeding has not stopped, pinching should be continued for a further ten minutes. If bleeding has not stopped after a third period of pinching, call the doctor or an ambulance.

SUMMARY

Try to control bleeding by nostril pressure. If this does not work, call for help.

Gums

This problem can occur after a tooth extraction or following an injury to the mouth. As for a nose bleed, the patient should sit forward holding a bowl to catch any blood dripping from the mouth. Get them to put a pad of clean gauze on but not in the tooth socket. This should be thick enough to squash the blood vessels in the gums when bitten on. The pad should not touch the socket, or it will pull the blood clot away when it is removed, and bleeding will restart.

Once the pad is in place, pressure should be maintained for ten minutes. Then gently remove the gauze, but if the bleeding has not stopped reapply the pressure for another ten minutes. If bleeding persists, ring the dentist or the GP.

SUMMARY

Control bleeding by gum pressure. If this does not work, call for help.

Varicose veins

An ambulance should be called, because the patient will need hospital attention. In the meantime, ask the resident to lie down, raise the leg and prop it up on a pile of books or a stool. Remove any tight clothing such as garters, support hose or girdles which could act as tourniquets and make bleeding worse. Cover the bleeding point with a pad of gauze secured with adhesive tape or bandage.

SUMMARY

Call an ambulance.

While waiting, keep the resident lying down with the leg raised; control bleeding by pressure on the bleeding point.

Blisters

These form on an area of skin that has been burned or been rubbed, for example by a shoe; the top layer of skin becomes separated from those underneath by fluid. If blisters are left alone, the top skin layer forms a natural, sterile dressing while healing goes on underneath. Eventually a new layer of skin forms on the raw area and the fluid is re-absorbed. Blisters should never be pricked, as this lets germs in. If padding is necessary to protect blisters from further injury, the covering should extend beyond the blistered area.

SUMMARY

Do not prick or burst blisters. Apply padding for comfort if necessary.

Bruises

A bruise happens when blood vessels are damaged and leak into the surrounding tissues. Placing a cold compress on a bruise will make the blood vessels contract and reduce swelling. (See under 'Stings', p 135, for how to make a cold compress.)

Occasionally bruising may conceal a more serious injury such as a broken bone or damage to internal organs, or the blood loss into the bruise may be sufficient to make the person feel faint and ill. If you think either of these things may have happened, or if the bruise is on the head, call the doctor.

SUMMARY

Apply a cold compress to minor bruises.

Seek skilled help:

- if the bruise may overlie a serious injury;
- if the person seems unwell;
- if the bruise is on the head.

Burns and scalds

Severe

A burn or scald is severe:

- if the burned area is more than an inch (2.5 cm) square;
- if it goes deeper than the outer layer of skin;
- if the burn was caused by electricity;
- if the burned person seems unwell or is very frail.

When someone has been scalded, immerse the affected area in cold water and remove soaked clothing when it is cool enough to handle. Then send for a doctor or ambulance at once.

If a resident's clothes catch fire, douse the flames with water or lie the person down and smother the flames by wrapping tightly in a coat or blanket. Do not roll the resident over and over, as this may burn previously undamaged areas. When the flames are out, soak all layers thoroughly so that smouldering clothing does not continue to burn the skin.

While waiting for help, cover any exposed burnt skin with clean, smooth fabric such as a sheet or pillowcase, but otherwise leave the burnt areas alone. If the sufferer feels cold, add a layer of blankets. Give only small sips of water or ice to suck for thirst, as larger amounts may cause vomiting and will delay treatment under anaesthetic.

SUMMARY

Cool and remove clothing soaked in boiling liquid.

Douse flames with water or blankets.

Call the doctor or ambulance.

Leave the burned area alone.

Minor

These can be treated at home. Cool the burnt skin at once with plenty of cold water, either by holding it under a running tap or by plunging it into a basin or bath. If water is not immediately available, use another clean liquid such as beer or milk. Remove the victim's rings, watches and tight clothing from around the affected area before it starts to swell.

Small burns should be left open to the air if possible. Clear fluid will ooze from the burnt area and dry to form a germ-proof dressing which should not be disturbed. If a protective covering must be put on to prevent clothes rubbing, use non-adherent gauze. Do not apply any proprietary lotions or creams, butter or bicarbonate of soda to a burn without first getting medical advice.

SUMMARY

Cool with plenty of cold water.

Leave open to the air if possible.

Apply nothing to burnt areas without medical advice.

Chemical burns

Burns caused by chemicals such as caustic soda or bleach should be thoroughly rinsed under a running tap for about ten minutes. Remove contaminated clothing without letting it touch undamaged skin.

SUMMARY

Rinse well under running tap.

Care is needed if chemicals are left on clothing – do not contaminate the resident or yourself.

Chest pain and heart attacks

Chest pain can have a minor cause such as a muscular strain, but it may be a sign of more serious heart or lung disease. Except in the most trivial episodes, call the sufferer's doctor.

Angina

This is a tight, squeezing chest pain which may extend from behind the breast bone into the throat or down the arms. First get the person with angina pain to sit down. He or she should take one glyceryl trinitrate (GTN) tablet or use a GTN spray, if these have been prescribed; the directions for use should be followed carefully. If the pain is not relieved in ten minutes, they should take another tablet or more spray. If the resident is not better within ten minutes of the second dose, call the doctor or the ambulance.

During the 20-minute period when the medicine is supposed to be working, call the doctor or ambulance:

- if the pain becomes very severe;
- if the person becomes short of breath;
- if the person starts to lose consciousness.

If angina attacks occur frequently, the resident should see the doctor in case the drug therapy needs adjusting or more investigations need to be done.

Heart attack

A heart attack in a young or middle-aged person produces crushing central chest pain, similar to the pain of angina but usually occurring during rest rather than during exercise. The person becomes pale, sweats and may vomit. If damage to the heart is severe, they may become rapidly unconscious and even die.

An older person who is having a heart attack may show the same symptoms, but in many cases will not. They may have no pain, but instead may become confused, develop the signs of a stroke, become short of breath, faint or have an epileptic fit. If these things happen, you should summon medical aid urgently.

Until the doctor or ambulance arrives, stay with the resident, give reassurance and make them as comfortable as possible in a sitting position, either in a chair or propped up on pillows in bed. If they become unconscious and no pulse can be felt, it is likely that the heart has stopped beating. If this happens – and only if you know how to do it properly – start mouth-to-mouth respiration and cardiac massage.

Pleurisy

This happens when a chest infection spreads to the membrane covering the lung. The pain will be sharp, stabbing and worse when breathing in. Call the doctor.

SUMMARY

Call the doctor for all but the most trivial attacks.

While awaiting help, assist the resident to take medicines prescribed for angina.

If the resident collapses and has no pulse, consider starting resuscitation.

Choking

This happens when a small piece of food or vomit enters the windpipe. In mild cases the sufferer will be coughing but still able to breathe. Take control of the situation. Tell the person to take a deep breath slowly and cough as hard as possible. If two coughs do not clear the obstruction, remove any false teeth, insert your index finger and attempt to dislodge the obstruction. It may also help the person to bend forward across your supporting arm with the head below waist level, while someone gives sharp slaps with a hand between the shoulder blades.

In more severe cases of choking the person may be unable to breathe and will become blue in the face. Get behind the resident and put your arms around them with one fist pressed into the stomach. Grasp your fist with your other hand and pull suddenly inward and upward. The force of the air being expelled from the lungs is usually enough to dislodge the obstruction from the windpipe, and the blockage will shoot out of the mouth. This technique, called the Heimlich manoeuvre, should be learned by attending a first aid class.

SUMMARY

Mild cases

Encourage coughing.

Remove the blockage by hand.

Bang between the resident's shoulder blades while they lean forward.

Severe cases

Use the Heimlich manoeuvre, described above.

Cramp

To relieve the pain of cramp, stretch the contracted and painful muscle until the contraction passes off. Cramped toes, for instance, will need to be uncurled and held straight, with the palm of the hand beneath the sole of the foot. Alternatively, get the person to stand one pace from the wall, put their hands on the wall and stand on the toes. If the cramp recurs, repeat the manoeuvre. If residents are much troubled by cramp, they should consult the doctor, as drug therapy is sometimes helpful.

SUMMARY

Stretch the painful muscle.

For recurrent cramp, consult the doctor.

Cuts, grazes and puncture wounds

A sharp knife causes a clean cut, whilst irregular objects tear the skin. A graze occurs when the superficial layers of the skin are scraped away, leaving a raw area which may be dirty. A puncture wound happens when a sharp pointed object such as a nail breaks the skin. Such injuries may have serious consequences if they are deep enough to damage internal organs or if the wound is dirty, as tetanus germs grow easily in the deeper layers of tissue.

Severe

Call the doctor or ambulance. In the meantime do not remove any object that is stuck in the wound, as it may be acting as a plug and reducing bleeding. Try to control the blood flow by pressing on the wound through a pad of clean material, or on the area around any object protruding from it. Help the person to lie down, and raise and support the injured part.

Minor

These can usually be treated by the injured resident – if necessary, with your help. After washing your hands and the area surrounding the wound with soap and water, the wound should be cleaned either by rinsing under the tap or by wiping with clean, wet swabs. Remember to wipe from within the wound outwards, and use a new swab for each stroke. If a blood clot has already formed, it should not be removed, or bleeding may start again. After cleaning, the wound area should be patted dry, and a small plaster and gauze or ready-made dressing applied.

A graze or cut that bleeds little and is not in an area where it will be rubbed by clothing is better left exposed to the air. If a dressing is necessary, it should be removed after a few hours or on the following day, when the bleeding has stopped. Check whether the resident needs a tetanus injection, and encourage them to see the doctor if tetanus protection is not up to date or if there is doubt about this.

If a wound becomes more painful, swollen and red, pus oozes from it or red lines or swollen glands are found nearby, it has become infected, and the doctor should be notified.

SUMMARY

Severe cases

Call the doctor or ambulance.

Press to control the bleeding.

Do not remove protruding objects.

Minor cases

Clean the wound with soap and water.

Apply a dressing if necessary till the wound is dry; then leave open.

Encourage a check on tetanus protection.

Diabetic emergencies

If someone with diabetes takes too much insulin, too many tablets or misses a meal, the blood sugar falls and they become hypoglycaemic. People with diabetes call this reaction a 'hypo'. The hypo sufferer feels faint, dizzy and confused, and sometimes irritable and aggressive. Because of these mental changes, they are often unable to take sensible action without help. They urgently need sugar, which you should give in the form of sugar lumps, sweets, glucose tablets or a heavily sweetened drink (a small bottle of Lucozade in the fridge is a useful standby). If the hypo is not quickly corrected, the diabetic will become unconscious. If this happens, do not try any longer to give sugar by mouth, but call the doctor or ambulance without delay.

Someone with diabetes may become drowsy and confused for other reasons than having a 'hypo'. However, giving sugar to such a person will in any case do no harm. If it does not produce a rapid improvement, call an ambulance at once.

SUMMARY

A diabetic with 'hypo' signs needs sugar urgently: watch for faintness, confusion, irritability and aggression.

Rapid recovery is usual; if it does not occur, call an ambulance.

Diarrhoea and vomiting

An older person with a 'tummy upset' should eat nothing and drink only clear fluids – not milk – until symptoms have subsided. It is probably advisable for the resident to stay indoors, and to rest in bed if they feel weak or sleepy. A light diet should be started cautiously with dry foods such as salty crackers, working gradually up to a normal diet.

The doctor should be called if diarrhoea and vomiting persist for more than 12 hours, or if the person develops abdominal pain or otherwise seems seriously unwell. A frail older person should see the doctor sooner as they may become seriously ill from fluid loss and need careful replacement of fluids (rehydration). Tummy upsets may take residents 'off their legs'; if this lasts for more than a few days, call the doctor.

SUMMARY

Clear fluids at first, then gradual return to normal eating habits.

Call the doctor if:

- symptoms persist for more than 12 hours;
- the resident is frail;
- abdominal pain develops;
- the resident is not soon back to normal.

Epilepsy

See 'Fits' (p 128).

Eye emergencies

Serious diseases

The symptoms of these include:

- sudden complete loss of vision;

- disturbances of the field of vision, such as the sensation of a curtain closing across it or of seeing black patches or 'floaters' in it;
- seeing flashes of light or coloured haloes around objects;
- pain and redness of the eye.

These require an urgent expert opinion, ideally from the emergency department of an eye hospital.

Major accidents

When a resident's eye is injured, for instance by a sharp object or a burning spark, call the ambulance. While waiting for help, ask the resident to close the injured eye; then cover it with a pad of clean gauze, secured with a bandage or adhesive tape. Tell them to shut the good eye too because if it moves the damaged eye will follow it. The resident will now be unable to see, so they must be guided if moving about.

Chemicals in the eye

Call the ambulance. While waiting for it, try to wash the chemical away by holding the person's face under a gently running tap, or by pouring water from a jug. Do not allow the contaminated water to run over the person's face. Once the eye has been fully rinsed, wipe it with a clean gauze pad.

Minor accidents

Particles of grit or an eyelash may stick to the eyeball or lodge within the lower lid. They are easiest to remove with a damp wisp of cotton wool or tissue, moulded to a point, and by working towards the inside corner of the eye. If this procedure is not rapidly successful, the eye should be covered with an eyepad or square of clean gauze and the person sent to the doctor or the hospital. Skilled help will also be necessary when an object becomes embedded in the eyeball or when it overlies its central part, the black pupil and the coloured area surrounding it; do not attempt to remove these yourself.

SUMMARY

Urgent expert help is needed if a resident:

- has lost the whole or a part of the field of vision;
- sees black patches, haloes, 'floaters' or flashes of light;

- has a painful, red eye;
- has been injured by a sharp object, a spark or a chemical in the eye.

Small objects in the eye can be removed with damp tissue if they lie over the white of the eye. If this is difficult, seek expert help.

Fainting

This is a sign that, for a short time, insufficient blood has been reaching the brain. It usually happens to someone who has been standing still for a long time, especially in warm surroundings. People who faint crumple gently to the ground, but 'fall soft' and are usually little hurt. They will appear very pale and will have a slow, weak pulse. They should be left lying down, as this will help to get the blood back into the brain. It is also useful to raise the legs and rest them on a stool or other suitable object. Loosen tight clothing at the neck or waist and allow them plenty of fresh air. Call the doctor if they are not soon better.

It is wise to keep a discreet eye on an older person who faints for a few days afterwards. Occasionally a faint can be a sign of illness; if you are concerned, consider calling the doctor.

SUMMARY

Leave the affected person lying down and raise the legs to restore blood flow to the brain.

Call the doctor if recovery is not rapid.

Falls

If you find someone on the floor unconscious, you should summon help at once, and in the meantime care for them as described on page 137. If the resident has been lying for some time in cold surroundings, care for hypothermia may also be needed (see p 132).

Someone who has fallen may not be seriously hurt but simply be unable to get up. Never attempt to lift someone by yourself as you may injure your back in the process. If there is no one else strong enough to help you in the scheme, you should call the ambulance.

Provided the person who has fallen can roll to a chair, you may be able to get them up unaided in stages, with rests in between. The resident should first get the stronger elbow into the seat of the chair; then, by putting the other elbow on the chair as well, they can pull up into a kneeling position. Then, by transferring weight to the strongest foot, they can get up to the level of the seat, twist round and sit down.

SUMMARY

Do not lift alone.

Help fallen residents to roll to a chair and get up in stages.

If the resident is unconscious, injured or cold, refer to the relevant sections of this book for further advice.

Fits (epilepsy)

This condition may start in childhood and persist into adult life, or begin at any age. Fits often follow a pattern. At the onset people may experience an 'aura', which is a feeling that a fit is about to occur. After this they will become unconscious and fall, sometimes crying out. They then go rigid and may stop breathing, becoming blue in the face. After this, their limbs will jerk, their breathing will become noisy and they may froth at the mouth. As this stage passes off, the muscles relax, breathing quietens and they gradually return to normal, though they are likely to be sleepy and confused for several hours.

If you are present at the beginning of an attack, try to break the person's fall and then put something soft under their head. Loosen any tight clothing and keep the airway clear by rolling the person onto their side and pulling the jaw forward. Do not try to put anything into the mouth, or to restrain involuntary movements.

If this is the person's first fit – as far as you know – call the ambulance as soon as possible. This may not be necessary for residents you know to have fits, provided they recover rapidly and completely. However, you should suggest that they let the GP know about the episode, as a change in treatment may be necessary to prevent a recurrence. Even people known to have epilepsy require urgent treatment if several fits happen one after the other, if they are injured during a fit or if they are slow to recover consciousness. People with epilepsy are well advised to wear a locket or bracelet giving details of their condition and medication. These are available from the Medic-Alert Foundation.

SUMMARY

Try to reduce harm by:

- breaking the person's fall;
- protecting the head;
- keeping the airway clear.

Call the doctor for:

- a resident's first fit;
- fits that occur one after the other;
- a resident who is injured or slow to come round after a fit.

Fractures (broken bones)

Old bones are fragile and brittle, and may break under an impact that would leave younger bones undamaged. Confused older people may not appear to suffer much pain from a fracture. It is therefore important to be suspicious that bones may have been broken even when injury seems comparatively trivial, and to seek medical aid accordingly.

Signs to look for

When a bone has been broken, the person may have heard or felt it snap. The affected bone will usually be painful and tender to touch, and it is usually difficult or impossible for the person to move the injured limb. This may be distorted into an unnatural position, and may also be swollen and discoloured by bruising. Moving it may produce a grating noise as the broken bone ends grind across each other. Try to prevent this from happening, as soft tissues around the broken bone may be damaged.

Fracture of the femur (thigh bone) is a common injury in older people, especially women. The person who suffers it is almost always unable to get up from the floor. The affected leg may look shorter than the normal one, and be lying with the toe pointing outwards, away from the other leg.

What to do

All suspected fractures need prompt medical attention, so call the doctor or ambulance. While waiting for help, remember that, in a serious accident, breathing difficulties and severe bleeding take precedence over broken bones – otherwise the end result may be a perfectly splinted corpse!

Do not move the casualty before medical help arrives unless they are in immediate danger. If you must move him or her, immobilise the broken bone by splinting. Ambulance staff are expert at this, so you need not be concerned with it except when you cannot get emergency help right away. Whatever object is available should then be used – for example, a board, a walking stick, a broom handle or rolled up newspaper. It should be firmly padded to prevent further injury. The splint needs to be applied so as to immobilise the joints above and below the broken bone, so that the bone ends cannot move about. For instance, with a break in the lower leg, the knee and ankle must be steadied.

Control bleeding from an open fracture by direct pressure on the wound, without displacing the protruding bone. If the casualty does not need to be moved, you can apply a sterile gauze dressing lightly over the wound, but do not interfere with it further. If movement is absolutely necessary, pad the bone ends with sterile gauze and support them to prevent pressure, movement and tissue damage from the sharp ends.

SUMMARY

Remember that old bones break easily, and call for help if suspicious.

Make sure that the airway is clear.

Control any bleeding.

Do not move the casualty unless absolutely necessary.

When movement is unavoidable, splint the break and pad the jagged ends of bone.

Headaches

These are very common and usually not serious. Suggest that the resident crushes two tablets of paracetamol before taking them with a good draught of water, or takes their preferred headache remedy according to the directions on the packet or bottle. The resident should then rest in a place with subdued lighting until the pain passes off. If the headache persists, or if the resident seems otherwise unwell (eg is confused or vomiting, finds light uncomfortable, or when the scalp is tender to touch), call the doctor.

SUMMARY

Suggest household remedies for mild headaches.

Call the doctor if pain persists or the resident seems generally unwell.

Head injuries

All but the most trivial bangs to the head require expert medical attention. Someone who has been knocked unconscious, even for a short time, may need to be admitted to hospital for observation. If you think the resident may have been unconscious, the doctor must be called, even though the person seems quite well at present.

A scalp wound will bleed very freely and this may be alarming. Try to remember that, because of the good blood supply to the scalp, the wound will also heal rapidly and well. While waiting for the doctor or ambulance, bleeding can be controlled by applying pressure to the wound. If underlying bone damage is suspected and this causes pain, press either side of the wound. If the person becomes unconscious, follow the guidelines on page 137.

SUMMARY

Call the doctor to all but the most trivial cases; residents who have been knocked unconscious must see a doctor.

Press to control bleeding from scalp wounds.

Hypothermia

This medical emergency can occur in sheltered housing if the heating fails or is turned off, or if a resident becomes ill.

In hypothermia the deep body temperature falls below 95°F or 35°C, measured with a low-reading thermometer; temperature readings taken with an ordinary clinical thermometer may be misleading. Normal body temperature fluctuates around 98.4°F (37°C). In someone with hypothermia, a covered part of the body such as the armpit or abdomen may feel cold to the touch. The colder people are, the less likely they are to be fully conscious. Many people become hypothermic because of injury or illness, and this may add to the dangers of the situation.

Hypothermic people need urgent medical attention, so you should call the doctor or ambulance. While waiting for help, the room should be warmed and the resident 'insulated' to keep in body heat. Wrap them in a 'space' blanket if you have one; if not, aluminium cooking foil makes a good substitute. They should then be 'over-wrapped' with blankets or whatever else is available, not forgetting the head and hands. Keep them lying down. Avoid putting hot water bottles round them; these may cause the skin blood vessels to open up suddenly and release a rush of cold blood, which could impair the heart beat. There is also the risk of burns. Do not give a hot drink to anyone who might need an anaesthetic.

SUMMARY

Remember the risk of hypothermia.

Call the doctor or ambulance to affected residents.

Warm the room and wrap up the resident to conserve their heat.

Avoid hot water bottles; be cautious with hot drinks.

Poisoning

This is sometimes accidental but may be deliberate (see 'Overdoses and suicide attempts', p 133). Do not waste time trying to decide which; instead, call the doctor or ambulance at once. While waiting for help, care for unconscious residents as described on page 137. Ask conscious residents what happened, so that if possible the poisonous substance can be identified and the container sent with them to the hospital. Someone should stay with poisoned residents all the time until help arrives, and should be ready to start resuscitation. It is unwise to try to make people who have been poisoned vomit.

SUMMARY

Call the doctor or ambulance.

Stay with the resident and be prepared to resuscitate.

Do not induce vomiting.

Send the poisonous substance to hospital with the person if possible.

Psychiatric emergencies

Overdoses and suicide attempts

If you believe an overdose to be deliberate, you must take the situation seriously. Unsuccessful suicide attempts are often later repeated and may then prove fatal. Call the doctor or ambulance and, while waiting for help, care for the resident as described under 'Poisoning' (p 132).

Acute confusion

Someone who becomes suddenly confused needs urgent medical attention. Call the doctor, stay with the confused resident and try to reassure them until help arrives.

Aggression

Some confused people may become violent. You should be aware of the risk of this, especially with people who have been aggressive in the past, or who abuse alcohol or drugs. Good management can often prevent outright violence and defuse the situation. Here are some suggestions as to how to cope:

- Make sure your whereabouts are known to others before you visit someone who may be aggressive.

- Keep your distance, and do not crowd the person.

- Do not be the first to touch: your would-be reassuring arm round the shoulders may seem like an assault to the confused person, who may hit back.

- Remember that the confused person is probably more frightened than you are. Try to appear calm and in control, acting neither in a threatening way nor as a nervous victim.

- Keep talking in a calm but firm voice. Avoid arguments and confrontation; distract attention from a touchy subject by talking about something else. Do not talk down to the confused person, but allow them to 'save face'.

- Watch for warning signs of approaching violence such as restlessness, pacing up and down, fist clenching, faster breathing, destroying objects or looking for weapons.

- Keep your escape route open behind you, and if violence is imminent, leave at once.

Aggressive, noisy and disruptive behaviour can be very disturbing to other residents in a sheltered housing scheme. Every attempt should be made to treat the underlying problem or to modify the difficult behaviour in the first instance. When these measures are unsuccessful, a move to more suitable accommodation may seem the only alternative; if this situation arises in your scheme, you may like to refer to the section on 'Moving in and moving on' (p 185).

SUMMARY

Call the doctor to people who become suddenly confused.

Remember the risk of aggression; reduce risk by using the guidelines above.

Splinters

When a small bit of wood or metal gets stuck in the skin, wash the area around it with soap and water. You can remove the splinter using forceps that you have first sterilised in a flame or cleaned with disinfectant. Pull in the opposite direction from the way the splinter went into the skin. If the splinter does not come out easily or starts to break up, you will need medical help. An anti-tetanus injection may be necessary if the splinter was introduced from an object out of doors.

SUMMARY

Clean the skin; remove the splinter with clean forceps.

Check whether an anti-tetanus injection is needed.

Stings

Severe

A sting can be serious if it is inside the mouth, as can happen if someone bites an apple with a wasp sitting on it. Stings are also dangerous in a person who is allergic to them, or if someone is stung by a great many insects at once – for instance, when clearing a wasps' nest. In these situations, call an ambulance at once. In the meantime do not leave the victim alone, watch them carefully in case breathing or circulation deteriorate, and give ice to suck to reduce swelling inside the mouth.

Minor

These are frightening rather than dangerous. Treatment will depend on the type of insect responsible. Bees leave a small sting embedded in the skin; this can be removed with a pair of tweezers held as close to the skin as possible. Avoid squeezing the sac at the top of the sting because this will force more poison into the skin. A wasp injects its irritant directly, as with a syringe and needle, withdrawing afterwards; you may be able to wipe away some of the venom from the surface of the skin.

Treatment

With both sorts of stings it may help to swab the skin with weak bicarbonate (baking soda) in water, and to apply a cold compress or icepack to reduce swelling. You can make a cold compress by soaking some absorbent cloth such as old towelling in iced water and then wringing it out until it is wet but not dripping. Then wrap the absorbent cloth in another cloth such as a tea towel and apply it to the affected part. Alternatively, you can make an icepack by putting ice cubes in a plastic bag and sucking the air out with a drinking straw. A packet of frozen peas also makes a good icepack.

A certain amount of pain and swelling are to be expected on the day when a sting occurs and for about 24 hours after. If the patient is frail or becomes unwell, the doctor should be notified.

SUMMARY

Severe stings (sting in mouth, allergy to stings, many stings)

Call the doctor or ambulance.

Stay with the resident until help arrives.

Mild stings

Remove the bee sting.

Swab away wasp venom.

Apply cold compress or ice.

Stroke

The usual signs of a stroke are the development of paralysis of the limbs and face on one side of the body, with slurring of speech and dribbling of saliva from the corner of the mouth. Stroke sufferers may also wet or soil themselves because of loss of control of the bladder and bowels.

Severe

The most severe cases of stroke prove fatal, and you may find the resident unconscious or already dead. Note the time and send for the doctor or ambulance without delay. Until help arrives, follow the instructions about unconsciousness on page 137.

Less severe

The patient may be found in bed one morning, unable to get up because of partial paralysis. Alternatively, sufferers may be confused and unsteady on their feet and have slurred speech. After examining the resident and verifying that a stroke has occurred, the doctor will usually admit them to hospital.

Transient ischaemic attacks (TIAs)

These produce stroke symptoms which disappear within 24 hours. The doctor must be told about these, as prompt treatment may prevent a later complete stroke from occurring.

SUMMARY

Call the doctor or ambulance.

If the resident is unconscious, follow the plan on page 137.

Sunburn

You should take the affected person to a cool place and give them plenty of water to drink, while sponging the burnt area gently with cold water. In severe cases, call the doctor.

SUMMARY

Cool surroundings, water to drink and cold sponging help.

Call the doctor to severe cases.

Unconsciousness

Anyone who has lost consciousness and does not rapidly regain it is severely ill, and you should call the doctor or ambulance at once. While waiting for help to arrive, the most important thing is to make sure that the resident is breathing normally. Put them in the recovery position, lying prone on the stomach with one arm and leg bent in support, and facing towards the side of the bent limbs. This position makes the jaw and tongue fall forward, keeping the airway open, and allows vomit or secretions to drain out of the mouth.

Someone should remain with the unconscious person all the time until medical help arrives, and should be prepared to start resuscitation if necessary. Control any bleeding, and cover the person with a blanket to keep them warm and prevent hypothermia. Never give an unconscious person anything by mouth; they will be unable to swallow it and may drown. If the person recovers consciousness while waiting, reassure them and allow them to rest until help arrives.

You can help the doctor to find the cause of the condition and start the right treatment by giving information as to how the present incident happened, how long unconsciousness has lasted and what the person's previous health has been like. If they are taken directly into hospital and you do not accompany them, you should give a short written account of medical details to the ambulance staff, to be shown to the hospital doctor.

Common causes of unconsciousness include head injury, heart attacks, strokes, epilepsy and diabetes.

SUMMARY

Call the doctor or ambulance.

Place the resident in the recovery position and keep the airway open.

Be prepared to resuscitate if necessary.

Cover the resident to keep in warmth.

Provide useful information to the doctor or hospital.

Finding someone dead

When you find someone dead, notify the GP. While waiting for the doctor to come, do not move the body or interfere with its immediate surroundings. However, it may be wise to lock the doors and draw the curtains if this will prevent someone else from happening upon the scene and being disturbed by it. If the death has occurred in one of the communal rooms of the scheme, it may be advisable to station dependable people outside the entrance to prevent accidental shocks to other residents.

Once the doctor has seen the body and confirmed that death has occurred, they will advise on the next step. A doctor who is the resident's GP and has attended them in the last illness can sign the death certificate without further delay. If the doctor says that the coroner needs to be consulted first, this does not necessarily imply that there is anything suspicious about the death. Some sudden deaths must be referred to the coroner in this way – for instance, if the death follows an accident such as a fall, or could be connected with the person's past occupation. Usually the doctor will be able to give the certificate after talking with the coroner. Occasionally, the coroner will order a post-mortem examination to establish the cause of death, and on rare occasions an inquest will be necessary. If you do not understand what is going on with these complicated legal arrangements, be sure to ask, as this may save needless anxiety for you and the relatives. You may also like to refer to the section on bereavement (see p 197).

SUMMARY

Call the doctor.

Do not move the body.

Prevent others from coming on the scene unexpectedly.

LEARNING FROM AN EMERGENCY

Many wardens expect too much of themselves when accidents occur, and scourge themselves with guilt afterwards, but you should resist both these temptations. After the emergency, however, comes the time to take stock. There is a lot to be said for writing down a full account of what happened while it is still fresh in your mind. You should set it down 'just as it comes', including feelings and difficulties; grammar and spelling can be tidied up later. This account may be of practical use to scheme managers, or to the police or the coroner if, sadly, a fatal incident has occurred. Writing everything down will also help you to come to terms with your feelings of distress. Talking about the incident is also useful; another warden is the best person to listen, and you will be able to do the same for them on another occasion. You should be able to attend wardens' meetings from time to time, and can find a suitable person there.

Be kind to yourself after a bad experience, and do not try to be too 'wonderful'. However, the return to normal should not be too long delayed, as following an accustomed routine can be very comforting to the spirit. After a few days have passed it will be sensible to go over the incident again yourself, looking for avoidable factors. This should not be done with the intention of finding a culprit or scapegoat, but so as to try to prevent the trouble arising again or to reduce the severity of the consequences if it does. For instance, you may find that useful equipment needs to be replaced or repaired, that your deputy needs clearer instructions or that residents' understanding of fire precautions needs to be improved.

This has been literally a chapter of accidents, and, taken in at a single gulp, makes alarming reading. In most schemes such dramatic events will be infrequent, but if you are wise you will be prepared both practically and emotionally for them to happen. Knowing what to do when things go wrong is obviously of practical importance, and the confidence this knowledge brings gives a feeling of security that benefits wardens and residents alike.

5 When Older People become Frail

REASONS FOR INCREASED FRAILTY

Sheltered housing residents as a group are frailer than they used to be, and this trend is likely to continue for the foreseeable future. There are two main reasons for this. Firstly, the age group eligible for sheltered housing contains more very old people and fewer who have recently retired. Though many individuals are active and independent in their 80s and 90s, considered as groups people over 80 and especially people over 85 tend to be less able and to need more help than people in their 60s and 70s. Secondly, community care legislation makes it likely that frailer residents who would previously have moved on to residential care will remain in their own homes for longer, perhaps until they die. The care they need will then be provided in a sheltered housing setting.

How you can prepare yourself

Your role as warden is bound to change, though the way in which you work will vary according to local circumstances. You will need to know how the more common sorts of frailty come about and what can be done to minimise their effects. Armed with this knowledge, you will be able to advise and help residents who ask for your assistance and to deal with caring agencies on behalf of those who are unable or unwilling to do this for themselves.

RESIDENTS WITH A TENDENCY TO FALL

Older people often fall, and this gets more common with increasing age. Those who have done so in the past dread doing so again, and rightly so. Serious injuries such as fractures of the hip and wrist and head injuries can threaten independence and even life. What is more, some people are uninjured but unable to get up; lying helpless while waiting to be found is not only distressing but can also be dangerous, as pneumonia, dehydration or hypothermia can result. Sometimes people fall in a position where they are unable to reach an alarm cord or bell. Residents who fall may only then understand the importance of these cords being within reach from floor level rather than being looped out of the way or pushed behind large pieces of solid furniture.

Causes of falls

Falls can be classified as 'trips' or 'turns'; trips are due to factors outside the older person, and turns to abnormalities inside the body.

'Trips'

Trips are common in people under 80 who often lead active lives. They are due to hazards such as torn and rucked-up carpets, dainty rugs that slip on polished floors and trailing electrical flex. People with poor sight are especially liable to trip, and poor lighting may make things worse.

Trip hazards are easy to spot but, as with looped-up cords, may be difficult to correct. You should recognise that older people, like the rest of us, have the right to decide how to organise their homes; your responsibility is merely to point out where risks are being run, leaving the resident to decide whether or not to run them. Bullying is likely to be counterproductive; in fact, residents seem more likely to put things right if they feel that the decision has been left to them.

'Turns'

Several factors often act together to produce unsteadiness and falls. The balance mechanism and the ability to right oneself after a stumble both tend to deteriorate with increasing age, and these tendencies unfortunately cannot be put right. However, other contributory causes may be remediable if health can be improved. You should suggest to residents who fall frequently that they consult the doctor to see what can be done to help; they can also ask to be referred to a hospital geriatrician for specialist advice.

Anything that reduces the amount of oxygen-rich blood reaching the older person's brain will make them unsteady on their feet; simply getting up from bed or chair too quickly is one common cause. Medicines may make this worse: sleeping tablets and tranquillisers are common culprits, as are diuretics, and the unsteadiness may improve or even disappear if the tablets are stopped. Things are more difficult when residents' falls seem to be linked to the tablets they are taking to lower their high blood pressure: a separate decision has to be made in each case as to whether the falls or the high blood pressure are more dangerous. Untreated heart disease may contribute to falls when the heart is pumping inefficiently or beating irregularly; these problems can often be put right with either drug treatment or a pacemaker. Anaemia is another treatable cause of falls. Arthritis of the neck may compress blood vessels and reduce the brain's blood supply, but it may also block the information pathways informing the brain about neck bending and head position which help in maintaining an upright posture. People with arthritic neck vertebrae should avoid sudden, sharp neck movements, and when unsteadiness is a severe problem a well-fitting support collar may be useful.

Good medical investigation and appropriate treatment may get rid of the falls entirely or at any rate make them much less frequent. Persisting falls will be less hazardous if the affected resident will agree to use a body-worn trigger for an alarm system. This avoids the unpleasant consequences of lying on the floor for a long time before help arrives.

Over-protection is dangerous, too

Though falls are risky, over-protection also poses dangers. Residents who are unsteady on their feet may prefer to run the risks of falling in their own homes and to take the consequences, rather than to accept the restrictions of residential care, and of course they have every right to make this choice. However, if you believe a resident to be in danger, it is sensible to protect yourself from the risk of criticism by informing your managers; it may also be appropriate for you to discuss the situation with the resident's family. On the whole, it is worth remembering that we tend to over-emphasise the risks of older people staying active; in fact, the tedium and depression resulting from too little change, excitement and risk are far more dangerous to the quality of life.

THE RISK OF HYPOTHERMIA

Ageing affects temperature control

As the years pass, the body's 'thermostat' may become faulty. For physiological reasons outside their control, older people become less able to increase their body heat production in cold conditions and are also less able to notice that they are becoming cold. Once the body temperature starts to fall, the brain becomes sluggish, and normally capable and independent older people become less able to take charge and put things right in their usual sensible way. However, the well informed can plan ahead to protect themselves by using room thermometers and making sure that the room temperature does not fall below 68°F (20°C). As warden, you may be able to obtain such thermometers and encourage their use.

Health factors in hypothermia – who is at risk?

Some people's state of health increases their vulnerability in the cold. This may happen because their thinking abilities are impaired by illness or alcohol abuse, because they are too disabled to produce much body heat by muscular exercise or because they frequently fall and are unable to get up. With these groups of people in mind, it may help you to construct an 'at risk from hypothermia register' as a useful step in its prevention. This list would include people to be kept a close eye on whenever the weather turns cold because they are mentally frail, have a tendency to fall, or are housebound and immobile because of arthritis or a stroke. Residents who drink heavily or those with flats or rooms that 'strike cold' are also at increased risk. Take note of someone who may have come into sheltered housing because of a previous hypothermic episode and find out the circumstances of that incident; this may help you to prevent it from happening again.

Helping residents to keep themselves warm

Encourage residents to keep one room in their flat or bungalow warm during the worst of winter weather, with a bed sited against an inside wall and supplied with enough blankets. Blankets may wear thin and need to be replaced; in an emergency, sheets of newspaper can be placed between blanket layers to provide helpful insulation. Try to persuade residents to raise the bedroom temperature above Arctic levels, by reminding them that cold air increases a tendency to cough as well as chilling the whole body.

Encourage residents to wear adequate clothing. Wool is best, and layers of garments provide insulating airpockets. Frailer people who do not move about much need to conserve heat with extra clothing even when indoors. Gloves or mittens, socks and even hats may be sensible wear, for considerable heat loss occurs from the head. Smart, warm clothing or thermostatically controlled heating appliances make good presents for Christmas or a winter birthday, and relatives may be glad of suggestions such as these from a knowledgeable person like a warden.

Ensure that a frail person can prepare hot food and drinks, perhaps, for instance, by using a divided saucepan to reduce cooking costs, or having a vacuum flask filled with hot soup or tea. Porridge can be made cheaply overnight by using a slow cooker. Where necessary, you should suggest that the resident seeks further help at home.

Check on the safety of heating appliances and be prepared to give advice and help where necessary. Electric blankets must be serviced regularly and used properly. You should also watch out for dangerous paraffin heaters or unguarded fires. Ventilation is important when the fuel used is coal or gas, and any room insulation should not interfere with this.

Be aware of the financial aspect of keeping warm, especially in a scheme where residents have to pay for fuel as a separate item from the rent, or in the community if you are a mobile warden. If one of your residents or clients has difficulty with heating bills, you could suggest that they pay by instalments or by a prepayment method such as by purchasing stamps from the electricity or gas board or the post office. The fuel boards do try to help their older consumers; older people who receive a bill they cannot pay should tell the fuel board concerned *at once*; supplies will not be cut off provided the supplier is informed. You or your residents can get further information or advice from gas or electricity showrooms, a Citizens Advice Bureau or Age Concern's Factsheet 1, *Help with Heating*.

You may be able to help the older people you care for to make sure they are getting all the state benefits to which they are entitled, especially if they are disabled or need extra heat because of illness. Age Concern's annually updated publication *Your Rights* will be useful for reference.

INCONTINENCE OF URINE

Spoils lives but can be curable

Incontinence or the fear of it has far-reaching effects on sufferers. They restrict their activities in order to stay within reach of a lavatory, and to avoid the embarrassment of leaving a wet patch on someone else's chair. Gradually they give up the attempt to live a normal life and may easily slip into depression and withdrawn apathy. The smell and unpleasantness associated with incontinence may lead to loneliness in a sheltered scheme; in many places, incontinence of urine may be the final straw that leads to the breakdown of care and a move to other accommodation.

This is a sad picture, when one considers how prompt investigation and treatment might have put things right. Too often, incontinence is accepted as being due to ageing, but this is never the whole explanation. It is true that as we get older we need to go to the lavatory more often (frequency) and cannot put off the visit for as long as we used to (urgency). Less has to go wrong to make a person 80 years old incontinent than one of 40. However, at any age the faults contributing to the incontinence may be correctable, and getting the person dry will enormously improve their quality of life.

Getting professional help

Most incontinent people can benefit from skilled medical advice, and you may be able to encourage them to seek help. This is never an easy subject to broach, and it may take several attempts before sufferers are prepared to admit that they have a problem. Experience suggests that it is helpful to explain how common incontinence is, especially in women: 50 per cent of women who have had one child and over 80 per cent of those who have had two children will have suffered from it at some time in their lives. It also helps to assure the person that their problem is not their fault; this is especially important if, as sometimes happens, other residents have unkindly labelled the incontinent person as 'lazy'. You should also try to convince the incontinent resident that help is worth seeking, as they may wrongly believe themselves to be incurable. Incontinent people can truthfully be told that improvement is likely and cure a possibility. Even when things cannot be put right completely, modern ranges of pads and pants can make the problem less obtrusive and life more tolerable than used to be the case.

Older people may find it embarrassing to discuss the private parts of their bodies with a young doctor of the opposite sex. You could then ask an incontinent resident who felt like this whether they would like you to speak to the doctor on their behalf. You could also encourage them to ask at the surgery for an appointment with a doctor or nurse whom they would find it easier to approach; it should be possible to arrange this. Any necessary tests can then be arranged so that treatment can be organised.

In some areas of the country there are out-patient continence clinics where doctors, nurses, physiotherapists and other health care workers co-operate in caring for incontinent people who have been referred by their GP. Continence advisers from such clinics also work in the community in some areas, and visit people in their own homes. They are nurses who have extra training and a special interest in this sort of condition. Your district nurse or the local Community Health Council will tell you whether there is a local continence adviser in your area. You can also get in touch with the Continence Foundation for advice and books and leaflets aimed at promoting continence. Publications are also available from Age Concern England.

Where the special services outlined above do not exist, an incontinent person may be referred to a urological surgeon, a gynaecologist or another specialist. The GP and the district nurse will help to look after the person in the community.

Common patterns of incontinence

Stress incontinence

This generally affects women as a result of damage to muscles of the pelvic floor during childbirth; these weaken still further after the menopause because of hormonal changes. Leaking of urine occurs with the 'stress' of lifting or straining to get up from a low chair, or with coughing, sneezing or laughing; being overweight worsens the problem. The after effects of nerve damage during labour or at delivery may make things worse.

Incontinence sufferers may not seek help because of embarrassment or because they think that nothing can be done. This is wrong, for a good deal of help is available. In mild cases, 'post-natal' type exercises can be helpful, as is hormone treatment either in tablet or patch form or in locally applied creams. Some women benefit from a ring pessary being inserted into the vagina. A simple menstrual tampon can be helpful in minor degrees of stress incontinence. Both these devices help to support the bladder and urethra in their correct position. In many cases, the answer is a formal operation, and the woman should ask the GP to refer her to a suitable out-patient clinic.

Urinary infection

Someone suffering from this condition has a marked desire to pass urine when the bladder contains only a small amount, though this may be less noticeable in older people. The urine often smells fishy and unpleasant, and may be frothy or even blood-stained. In younger people the passage of infected urine is painful and burning, but in an older person this is often less marked.

Someone who thinks they may have a urinary infection should consult the doctor, so that a specimen of urine can be collected and sent to the laboratory for examination. An antibiotic will usually then be prescribed. A urinary infection may be solely responsible for incontinence, and it will worsen incontinence due to another cause, so every incontinent person needs to have a urine test.

Unstable bladder

This is very common in people who have had a stroke, who develop a dementing illness, who have Parkinson's disease or who suffer from multiple sclerosis. The muscle of the bladder wall becomes over-active, leading to an urgent and frequent need to pass urine. If the visit to the lavatory is delayed, incontinence is likely, and the situation will be aggravated by immobility or a urinary tract infection.

Treatment can often be managed by habit training. A well-motivated person with good nursing support may be able to benefit from this at home; alternatively, the sufferer can be admitted to a hospital geriatric ward. The techniques used are quite simple. Very often, just reminding someone to pass water or assisting them to the lavatory every two hours or as necessary is enough to correct the problem. A simple chart can be used to record whether the patient was wet or dry at the two-hourly checks; ideally, people should take charge of this and fill it in themselves. When wetness persists, the times of checks and visits to the lavatory can be suitably adjusted.

The person's morale lifts as soon as the incontinence starts to improve, and a great sense of achievement is felt on marking the chart as dry. After this, the bladder can be retrained to go a little longer between visits, and reminders can eventually correspond to events of the day, such as meals and outings, rather than being prompted by the clock. Occasionally, drugs are also used to help control this kind of incontinence, but unwanted effects from these can be troublesome. Sometimes the 'insurance' provided by wearing an incontinence pad will also be necessary to make the person feel secure.

Mechanical obstruction

In men this often happens because of an enlarged prostate gland which interferes with the free passage of urine. An affected resident will have a poor urinary stream, with difficulty in starting to pass urine and dribbling as he finishes. This leakage stains clothing and bedding and causes smell. Because of the partial blockage, the bladder becomes unable to empty itself completely; a stagnant pool of urine accumulates, becomes infected, and thus makes incontinence worse. Eventually the man becomes unable to pass urine at all, and needs admission to hospital for this retention to be relieved.

In prostatic enlargement the combination of back-pressure and increased liability to infection can damage the kidneys, so someone with this condition is at risk of developing kidney failure. The condition is thus a threat to general health as well as a cause of the tiresome symptom of incontinence. Because of this, someone with an enlarged prostate should be encouraged to see the doctor with a view to receiving surgical treatment. The necessary operation is now a much simpler undertaking than it used to be, and can be safely performed on quite frail people.

In women, gynaecological conditions such as fibroids can obstruct the bladder outlet and cause incontinence; this can be treated surgically.

In both men and women, severe constipation can cause mechanical obstruction and incontinence. Someone suffering from this will require nursing or medical help to remove the mass of faeces. After removal, the person should take steps to avoid constipation developing again; you may be asked for advice, in which case you can recommend increased fibre and fluids in the diet.

Contributing factors

Once a person has developed a tendency to incontinence, many things can aggravate the situation.

Immobility

A condition such as osteoarthritis or Parkinson's disease that slows up movement will make older people more likely to wet themselves while trying to get to the lavatory. Treatment of the condition and improving mobility will improve their continence. Another solution is to shorten the distance to be travelled by providing a commode or a urinal near at hand. Anxiety probably strengthens contractions of the bladder wall muscles, so anyone who is 'caught short' will have a better chance of reaching the lavatory in time by pausing to take a few deep breaths, rather than by rushing.

Clothing

When the need to urinate is urgent, having to undo complicated clothing can result in incontinence. Wrap-over or gathered skirts are easier to manage in a hurry than tight ones. In men, difficult fly buttons can be replaced by Velcro. Advice about clothing for people with various types of disabilities can be obtained from the Disabled Living Foundation.

Lavatories

Attractive toilet facilities are an essential factor to prevent someone with incontinence from putting off a visit to the lavatory until near the danger point for an accident. This may happen, for instance, if a partially sighted person who has to share a lavatory unwittingly sits down on a soiled seat; understandably, a possible recurrence of the situation will be postponed for as long as possible.

Diuretic drugs

A tendency to incontinence can also be affected by diuretic drugs which increase the amount of urine passed. The prescribing doctor may be unaware of the urinary problem if the person is too shy to mention it, even though it is often possible for a diuretic to be stopped without the person's health suffering. You should ask the resident if they would like you to inform the doctor, if you think this may be happening. People with untreated diabetes also pass large amounts of urine. Incontinence resulting from this is quite commonly what brings the elderly undiagnosed diabetic to the GP for an examination. Once the diabetes is brought under control, the incontinence will improve.

Helping people with incontinence

Managing fluid intake

There is a tendency among incontinent elderly people to restrict the amount of fluids they drink. However, this is a mistake, because dehydration is dangerous for elderly people, and, paradoxically, may worsen the incontinence. The timing of drinks may be adjusted to promote continence provided the total daily amount remains adequate: for instance, if the person commonly wets the bed, the daily fluid requirements can be taken before 6.00 pm. Occasionally this strategy does not work, and the more concentrated night-time urine so produced irritates the bladder and causes a wet bed. In these circumstances, a late-night drink may prevent incontinence. The sensible course is to experiment with timing of drinks that together total the volume of fluid needed over the 24-hour period, for no two bladders – or their owners – are alike.

Washing clothes and bedding

The smell of incontinence is probably the most distasteful thing about it. Deodorants such as Nilodor can be used in appliances or on padding or can be added to the water used for shampooing stained carpets. However, the most important factors in the prevention of smell are the speed and efficiency with which wet clothing and bedding are changed and laundered. All clothes should of course be washable, and if they become wet or soiled, should be sluiced off at once in cold water. Dirty laundry or used incontinence pads should be stored in sealed plastic bags.

An incontinence laundry service may be available locally; the social services department or Age Concern will know whether this is so. Note that the provision of a laundry service varies in different areas of the country. If you think there is an unmet need for this service where you work, you should discuss the situation with the staff of your local Community Health Council.

Protecting furniture and bedding

Plastic sheeting over the mattress is not usually sufficient, and will in any case have a bad effect on the sufferer's skin. The standard Inco pad is often useful but is inclined to leak around the edges. The Kylie Sheet is a useful newer product, but a washing machine and tumbler dryer need to be available. Your continence adviser should be able to tell the resident or their helpers which equipment will best meet individual needs.

Modifying toilet facilities

Where an older person has difficulty in standing up and sitting down safely in the lavatory, extra support rails and a raised lavatory seat may be helpful. The occupational therapist at the social services department will be able to arrange for this, but in some areas there are long waiting lists for this service. People in wheelchairs will have to learn to transfer from chair to lavatory or commode, so the seats will need to be at the same height. A physiotherapist will be able to teach transferring skills and advise about seating.

Stroke patients with restricted use of one hand or arm may have difficulty in cleaning themselves. Moving the toilet paper holder or supplying a pad of interleaved sheets rather than a roll may make this operation easier. A bidet may occasionally be useful; a portable form is available which fits over the lavatory bowl and can be emptied into it.

Using equipment

Catheters

A person with irreversible incontinence may wear an in-dwelling catheter. This is a plastic tube passed up the urethra and into the bladder, containing an inflatable balloon that expands and keeps the catheter from falling out. The urine drains through a hole at the end of the catheter down the outer section of tubing and into a plastic bag that is secured to the waist or leg. The bag must be fixed below bladder level to help drainage and reduce the risk of infection from backward flow. If the tube is sat on or kinked, drainage will be blocked and urine will leak where the tube joins the bag.

Occasionally a catheter will become blocked, and its wearer will be in pain because they cannot pass water. A temporary block can be relieved by milking the tube. If this does not work, the doctor or nurse should be called. If it is not possible to unblock or replace the catheter rapidly, the best course of action is to remove it by first cutting off the end to deflate the balloon and then gently pulling it out. The person will then be out of pain, but incontinent until a new catheter can be inserted.

Catheters are either changed by the district nurse in the person's home or in the catheter clinic at the local hospital. The person should know whom to call in case of emergency, and should carry a record card so that a strange doctor or nurse can read the circumstances of the particular case. Ideally, someone with a catheter should also keep a spare catheter and the sterile pack needed for its insertion in case of need.

If the person wishes to have a bath, this is possible with the bag in place or if the bag is removed and the end of the catheter is corked with a conical spigot. If the bag is left on, it must not be raised higher than the patient's bottom, as there is a risk of infection if urine from the bag flows back into the bladder.

Sexual intercourse is possible for people who are catheterised. Some prefer to have the catheter removed before sex and replaced afterwards, but others find the arrangements for this an intrusion on their privacy, and prefer to manage with it in place. Advice from the organisation SPOD can be helpful.

Self-catheterisation

In a few cases, patients or their carers learn to pass a catheter whenever the need to pass urine arises. You are most likely to meet this with a younger resident who has a condition such as multiple sclerosis. People who use these techniques are likely to cope well in normal circumstances, but you may want to check that you know whom to get in touch with in an emergency.

External appliances

These are sometimes worn by men. The newer ones are quite satisfactory, and maintain a good fit without being uncomfortably tight round the penis. Both the appliance and the underlying skin need to be kept scrupulously clean to prevent soreness and smell. Padding or similar precautions may need to be used instead of, or as well as, the appliance during sleep.

Urinals

Many older men find a bottle urinal useful, especially at night. These are easier to use if the man sits up and dangles his legs over the edge of the bed. Some are available with a non-return valve at the neck, and this prevents accidental spillage.

The female anatomy is more difficult to accommodate with a urinal, but there is the commonly used 'St Peter's boat', or a disposable urinal with its own plastic bag designed to fit into a handbag.

Further information about incontinence can be obtained from the local continence adviser or the Continence Foundation.

BOWEL PROBLEMS

Constipation

Many of the generation who are now elderly learned in childhood that all sorts of medical and even moral dangers lay in wait for anyone who did not have 'a good clear out' every day. This is not so: the natural frequency of passing stools varies considerably from person to person. Provided that there has been no recent change in habit, there is no bleeding from the back passage and the stools are not hard or difficult to pass, a daily bowel movement is not necessary for health. However, the onset of sudden constipation or an increased frequency of passing a motion, especially when blood is also passed, may be a sign of serious underlying disease and should always be reported to the doctor. On the other hand, as well as being uncomfortable, constipation may aggravate a tendency to urinary incontinence and may make confusion worse in someone who is mentally frail.

The intestinal muscle seems to become less efficient with increasing age, so it takes longer for food residue to travel the full length of the digestive tract. The bowels of anyone on a low-fibre diet or who does not drink enough will become sluggish. Some drugs also cause constipation; some cough mixtures and cold medicines bought over the counter can do this. If someone has painful piles or a fissure, going to the lavatory may become a very painful business: faeces will be retained and become hard, so the next attempt to move them will be even more painful and a vicious circle will be set up.

While severe cases require medical advice, commonsense home remedies are useful in milder ones. Someone who tends to be constipated will be helped by increasing the fibre intake in their diet, as well as the daily amount of fluids. Three to five pints per day (one and a half to two and a half litres) at least is recommended. See pages 30–31 for suggestions on encouraging residents to drink more. Also, bowel activity seems to increase in people who take more exercise.

Laxatives should be avoided as far as possible, as they impair the normal bowel-emptying pattern. When necessary, the doctor or nurse will advise on a suitable preparation.

Faecal incontinence

Though it often happens in confused people, faecal incontinence is rarely the result of mental frailty alone, and a medical search for a cause is always indicated. Sometimes the person may be suffering from diarrhoea and has simply been unable to reach the lavatory in time. The situation will be resolved when the cause of the diarrhoea is identified and treated – for instance, the over-use of laxatives or food poisoning.

The commonest cause of faecal incontinence is spurious diarrhoea, when the person is really severely constipated and liquid faeces leak past the obstructing mass. In these circumstances the sufferer requires a simple medical examination, which will usually reveal the cause and indicate appropriate treatment. Some very frail older people have bowels loaded with soft faeces which they are too weak to push out. Again, these people can be helped if they are examined and treated.

Even with the occasional persistent case of faecal incontinence, it is still possible to contain the condition. The district nurse gives the individual an enema about twice a week to empty the bowel. Between times, the patient takes constipating medicine to restrict bowel action. Protective clothing can be worn in case of accidents. Provided these measures are followed, the situation should become tolerable for people with faecal incontinence and their carers.

VISUAL HANDICAP – MAKING THE MOST OF REMAINING SIGHT

Registration

A visually handicapped person should register as partially sighted or blind. This is done by an ophthalmologist (a hospital specialist) on referral from the GP, and entitles the person to special benefits. The Benefits Rights Office at the RNIB (Royal National Institute for the Blind) produces leaflets describing these.

Services for visually handicapped people

These vary in different parts of the country. You may be able to find out about them from the social services department, where there may be a special social worker for visually handicapped people. If there is no such service in your area, other sources of information are the RNIB, and the Low Vision Adviser at the Partially Sighted Society. In addition, there is the weekly Radio 4 programme 'In Touch'. Some very useful books and booklets are produced by Broadcasting Support Services in connection with this programme, and your visually handicapped residents may benefit from these; if necessary you could help them write for a publications list (see Further Reading). In many public libraries there is a directory of agencies for the blind.

Low vision aids and partially sighted people

The ophthalmologist who has registered someone as partially sighted may also refer them to a specialist in low vision aids. The Partially Sighted Society produces a list of Low Vision Clinics and also of optometrists and opticians who perform low vision assessments and stock low vision aids. These aids include magnifying devices such as a small telescope, neat enough to be hidden in the palm of the hand, which can be used for identifying friends in the street or reading bus numbers and street names. For close work, magnifying glasses of various designs are available. Hand-held ones are useful to carry about for occasional use; there are also spectacles with very thick lenses, and tiny binoculars to be held very close to the eyes when reading. Some low vision aids incorporate a built-in light.

Light and colour

Good lighting can be very helpful to visually handicapped people. Someone with failing sight should be sure to sit sideways on to a window when using a low vision aid, and at night should use a reading lamp on an adjustable arm with the light directed over the left shoulder on to the written page or other close work. Contrasted dark and light colours around the home will also help a partially sighted person to use stairs safely and to find light switches or door handles. Someone with poor sight may still be able to read short messages if they are written in large, bold letters with a thick black felt pen.

Help with daily living and getting about

The social services department may be able to arrange for training in daily living skills and in getting about independently, either by using a long cane or in some cases with the help of a guide dog. In some areas of the country there are technical and mobility officers for the blind, also attached to the social services department, who will visit people at home to help them adjust to difficulties. There are also a few day centres that specialise in work with blind people. The RNIB has a number of useful publications.

Listening and reading

A registered blind person who needs a radio can get one through the British Wireless for the Blind Fund, and the local social services department can advise about the procedure. The BBC Radio 4 programme 'In Touch' is likely to be of special interest. Reduced rate television licenses are also available; and the RNIB sells a television device that receives only sound and no picture, and for which no licence is needed.

Learning to read the Braille or Moon system is an important part of a newly blind person's rehabilitation, and some determined people in their 80s have done this. There are special editions of newspapers and some periodicals in Braille and Moon, and some official leaflets can be obtained in these scripts. Registered blind people are eligible to become members of the Braille National Library for the Blind and the RNIB's Talking Book Library, and so are those who have poor reading vision, as certified by their GP, an ophthalmologist or an optician. The subscription for the Talking Book Library includes the cost of hiring a playback machine as well as cassette tapes. The Talking Newspaper Association produces editions in most areas of the country to be 'read' by the playback machines.

An excellent leaflet to transfer on to tape for a blind person would be the one published by the RNIB on running your home. The RNIB can also advise about the choice of standard cooking equipment and cookbooks. In addition, a fully equipped kitchen designed for use by visually handicapped people has been set up at the Disabled Living Foundation, and can be visited by appointment. Some instruction booklets that are supplied with domestic equipment are available in Braille, and taped cookbooks can be obtained from the Talking Newspaper Association.

Social contact

Be sure to tell a blind person when you enter and leave a room, as they cannot see you and should be spared the embarrassment of talking when no one is there. Unless your voice is familiar to the person, say who you are, and in any case explain what you are doing – whether you are bringing a letter or are letting in the electrician, for instance.

When introducing a blind person to a group of residents in a sheltered scheme, explain the disability in a matter of fact way. Otherwise the person may be thought to be unfriendly and standoffish when he or she is simply unable to see and respond to smiling faces. Remember that many of the early stages in the establishment of a relationship involve eye contact, which a visually handicapped person cannot achieve. The RNIB produce a leaflet 'Meeting Blind People' which is reassuring to people who are unfamiliar with anyone with this disability.

Acting as a guide

A partially sighted or blind resident will need to be given a careful tour of the scheme, with specific directions being given along the route from the person's flat to the lounge, the laundry room, the public telephone, etc. Acting as guide is sometimes difficult and can be frustrating for both parties, so it is helpful to know a few principles. For instance, blind people usually prefer to hold the arm of their guide, rather than to be frog-marched by someone holding on to them.

When walking on a flat surface, hold your arm (the grip arm) straight with fingers pointing towards the ground so that the blind person can grasp your upper arm, with their grip hand, on the inside. They can then walk slightly behind you, and can detect changes of direction by noticing your body movements. When it is necessary for the two of you to walk in single file, put your grip arm in the middle of your back, so that the blind person can change their grip hand if this is more comfortable.

When the blind person needs to walk on your other side, they should slide their grip hand across your back to catch hold of your other arm which will then become the grip arm. The techniques for helping them to sit down vary with the type of seating involved.

A novice guide may like to practise guiding techniques with a blindfolded volunteer, and it is useful to take a turn under the blindfold yourself to discover what it feels like to be guided. The RNIB produce an excellent illustrated free booklet called 'How to Guide a Blind Person'.

It is useful to know about services for visually handicapped residents, as they may find it difficult to gather this information for themselves. Imaginative use of available equipment and aids can increase independence and help visually handicapped people to continue to enjoy life.

IMPAIRED HEARING

Diagnosis first

Someone with difficulty in hearing should first go to the GP. If no simple cause, such as a build-up of wax, is found to be the problem, the person will then be referred onwards to an ear, nose and throat (ENT) specialist at the local hospital, where tests will be organised. These tests usually include an audiogram, which is a map of the pattern of hearing loss. A treatment plan can then be designed.

Getting a hearing aid

After treatable causes of deafness have been attended to, a hearing aid may be prescribed, available on the NHS at the ENT (ear, nose and throat) department of hospitals or at commercial hearing aid centres. The usual NHS aid is worn either behind the ear or on the body. Behind-the-ear models have all the necessary equipment in a small and inconspicuous case, but they are less powerful than the body-worn types. The latter also have large controls which may be easier for someone with arthritic fingers to manipulate. Both types have an earmould, and an impression of the ear is taken by the technician so that the aid will fit properly.

Privately supplied aids may also be worn on the body or behind the ear. There are also models enclosed in the earpieces of spectacle frames and some worn within the ear itself. These aids can be expensive, and the purchase price does not cover the cost of repairs. They are sometimes bought on hire purchase, but residents should be very careful about signing any HP documents; they may want to get advice first from a relative or friend, or the Citizens Advice Bureau. Some commercial devices are advertised as hearing 'correctors' or 'adjusters', but these are still only amplifying hearing aids. In general, an elderly person is best advised to obtain an NHS aid; but in some areas they will have to wait.

Very elderly, infirm people who have difficulty in adapting to a hearing aid may sometimes benefit from an old-fashioned ear trumpet or conversation tube. Various types are obtainable on the NHS; whilst they are less efficient and more conspicuous than conventional aids, they need no upkeep, no batteries and no adjustment, and are comparatively easy to get used to. The RNID or hearing clinic should be able to advise.

Adjusting to an aid

Among publications from the Royal National Institute for Deaf People (RNID) are two booklets, 'Hearing Aids – Questions and Answers' and 'Understanding Hearing Aids'. Both would be useful to a resident with a new hearing aid, and you might like copies for reference. NHS hearing aids always come with their own explanatory booklet. You can help by encouraging residents to read this, and may want to refer to it yourself.

In some areas of the country there are specially trained hearing therapists attached to the hearing aid clinic to help people to adjust to hearing loss and to get the most out of an aid. This can require a lot of effort. Many people do not realise until they wear one that a hearing aid amplifies all round, background noise as well as conversation. If the person has heard little for the past few years, the sudden din can be upsetting and difficult to accept. Getting an aid adjusted properly and learning to use it to best effect may require several clinic visits. Some older people may find this so tiring and disheartening that they give up trying to use the hearing aid. As a warden, you may be able to help by encouraging perseverance and, whenever possible, by reducing the practical problems of clinic or hospital attendance. For instance, the time spent waiting around for transport can be reduced if taxis or volunteer drivers are used instead, and a volunteer escort may also help. Some wardens have arranged for hearing services in their schemes, and you might want to find out if this is possible in your area.

When trying to help people adjust to an aid, you should suggest the following technique. Firstly, they should start using it in a quiet room with someone else sitting opposite, about five or six feet away, with sufficient light for lip movements to be clearly visible. When they have become accustomed to this controlled situation, they can then progress to group conversation, remembering to turn the hearing aid down when surroundings are especially noisy. Many hearing aids have a switch marked 'T' which receives magnetic signals rather than sound and can be used with the telephone (if adapted), with some TV sets and in buildings that have an induction loop system fitted. Theatres, cinemas and churches that operate loop systems usually display an ear symbol or 'T' sign to indicate that they have this facility. Loop systems can be fitted in residents' flats at social services department expense. They are useful in public rooms too, but the money for this has to be found privately. You can find out more about loop systems from the RNID or from the British Association for the Hard of Hearing.

Sources of help

The social services department may have a social worker for deaf people, who can advise about hearing aids and equipment. Clubs for deaf people and those who are hard of hearing are a good means of maintaining social contact for those who enjoy them. Information about aids, learning lipreading, the induction loop system, specially designed articles such as visual doorbells, and rehabilitation and residential services can be obtained from the Royal National Institute for Deaf People. The Association of Teachers of Lipreading to Adults has details about learning this technique.

Talking with a deaf person

When doing this, you should make sure that the deaf person can see your face clearly so that they can lipread. Face the person, remove sunglasses, and do not talk with a pipe or cigarette in your mouth. Good lighting is of course essential. A pad and pencil will be useful not only to indicate conversation subjects at the outset, but also to convey any information that must be accurate such as 'Hospital Appointment, August 6th, 2.30pm'.

Before starting to speak, try to attract the person's attention so that they do not miss the beginning of what you say. Speak a little slower than normal and concentrate on being clear rather than loud; be aware that the natural rhythm of speech is destroyed if you speak too slowly.

If the hearing-impaired person does not understand you at first, it may help to rephrase what you say. For instance, the sounds making up the word 'August' are invisible to the lip reader, whilst the word 'summer' is easily read. Place yourself five or six feet away from the person, unless their sight is poor, in which case it may be appropriate to move closer. Of course, when a person is distressed and needs comforting, the communication received from touch and physical contact may be more important than what is heard.

IMPAIRED SPEECH

Speech difficulties are much less common in elderly people than are problems with sight or hearing. Poorly fitted dentures are one simple cause, which can be put right if the dentist adjusts the fit. People getting used to a new set of dentures may gain confidence and improve their speech by reciting in front of a mirror until they are confident that the new teeth will not slip.

If you have a number of frail and housebound residents with dental problems, it may be worth enquiring from the district health authority whether they run a community dental service. Age Concern produces a Factsheet called 'Dental Care in Retirement', and you or your residents might like to send for it.

Hoarseness or loss of voice may occur with an upper respiratory tract infection such as a cold, but it should get better within two or three weeks. If it persists for longer than this, the GP should be consulted, as very occasionally something serious is amiss.

Stroke, Parkinson's disease and conditions such as motor neuron disease can also affect a person's speech. It helps if the affected person can see a speech therapist, both to receive treatment and so that relatives and carers can be advised how best to help the speech-impaired person. The self-help organisations for these diseases are a good source of information about the speech difficulties involved.

CONFUSION, DEMENTIA AND MENTAL FRAILTY

Physical illness causing confusion

When older people get ill, they may become mentally confused. This can occur at any age but, because of ageing changes in the brain, it happens more easily in sick older people. Confusion of this sort is called a delirium or a toxic confusional state. It can result from a number of treatable medical causes such as chest or urinary infections, poorly controlled diabetes, or dehydration and the chemical upset due to diarrhoea or vomiting. It can also occur as the unwanted effect of medicines.

A physical cause is likely if the older person's muddled state has come on quickly – often over as little as 24 hours. Sometimes the illness at the root of the trouble is obvious, but sometimes a careful examination and investigations will be needed before it can be identified.

A doctor who does not know the sick resident well may not be aware that they are not usually confused. It is therefore very helpful if you, with your superior knowledge of the resident's abilities, can tell the doctor that something seems to have gone suddenly wrong. If the cause can be found, it will usually be possible to put things right, though recovery is often slow and jerky.

Poor sight and hearing, not confusion

It is also worth remembering that someone who cannot see or hear well may appear to be confused when they are not. You should try to make sure that your residents know how to get help with sight or hearing disabilities; if asked, you should give practical assistance in getting this.

Depression mistaken for dementia

People who are slowed down by a severe depressive illness may seem to have dementia. When there is doubt as to the cause of an older person's abnormal mental state, the GP may arrange for a psychogeriatrician (sometimes called an old age psychiatrist) to visit to give a specialist opinion. Community psychiatric nurses may also be very helpful.

Dementia – permanent confusion

Some people who become confused do not have a physical illness of this type, and do not get better. This is not due to old age, but to one of a group of illnesses called dementias. There are two common types in the UK – Alzheimer's disease and multi-infarct dementia.

Which word to use?

'Dementia' and 'demented' are words best used in medical circles only, for two reasons. One is that, to many people, someone who is 'demented' is seriously disturbed, raving and probably dangerous. Very few older people with dementia fit this description, and many relatives would be understandably distressed if the word were applied to their elder. The other reason is that, because the dementias are incurable illnesses, it is important that before one of them is diagnosed, all likely curable causes of confusion have been carefully considered and discarded.

In general, it is probably best to describe people who are permanently confused because of a dementing illness as 'mentally frail' or 'mentally infirm'. It is often wise, however, to make sure that the person you are talking or writing to means the same thing as you do by the words you use, as awkward misunderstandings can otherwise occur.

Common types of dementia

Alzheimer's disease (AD)

This can happen at any time in adult life. In a few early-onset cases (before the age of 60) there is a clear family pattern, the disease being passed genetically from parent to child. However, most Alzheimer's disease occurs in later life, usually past 75 and often around the age of 80.

This late-onset form does not seem to be inherited, and we do not know yet what causes it. It is sometimes called 'senile dementia of Alzheimer type' or 'SDAT'; however, 'senile dementia' is a term best avoided as it implies that the person's mental confusion is the result of ageing, which is not the case. Whenever in life it happens, Alzheimer's disease attacks the brain substance, replacing useful nervous tissue with plaques and tangles of a useless substance called amyloid. The pattern of this destruction can be recognised if a piece of brain from an Alzheimer's sufferer who has died is examined under the microscope.

People with Alzheimer's disease do not get better and usually get worse, though the rate at which this happens varies from one person to another. The beginning of the disease can be difficult to notice, and it may come to attention because of changed social circumstances – for instance, the affected person's carer may be taken suddenly ill. AD sufferers often seem unaware of their deteriorating mental function. Their disease often affects judgement skills and may change their personalities. It also shortens their lives compared to people of the same age who do not have AD. However, it is not possible to predict how long any one person with AD is likely to survive.

Multi-infarct dementia

Here the cause is very clear. It happens because diseased brain arteries block and fail to supply blood to the brain tissue. Starved of oxygen-rich blood, these sections of brain die, and the functions they control are lost. Death of tissue because of lack of blood is medically known as 'infarction', and so the condition is called 'multi-infarct dementia' (MID). As the brain arteries block at irregular intervals, the MID sufferer tends to deteriorate in a jerky fashion, rather like going down an uneven flight of steps. This contrasts with the smooth downhill course of the person with AD.

People with MID commonly have other sorts of blood vessel disease, such as angina, heart attacks or arterial disease in the legs. They are also prone to major strokes. MID is in fact due to the effects of many tiny stroke episodes, and MID sufferers often show stroke signs when a blockage happens. These include sudden worsening of confusion, slurred speech, weakness down one side of the face and body, and epileptic fits. People with MID may be aware of what is happening to them, and because of this they may become depressed. Personality and judgement skills are usually affected less in MID than in AD.

Because of the generally poor state of their arteries, people with MID do not live long. They usually die of a heart attack, major stroke or other vascular catastrophe within two to five years of the diagnosis of MID being made.

Diagnosis and treatment of Alzheimer's disease and multi-infarct dementia

There are as yet no simple and certain ways of telling whether someone has AD or MID before they die and the brain can be examined. The most sophisticated sorts of brain scanning equipment can give a right answer in about 80 per cent of cases. At the moment these scans are mainly done when there is doubt as to whether the patient has a dementia or another, possibly curable, condition causing confusion. However, once a treatment for AD is available, it will be very important to make a certain diagnosis. There is no effective medical treatment for AD at the time of writing, but research suggests that there is real hope of one being found before long.

Little can be done for MID once it is established. Sometimes its progress can be slowed a little if the sufferer will stop smoking and if conditions such as diabetes, anaemia and heart disease are managed carefully. A small dose of aspirin sometimes helps, but some people cannot take this because of the risk of bleeding. Young or middle-aged people can reduce their chances of getting MID in later life by not smoking, by taking exercise, keeping their blood pressure within normal limits and eating a healthy diet.

What dementia is like

With a few exceptions, people with AD and MID have similar mental difficulties.

Loss of memory

Forgetfulness becomes severe enough to interfere with daily life. The sufferer forgets to light the gas they have turned on, or forgets that they have already paid the rent and goes out to do so, perhaps missing an important prearranged appointment with a visiting social worker or doctor. People with dementia hide things and forget where they have put them. They then accuse visiting helpers such as wardens and home carers of having stolen from them. Others tire out their carers by asking them the same question, over and over again; they have already forgotten the answer, and to them it is a new question every time. The memory for recent events is usually much worse than that for the remote past: the affected person can tell you what happened the day war broke out, but not what they had for breakfast this morning.

Loss of contact with reality – disorientation

Mentally frail people become disorientated, losing contact with reality and becoming very distressed. The sense of place is often lost first: they do not recognise their surroundings and find it very difficult to adapt to a new environment. This is why it is usually a mistake for a mentally frail person to move from familiar surroundings if this can possibly be avoided.

Loss of sense of time can cause great difficulties in sheltered housing where people live close together. A mentally frail resident may wake at 2.30am and noisily prepare breakfast before setting out for the shops at 3.00am, causing great disturbance to others.

Mentally frail people who no longer identify other people reliably may fail to recognise close relatives or carers. A remark such as, 'Go away, you're not my daughter!' can be very hurtful to a conscientious carer. On the other hand, mentally frail people may think that they recognise total strangers, and trustingly invite them into their homes.

Loss of abstract thinking

People with dementia lose the ability to think in the abstract and make 'if . . . then' connections. 'If I do not lock my door, then I may be in danger.' 'If I walk into the road without looking, then I may get run over.' These are examples of the sort of abstract thinking that mentally healthy older people do all day and that people with dementia cannot manage.

Loss of judgement skills

Mentally frail people also lose the judgement skills needed to put thought into practice. 'I don't know this caller – if I let him in, he could rob me. Therefore I will leave the chain on the door unless and until he identifies himself satisfactorily.' It is easy to see how the loss of abstract thought and judgement skills make mentally frail older people vulnerable to exploitation by unscrupulous people. Because of their loss of grasp on current reality, a mentally frail person may return to a garbled version of behaviour that served them well in the distant past; one example of this might be the older person who tries to boil an electric kettle on the gas ring.

Personality change

The personality of the dementia sufferer may change. This is more noticeable in people with AD, and is very distressing for relatives and friends to watch. While some mentally frail people become overactive, others become slow and apathetic. They lose all their previous interests and enthusiasms, and do little but sit around. It can be difficult to tell the difference between someone like this and someone badly slowed down by severe depression. The sufferer may need to see an old age psychiatrist to establish what is wrong.

Sudden tears and laughter

Some mentally frail people are very easily moved to laughter or tears, but the cause of the emotional outburst is soon forgotten. Incidents like these often seem to be more upsetting to carers than to the mentally frail people themselves.

Loss of inhibitions

As dementia progresses, 'inhibitions' tend to be lost. 'Disinhibited' mentally frail people are no longer able to control their feelings. They start to behave in ways that those around them find difficult to accept. Private things such as nose-picking or masturbation may be done publicly. Someone who feels angry may become aggressive, and if sexually aroused they may harass other people. It is important to remember that the person's feelings are normal: it is the way in which they are expressing them that is not.

What the person was like before the start of the dementing illness affects the way they behave when they become mentally frail. Someone who has always had trouble controlling a quick temper is more likely to become aggressive than someone who is by nature sweet-tempered and placid.

Confusion level varies

Someone with dementia is more confused at some times than at others. Carers often find this difficult to understand and to cope with. People with MID are most confused at the time a brain artery blocks, get a little better as swelling goes down and then worsen again when another blockage occurs. How well they function mentally will depend on how long it is since the last blockage happened, as well as how badly the whole brain has been damaged.

People with AD have good and bad days, so what they can understand and how much they can do for themselves genuinely varies from day to day. When tired, upset or unwell they may perform very poorly. On the other hand, they can with an effort appear almost normal if they want to impress. An inexperienced person can sometimes be deceived by this, and it may be a great help to a visiting doctor or social worker if you are available to explain the true state of affairs.

'Dementia? I don't believe it'

People almost always deny bad news when they first hear it, and often have to be told the same thing several times before they take it in. Relatives will sometimes appear to shrug off the very bad news that their elder – your resident – is showing signs of dementia. If this happens, it does not help for you to press them harder. It is more useful to keep them on your side by explaining the need for help gently but clearly, without harping on the reason why the need has arisen. Relatives will be more likely to acknowledge the nature and severity of their elder's illness if they are not forced or hurried into doing so.

Mentally frail residents themselves will also refuse to admit there is any-thing wrong. They will insist that they are perfectly able to look after themselves when it is obvious that this is not so. They will sometimes tell elaborate and superficially convincing false stories about their daily pat-tern of life – what psychologists call 'confabulation'. If pressed to do tasks or perform mental tests to the point at which they fail, they become very distressed or extremely angry – a 'catastrophe reaction'.

It is important to realise that someone behaving in this way is not deliberately trying to deceive. To people with dementia the world is a mysterious and terrifying place. They have no grasp of current reality and cannot remember recent events for long enough to help them cope with the problems of the present. They fall back on their memories of the past – of themselves as caring and coping people, who were able to do so much, so well, years ago.

CARING FOR MENTALLY FRAIL RESIDENTS

Though the underlying illness cannot be cured, good care for people with dementia makes a great difference to their lives. This section gives suggestions on coping with some of the more common difficulties wardens encounter when they try to do their best for their mentally frail residents.

Balancing rights and risks

On the one hand, older people have as much right to keep control of their own lives as anyone else has. On the other hand, people who for any reason cannot look after themselves properly have a right to be protected from danger. Trying to balance these rights is an uncomfortable task for a warden or anyone else close to a mentally frail person. Clear thinking on the lines suggested below will not make the problems disappear, but may help carers to retain their peace of mind while allowing mentally frail older people maximum freedom with minimum risk.

Too much safety can be dangerous

No life can be altogether risk-free: everyday activities such as using electrical equipment, crossing roads and travelling by public transport all have their small dangers. Oddly, though, young and middle-aged people worry more about the dangers their elders run while being active rather than being passive. There is great concern about the risk of falls when old people move about freely. Much less is said and written about the grave health risks of not being mobile, especially when such false 'safety' is brought about by sedation or restraint in a chair with a locking tray. Older people have not had safe lives; if they enjoy life more by continuing to live a little dangerously, it is stupid and unkind to stop them.

Protecting others

In general, we all expect to be allowed to choose the risks we run ourselves, but not to be permitted to endanger other people. Older people in poor health may choose to live alone because they consider the danger a small price to pay for independence; this action is justified because no one except the older people themselves is put at risk. On the other hand, someone whose driving ability is impaired is banned from driving because of the risks of accidents to other people; this applies whether the cause of the disability is poor sight at 50 or dementia at 80.

Covering ourselves

Those who care for mentally frail older people often worry that they will be blamed or disciplined if someone they look after comes to harm. Staff do have a right to protect their reputations, and it is usually possible for us to 'cover ourselves' without necessarily restricting the old person's activities. In fact, if we do not recognise our worries in these situations, our unconscious anxieties will make us more likely to restrict mentally frail people, without realising that we are doing this for our benefit rather than for theirs.

Thinking it through

When considering possibly dangerous behaviour, it helps to list carefully the three sorts of risks that concern us. These are:

- risks to the mentally frail people themselves, or to their property;
- risks to other people;
- risks to ourselves.

The next step is to consider whether these risks can be reduced, or whether the dangerous behaviour can be modified in any way. For instance, it may be possible to reduce the risk of a fire or a gas explosion by turning off the gas supply so it can be used only under supervision. Alternatively, the need to cook may be avoided if appropriate home care and a luncheon club or Meals on Wheels can be arranged.

Once this has been done, the three sorts of risks can be re-evaluated, and the conclusions used as the basis for a future plan. This plan should be put together in consultation with the mentally frail resident and all those who have an interest in their welfare. A meeting to do this should give everyone a chance to exchange information and also to express their feelings; it is entirely understandable that residents and professionals such as wardens should want to protect an older person they are fond of, but they must not be allowed to do so unless it is in the best interests of the old person. (An advocacy service may be useful here.) It is sometimes helpful to remember that it is very different to decide that risk taking is justified to improve quality of life, rather than just to let things slide and hope for the best.

'Wandering'

Mentally frail residents who 'wander' – that is, leave the scheme and cannot find their own way back unaided – are often a source of anxiety to wardens, and the approach to risk taking described above can usefully be applied here.

The risks are almost certainly over-estimated: the evidence shows that the chance of a 'wanderer' coming to harm are very small indeed, and no risk is posed to anyone else.

Identifying patterns

It is often possible to work out ways of improving older people's safety without making their lives miserable with undue restraint. To do this it is necessary to find an underlying pattern to the wandering behaviour, and knowing the resident's background and past history will help in this. Some people have a 'target' that they always make for – an old home or place of work, for instance. The jaunt can be made less risky if the people at the target destination recognise the confused person and are able to let those who look after them know where they are. Other mentally frail old people revert to an old pattern of behaviour. They may, for instance, get restless around tea time because of a long past need to take the dog for a walk in the early evening. If a short, accompanied walk can be arranged at the appropriate time, the old person will often settle happily, and have been perfectly safe throughout.

Other patterns include the sensible errand that goes wrong: the confused person reaches the post office or shops, but, being disorientated, cannot find the way home. A companion on the outing can ensure a safe return, and relatives or other residents may be prepared to accompany the older person. Some 'wanderers' are seeking stimulation, avoiding noise or trying to 'walk off' pain or discomfort; if the cause can be identified and eliminated, the problem may disappear.

Sensible precautions

It is usually sensible for mentally frail people who may wander to have their names and a contact telephone number about their persons. Identity bracelets and Medic-Alert lockets are now sufficiently widespread to be an acceptable and non-stigmatising way of doing this. Do not include the older person's living address in case the information falls into the hands of criminals. A recent photograph may help passersby to give you accurate information if you are out looking for a lost resident. It may also help to give the person's details to the local police station to help officers bring them safely home. The need to do this should of course be explained to the resident concerned and their consent obtained whenever possible.

To protect yourself, you should arrange to meet the resident's concerned relatives or friends so that you can explain the facts carefully to them. Make sure they understand that, though you will do your best to help reduce the risks their elder is running, you are unable to control the daily comings and goings of your residents. You can use this opportunity to listen to the family's worries about the older person's welfare and to reassure them when they over-estimate danger. You should also write to your managers with details of the situation, including a brief description of your dealings with the relatives.

You will find suggestions for further reading about risk taking in general and wandering in particular on page 228.

Wrong ideas, muddled behaviour and confused talk

Sometimes a mentally frail resident seems to be talking nonsense, or wants to act in a foolish way on the basis of a wrong idea. This is especially common during the dark hours when there are fewer outside clues to events in the real world, and when carers are often too tired to feel at their best. Here is a simple and easily remembered plan for coping with incidents like these.

Is it true?

First, beware of the unlikely truth. A personal collection of examples includes a man of 88 who was thought to be confused when he asked ward staff to tell his mother he had been admitted to hospital. She proved to be alive and in good health at the age of 112. It is usually wise to check on the facts of the case and to visit the scene; as well as alerting you to improbable facts, this will also help you to recognise misunderstandings and misinterpretations (see below).

Neither support nor confront confused thinking or behaviour

Never support a wrong idea or statement by agreeing with it or behaving as if it were true. Do not, for instance, chase out imaginary intruders or wild animals. Mental state tends to fluctuate, and when the fog of confusion lifts a little, the mentally frail person is likely to remember what you said and did and to feel puzzled and distressed by it.

On the other hand, there is no need to upset or annoy the confused person by confronting them with their mistake and a bald recital of the true facts. It is rarely necessary to comment on the objective truth of what is said. Remember that to the confused person it is a true account of what they think is going on, and listen carefully to what they say, bearing in mind what you know of their past lives and present circumstances.

Why it happens – misunderstandings, misinterpretations and feelings

Good observation and attentive listening will help you to work out the background to a confused resident's seemingly irrational behaviour. Some problems arise from misunderstandings: one old man was reported to have 'attacked the bath nurse' when from his point of view he had awakened suddenly from his afternoon sleep to find a strange woman trying to tear his clothes off. It is important to keep in mind that mentally frail people have a short memory span and a poor grasp on reality. This means that they need more, rather than less, explanation of who visitors are and what they have come for.

Many people with apparent 'hallucinations' are in fact misinterpreting things they really see and hear. Real events are distorted by confused understanding, poor sight and hearing. Also, the extra noises of tinnitus may be thought to be coming from outside the person. They may then be wrongly interpreted as, for example, noise from the neighbours or from squatters in empty flats. Removing the stimulus can sometimes make the problem disappear. In one case a resident's complaint of 'a man in my room' was traced to a misperception of her own image in a mirror; moving the mirror to the inside of the wardrobe door got rid of the intruder and of her distress. Again, if a resident can be persuaded to accept treatment for tinnitus, the wrong ideas based on it may disappear.

Mentally frail people often express their feelings in a confused way. Half-remembered wartime horrors or a half-forgotten nightmare may be at the root of the trouble when shadows or dimly seen objects are perceived as wild animals or lurking intruders. Some people may be helped by talking about the events underlying these feelings, but this needs some care and skill; you may want to discuss this with a community psychiatric nurse. When you do not know the underlying cause, it is best simply to deal with the feeling – to calm the fears and soothe the agitation. Confused people can be comforted more easily if they are separated from the apparent cause of the trouble, so moving to a different but still familiar room may help.

Restore contact with reality or distract

Whenever possible the confused person should be brought back to reality, with as much understanding and respect as possible. An example might be, 'That hat and coat over the chair did look like a burglar, Mrs Jones – it had me fooled too for a minute. Still, there was no one there really.' This will work only if the mentally frail person knows the speaker well and trusts them. In general, therefore, a resident warden is likely to find it easier to bring a confused resident back to reality than a less familiar mobile warden, though this may still be impossible when the older person is either very confused or very upset. In these circumstances, it is best to try distraction – perhaps some conversation on a topic known to interest the resident, conducted over a cup of tea. Later, when trying to settle the resident, a useful phrase is 'everything is all right now'. This provides reassurance without risking an argument about what did or did not happen earlier, often now disappearing into hazy memory. In a similar way, someone on a mistaken errand can often be stopped for long enough to forget about it if told 'There's time for a cup of tea'. By the time the tea is drunk there is no longer a need for a confrontation about whether, for instance, the long-adult children really need fetching from school, and the confused person can easily be persuaded to go back home.

Here is an example of the system in action. A hospital patient, an old man with moderate dementia, left the ward during a thunderstorm. He was eventually found in the coal cellar, which he refused to leave. The doctor called to him found that he thought the bangs and flashing lights were the effects of an air raid, and he would not 'come out of the shelter' while it was going on. The doctor stayed with him, reassuring him he was safe until the storm passed. The patient was then happy to accept the assurance that 'everything is all right now', and was accompanied back to the ward.

Here is a summary of what to do:

1 Find out if there is a basis of **truth** in the apparent confusion.
2 **Do not support** the confused behaviour.
3 **Do not confront** the older person with their mistake.
4 **Ask why** this is happening. Look for **misunderstandings, misperceptions** and **feelings**.
5 Bring the person back to **reality** if possible.
6 If this is not possible, use **distraction**.

Stimulating a failing memory

Dementia interferes with the memory for recent events. This means that a mentally frail old person will find it difficult to retain new information: having been told the doctor will call, the confused resident soon forgets about the planned visit and goes out for the day. People with dementia find it difficult to learn new skills: however easy the controls of the central heating or the microwave seem to us, the mentally frail person is unlikely to be able to master them.

Using memory cues

Mentally frail people can often be helped by the same sort of memory joggers we all use, especially in the early stages of the disease. A mentally frail old man may, for instance, be able to act on the information on the card in his pocket which reads, 'If lost, ring May on this number'. An up-to-date noticeboard in the scheme is useful for mentally frail residents to consult. The board should include the name of the scheme, a perpetual calendar reading, for example, 'Friday 4th December', and a list of today's events, with whatever other information seems appropriate.

Helpful scheme design and equipment

Ideally, sheltered housing schemes should be designed with the needs of mentally frail residents in mind. Clever use of fittings and decoration can also be helpful. Colour-coding the carpeting on different floors and attaching personally chosen pictures to otherwise identical front doors can help confused people to find their way to their own flat. The two ends of a corridor can be made obviously different by displaying plants, pictures or ornaments to act as landmarks.

There is considerable scope for mental prompting inside individual flats or bungalows. A carefully sited clock with a clearly visible face and hands helps the resident to keep track of time. Door labels and direction arrows assist someone with poor bladder control as well as a faulty memory to find the lavatory in time to prevent an accident. Labels on photographs saying, for example, 'Granddaughter Jane with great granddaughter Sarah' may help the resident to keep track of generations of relatives. If brought out beforehand, such photographs can help the resident recognise infrequent visitors or identify the writers of letters or callers on the telephone. Confused people who become distressed as soon as a caring relative is out of sight are sometimes reassured by a memo board reading, for instance, 'Jack at shops – back 10.30'. Muddled residents who spend a large part of the day in a chair will find it easier to keep in touch with the world around them if they can see out of the window. You may want to experiment with these ideas or with others of your own to find out what will help your residents.

Useful ways of talking

Callers who talk in an information-giving way reinforce links with reality. 'Good morning, Mrs Smith, have you had your breakfast? It's a cold morning, but that's only to be expected with Christmas three weeks away.' This sort of talk can help a confused person to understand what is going on around them and to cope better with life. You will need to adjust the speed and level at which you give information to match the resident's varying mental state: sometimes you will need to go slowly, whilst on good days little prompting may be needed. It always helps to point out things that the resident can confirm by their own observations, such as the weather, the colour of the sky or the state of the plants in the garden. Seasonal music, food smells or objects are helpful: conkers mean autumn, mince pies Christmas, and daffodils spring, for instance. When the resident comes from a different ethnic or religious group from your own, you may want to ask advice from their relatives, friends or community leaders as to what would be appropriate here.

Accusations of theft

These may be true

Mentally frail people quite often accuse other people of stealing from them. Occasionally these accusations are justified: unscrupulous people do sometimes take advantage of older people who are too confused to notice and complain, or who are unlikely to be believed if they do. More often the lost property has not been stolen, but misplaced or hidden and its whereabouts forgotten.

Why false accusations are made

Confused old people who make false accusations of this sort are not deliberately trying to make trouble for their relatives or for people such as home carers or wardens who have access to their homes. 'I've been robbed' is the conclusion the muddled brain comes to when it attempts to make sense of what seems to have happened: the lost article is not where it ought to be, so someone must have taken it away. Everyone loses things, but only mentally frail people allege that burglars have stolen their false teeth. In other words, it is not the act of misplacing the object that is abnormal, but the bizarre explanation given for the loss.

Finding lost property and protecting yourself

If you are wrongly accused of having stolen a resident's property, it is best not to argue but to sidestep confrontation by saying 'I'll help you look for it'. It is often useful to know where the resident has previously put things they regard as precious, as people often use the same or similar hiding places over and over again.

It is always wise to notify your managers about these incidents, in case a complaint is made against you. In most cases you should speak to the relatives as well, and make a note of the conversation. This is not only for your own protection, but also to enable relatives to take steps to care for their elder's property. If you think it possible that money or property really has been stolen, you should let your managers know at once, as the police should be called in.

Needs of carers

A mentally frail resident may have a spouse or adult child living with them as carer. Carers of this sort may be elderly themselves and are sometimes in poor physical health. They too have needs which, if met, will help them to go on caring for as long as they wish to do so.

Emotional support

Carers have feelings – tiredness, strain, exasperation, pity and love for the sufferer, and a great deal of anger. This may be directed at the confused person, at the professionals providing inadequate services or at the whole world. These feelings need to be expressed, and the best place to do this is within a carers' group. Try to find out about such groups in your area. They may be organised by the social services department, at the health centre or surgery or in connection with voluntary agencies such as the Alzheimer's Disease Society. You could also put carers in touch with the Carers National Association.

Puzzling behaviour may be easier to understand and to cope with when the carer knows it is a symptom of the dementing illness. The Alzheimer's Disease Society is a useful source of information, or you may want to lend this book to the carer. Practical help is very important, and your knowledge of equipment and services available locally will be very useful. You may also be able to help elderly people be assertive when asking professionals for information and help, or to act as an advocate on their behalf if asked to do so.

Respite care

Respite care, giving long and short breaks from caring tasks, is often essential if carers are to keep going. Some or all of the following may be available in your area:

- A night-sitting service in the person's own home, provided by volunteers or by a paid care attendant from an organisation such as Crossroads.

- Overnight accommodation in a centre or a residential home. This allows a carer an undisturbed night's sleep, secure in the knowledge that the confused person is safe and well looked after, but will not disturb them.

- Day-sitting, for the whole or part of the day. This can enable a carer to attend to essential tasks such as shopping and visits to social security offices or hospitals, or to have a little time to themselves at a club, visiting friends or pursuing a hobby or interest.

- A complete break to allow a week's or a fortnight's holiday. During this the confused person may be looked after at home, or may move to special sheltered housing, a residential home or hospital. Residential places of this sort are scarce, and it is often necessary to book well in advance for the popular summer months.

Carers may feel guilty about taking a break. If so, they should be reminded how important their continued health and fitness are to the person they care for; the doctor may be a useful person to reinforce this message. Uncomfortable guilt feelings may sometimes emerge as anger at whoever provided the respite, and this may lead to complaints out of all proportion to trivial mishaps. Whilst important shortcomings in services should always be pointed out, minor complaints are often best listened to without comment. Carers badly need to think that they do the job better than anyone else, and very often this is so.

Repetitive questioning

Some mentally frail people ask the same question repeatedly, over and over again. This is particularly exasperating for a relative such as an elderly spouse who spends a great deal of time with the confused person. There are no magic solutions, but the suggestions below may help.

It sometimes lowers the emotional temperature to remember that this behaviour is another symptom of the dementing illness. Mentally frail questioners are not trying to be irritating: because of their short memory span, it is a new question every time to them. Sensing the carer's irritation often makes things worse, because they feel even more unsure of themselves; they may then be asking as much for reassurance as for information. It is always sensible to give the requested information clearly and fully once. It sometimes helps to write down the answer and give the paper to the confused person for reference; for instance, someone who repeatedly asks, 'What's for tea?' can be given a 'menu'.

If this does not help, the person's attention can sometimes be distracted to an easy task that they are able to perform, such as putting plates on the table. Reference to an old and pleasant memory can also break the cycle of repetition. An example might be 'Do you remember when we were kids, Mum, and we used to listen to "Children's Hour" round the fire at tea time?'

When older people stop repeating themselves and talk of other things, this should be 'rewarded' with extra attention. General reassurance is always worth persevering with, such as 'Everything's all right, Mum, and the kettle's just boiling.'

Poor personal hygiene

Many of those who are now confused residents of sheltered housing schemes have in the past worked hard under difficult circumstances to keep themselves and their families clean and decent. This makes it all the more poignant when such people neglect themselves and their homes, becoming dirty and smelly. Confused people are often unaware of their unhygienic state, but the warden may be besieged by other residents and their relatives, all demanding that 'something must be done'.

Why does it happen?

There are several reasons why someone with a dementing illness can get into this state. Loss of recent memory means that they forget the recurrent need to change clothes and to wash. Having forgotten where clean underwear is kept, they keep to those whose whereabouts are known – the ones they have on. Loss of reasoning and judgement skills make it difficult to run a bath successfully, or to assemble the towel, soap and face flannel needed for a wash. In addition, loss of contact with reality means that the days slur into one another. Taken together with memory loss, this disorientation makes it difficult for confused people to keep track of when or whether a bath has been taken or the laundry done.

When to intervene

Keeping clean is a very personal matter, and wardens often wonder when, if ever, it is proper for them to interfere in this aspect of their residents' lives. Wardens know they are not supposed to function as a sort of hygiene police force, enforcing high standards of personal care and housekeeping, whether residents want to co-operate or not. Loss of insight and inhibitions can mean that mentally frail older people are bliss-fully unaware that they are unpleasant to be with; pointing out that they are dirty forces them to confront their own inadequacies, and this can make them very angry and upset. Even so, it is sometimes right to inter-vene: perhaps when a neglected person is increasingly lonely because others do not want to get too close, or has become the puzzled butt of unkind jokes. In the close quarters of some sheltered housing schemes, one resident's poor hygiene may well affect the comfort and wellbeing of others. This is especially likely if the confused person's neglect of them-selves or their surroundings is leading to bad smells and invasion by vermin.

Offering acceptable help

It may fall to you to broach the subject of personal and/or household hygiene with the resident. Your tact and knowledge of their personality will be important if your message is to be heard and accepted. Every effort must be made to preserve the resident's self-respect, as under-mining this will make things worse. It may help to describe the help avail-able in your area for personal and home care, emphasising that you know someone like the resident would prefer things 'just so' and would be con-cerned if it were becoming difficult to do everything themselves as they would like to. Bathing help or personal care often seems to be acceptable as a 'package deal', offered together with hairdressing and an outing to buy new clothes, if this can be arranged. If the resident is incontinent or if you think a physical illness or problem with medicines might be wors-ening their confusion, you might like to suggest a consultation with the doctor.

One common source of failure is the tendency of would-be helpers to try to impose their own hygiene methods on unwilling residents. Many of those who are now elderly and confused grew up in homes without bath-rooms, and even in middle life will have been accustomed to getting into a bathtub only once a week. Though showers are becoming much more familiar and acceptable, many older people still regard them as new-fan-gled, chilly and likely to gush steam or ice water in an unpredictable way. In the past, many ordinary people seem to have relied on a leisurely and thorough daily strip wash as their basic way of keeping clean. In later life, a return to their old habits may be the easiest way of improving their per-sonal hygiene. A reminiscence session may be an easy and acceptable way of finding out what is likely to work, and relatives may also be able to give useful information.

Making things easier

It helps to make the process of washing, showering or bathing as easy as possible, both physically and mentally. The occupational therapist will be able to advise about and arrange for equipment such as tap turners and rails round baths, but the resident may have a long wait both for assessment and for the aids to arrive and be fitted. Useful articles such as bath seats can be borrowed from the Red Cross, and most can be bought privately if funds permit. A Disabled Living Centre such as London's Disabled Living Foundation will be able to help the resident decide what equipment will be most likely to help them.

Tactful prompting

Verbal reminders may be more necessary for some confused residents than actual physical help. Unobtrusive replacement of dirty clothing with clean, or the request for more washing for the machine 'to make up a load' are tactful ways of getting clothes changed without a confrontation. In normal circumstances, Category 2 scheme wardens will be unlikely to provide 'hands-on' care, though this may happen in very sheltered schemes, or anywhere in a short-term emergency. Any warden may be in a position to advise relatives or other carers how best to help a confused person to keep clean and may draw on the information in this section for guidance.

The type of personal and bathing care and how often it is available varies round the country. To find out what is available in your area, you should ask at the health centre or surgery, the social services office or the community health council.

Medicines and confused elderly people

Medicines causing confusion

Almost any medicine causes confusion, but the commonest culprits are sleeping pills (hypnotics) and tranquillisers, which tend to accumulate in the body. Occasional causes include antidepressants, some medicines given for Parkinson's disease, some ulcer-healing medicines and high doses of steroids.

An older person can also become confused if the sleeping pills or tranquillisers they have been taking for some time are stopped suddenly. It is often a good idea for such medicines to be stopped, but this should be done gradually, under medical supervision. Stopping the medicines used to treat conditions such as thyroid disease or diabetes can also cause confusion if the underlying disease gets out of control.

Someone who has had a long-established problem with their medicines may appear to have a dementing illness, but may recover completely if things are put right. It is always important to consider medicines as a possible cause of confusion.

Medicines used to treat confusion

Confusion can sometimes be cured by getting rid of its physical cause: for instance, if someone becomes acutely confused because of pneumonia, the antibiotics that clear the chest will also clear the head. Less often, chronic confusion has a treatable physical cause: an example is the replacement of missing thyroid hormone in thyroid deficiency.

At the time of writing there is no effective treatment for Alzheimer's disease, though research is promising. Various medicines are offered as treatment for multi-infarct dementia, but there is no evidence that they help.

Some people with dementing illnesses seem upset, or behave in ways that make them difficult to care for. Agitation, restlessness, insomnia, hallucinations and delusions are examples of symptoms that can be helped with the right sort of medicines, such as thioridazine (Melleril) and promazine (Sparine). However, the dosage and timing need to be carefully adjusted to the particular patient's needs if unwanted effects are to be avoided: these include drowsiness, incontinence, poor co-ordination, falls and disturbances of movement.

Alcohol and confusion

Acute confusion can follow a drinking bout. Because tolerance of alcohol decreases with age even in life-long drinkers, the amount consumed may not seem large.

If a regular drinker stops suddenly, the abrupt alcohol withdrawal can also cause confusion. In really severe cases the terrifying and dangerous condition of delirium tremens (DTs) can occur. Withdrawal of alcohol from habitual drinkers is best done under medical supervision.

Long-term alcohol abuse can lead to brain damage. This happens partly as a direct toxic effect of the alcohol on the brain and partly because of nutritional deficiency, especially of vitamin B_1 (thiamine). Another factor is the high risk of head injury in people who fall over when drunk.

Some people who have drunk moderately all their lives lose control of their drinking when they develop a dementing illness. This happens because of both loss of self-control and loss of memory – they may truly think that the drink in their hand is the first today because they can remember no other. Because alcohol causes further loss of inhibitions, dementia sufferers who also drink are particularly likely to show inappropriate sexual behaviour or to become aggressive. Such people are very difficult to help, and often the best that can be done is to limit damage as far as possible.

Moving in and moving on

Established residents do better than new ones

People who develop a dementing illness when already living in sheltered housing do better on the whole than those who move in when they are already confused. This is because after living in a scheme for some time, many of the coping skills necessary for day-to-day life are safely locked in the long-term memory stores, rather than being held precariously in the leaky short-term memory. In addition, many such confused people will have made friends and given help to other residents in earlier and better days. Eccentric behaviour due to the dementing illness is more likely to be tolerated in an old and valued friend than in a comparatively unknown resident new to the scheme.

People who move into sheltered housing when already confused usually do badly. They cannot learn their way round their new surroundings or remember how to use new equipment, however often it is shown and explained to them. They often behave dangerously, disturb and upset other residents and become rapidly more and more confused and unhappy themselves.

Mentally frail applicants for sheltered housing

It is usually sensible to discourage people with dementing illness from coming into sheltered housing, unless they have a fit and mentally intact carer who proposes to move in with them. Such people may function well together, but it is worth remembering that if the 'fit' person dies unexpectedly, the mentally frail person will almost certainly be unable to manage without them.

Mentally frail applicants for sheltered housing schemes should either be referred to more suitable accommodation offering a greater degree of care, or shown how to obtain more care and supervision while remaining in the familiar and reassuring environment of their long-established home.

Moving on and its alternatives

Some residents who become confused choose to move on to residential care. They may decide on this because they know that they are becoming less and less able to cope with daily life, or because they are becoming increasingly lonely as they find it more and more difficult to keep up a social veneer. Many of these thrive in their new homes, becoming happier because of increased social contact as well as benefiting practically from tactful supervision and care. However, other residents in similar situations may not want to move, and wardens as well as other carers often wonder whether it is right to try to change their minds. There are worrying reports that people who are persuaded against their will to move into residential care are at high risk of dying soon after the transfer. If a change shortens a confused old person's life, it is obviously silly to push for it for safety's sake. All the same, there are times when a move seems in the best interests of the confused resident, because it is likely to improve their quality of life, or when it seems necessary to protect the interests of other vulnerable residents. If confused residents want to stay where they are, various ways of making this possible should be tried.

Every effort should be made to improve their mental state and coping abilities, and to modify dangerous or challenging behaviour; a community psychiatric nurse or clinical psychologist may be able to advise about this. It may also be possible to make such residents pose less danger to themselves and those around them. For instance, disconnecting the gas supply or turning it off when the resident is alone may abolish the risk of an explosion, and other arrangements can be made to keep the confused older person warm and well fed.

Speaking up for mentally frail residents – advocacy

Wardens are often in a good position to act as advocate for their residents. You may, for instance, be able to give information about useful services or explain how to use them to the best advantage. Residents may need encouragement to push themselves forward, or your support in making themselves heard. However, sometimes you may find yourself in a difficult situation. Perhaps the confused resident would like to stay in the scheme, but other frail residents are troubled by their behaviour and would like them to move; unsurprisingly, you feel unable to put forth a good case for each opposite point of view. In these circumstances an outside person can usefully act as the confused person's advocate. You may be able to find out about advocacy services in your area from local or national branches of organisations such as Age Concern and MIND, or by asking at the Citizens Advice Bureau.

Compulsory removal – the last resort

Compelling someone to move against their will is a last resort, and is only very occasionally necessary. Someone who is causing disturbance or distress to other residents may be in breach of their tenancy agreement. In theory, such a person could be evicted, making them homeless, when it would become the responsibility of the local authority to provide housing. In practice, agencies providing sheltered housing for older people rarely resort to the law in this sort of situation, both out of compassion for the confused person's plight and to avoid undesirable publicity. Moves to residential care in these circumstances are more often made informally, with the co-operation of social services and the older person's relatives. Variable amounts of 'persuasion' may be needed; no one feels comfortable about this, but it can sometimes be very difficult to see an alternative.

The Mental Health Act Occasionally a mentally frail old person is sufficiently unwell to be admitted to hospital compulsorily under the Mental Health Act. This 'sectioning' procedure is also used to get proper, safe care for some older people with mental illness such as severe depression or paranoid psychosis. The requirement for compulsory admission is that, by reason of mental illness or impairment, the person is a danger to him- or herself or to others, or that he or she will become worse without proper treatment. The application is made by an approved social worker on the recommendations of two doctors, usually the person's GP and a psychiatrist recognised under the Act. The way in which the people responsible interpret the Act varies a little from place to place around the country.

Section 47 Another relevant piece of legislation is section 47 of the National Assistance Act. This states that people who cannot look after themselves and are living in insanitary conditions can be compelled to receive care and attention. Section 47 can be used either when neglect has continued over a long period or when the person concerned has developed an acute illness or suffered a sudden injury and is refusing treatment. What usually happens is that the GP of the person concerned calls in the consultant in public health medicine (previously known as the Community Physician). The consultant certifies to the local authority that the person needs to be put into institutional care, either in their own interests or to prevent risk to the health of others or serious nuisance to them. The local authority then applies to the magistrate's court for an order committing the person to institutional care. Such people are sometimes, but not always, suffering from a dementing illness.

Many people find section 47 very distasteful, and it is certainly a grave matter to use it. Eighty-five per cent of people subject to such an order never return home, and most are dead within two years of the incident. However, though this could mean the forced transfer had hastened the person's death, it could also mean that people who are ill enough to meet the requirements for section 47 are not likely to live long in any case. Also, frail and vulnerable older neighbours may need to be safeguarded from real and distressing squalor; people admitted under section 47 usually leave behind them piles of rat-infested rubbish, rather than surplus dust on the mantelpiece.

Some local authorities use section 47 more than others. Of course, a low rate of use could reflect excellent services and an enlightened attitude, but it could also conceal less open and equally unpleasant forms of coercion.

In many cases such moves would seem likely to be unnecessary if adequate community services were available. Some older people, for instance, would be quite happy to be cared for at home though they refuse to go into hospital; make sure that you know what can be provided, and help your residents to negotiate for services they will find acceptable.

You may want to think further about these difficult problems, and will find suggestions for further reading on p 228.

Caring for mentally frail older people is never easy. Though cure is not yet possible, good care can make an enormous difference to the quality of life of people with dementia, and it is well worth while to acquire the necessary skills.

6 Terminal Illness and Bereavement

Deaths in sheltered housing are not rare nowadays, and it is even more common for residents to spend part of their terminal illness at home, moving to a hospice or hospital only in the final stages.

As a warden, you are likely to be involved with the care of dying people and with bereavement. This chapter covers practical aspects of care and also includes basic information on common patterns of behaviour in dying people and in mourners. It aims to make you feel a little more comfortable in what is inevitably a distressing situation.

CARING FOR SOMEONE WHO IS DYING

Dying at home

Until comparatively recently most people died in their own homes, and in some cases this is still the best place. Many people say that they would like to die in their own beds – home is familiar, we print our own personalities on it and keep the things we want to have around us there. Home life is not structured by routine; relatives and friends can visit when they like and sit on the bed if they want to. Home is private and one can do private things. Children and wives, husbands and lovers can creep into bed for a cuddle and mutual comforting when there is no one outside the intimate circle to see.

However, caring for a dying person at home is always difficult. It may be impossible if a great deal of attention is required, especially if the person doing the caring is frail and local back-up services are poor. When the resident and others are willing and the idea seems feasible, you should encourage home care; even if the experiment fails, it may be psychologically necessary to all concerned that it should have been tried.

Mobilising community care

Sick residents being cared for at home have to pay from their own pocket for many services hospital patients get free. Make sure that residents know about benefit entitlements, and help them to claim if necessary. There is a special system for obtaining Attendance Allowance quickly for a terminally ill person; the GP should know about this. Useful home nursing equipment can be borrowed from the Red Cross.

Where these services are available and would be useful, the resident may value your help in arranging for personal care at home, Meals on Wheels or the incontinence laundry service.

Relief for pain and other symptoms

If pain or other symptoms are distressing, the district nurse and the GP will be an important source of help, but they may need to supplement their knowledge and expertise by calling in the nearest hospice outreach team. The Hospice Information Service will tell you where this is. An outreach team can also be a great support to family and friends during the last illness and afterwards. If in-patient care eventually becomes necessary, families can be consoled by knowing that the decision to move the resident from home was made by people who know those involved and understand the situation. A short hospice or hospital admission to get symptoms under control and give relatives a breathing space may enable the resident to remain at home thereafter or, at any rate, prolong the home care period.

Help with nursing

In some places home nursing is available from Macmillan nurses via the National Society for Cancer Relief or from the Marie Curie Memorial Foundation. In addition, the local authority may run a home care service to help with getting up and going to bed, and 'twilight nursing' or night-sitting may be available. Get details of these services from social services departments, local Age Concern groups or a hospice. As always, the principle in organising and co-ordinating these arrangements is to identify the need and then find someone to supply it.

Hospital care

Some sick residents will be in hospital already when they reach the final stage of their illness, and some will need to be moved there, perhaps because the family and support services cannot cope with them at home. Many hospitals, despite limited resources, still manage to do their best – and a very good best – for terminally ill patients. Some have a team of specialists who will advise general ward staff on particular problems of medical and nursing care.

However, in general, the acute medical or surgical ward is not an ideal place for someone who is about to die, as it requires different skills from those needed for the proper care of someone who is terminally ill. Acute wards are like garages, geared to a rapid in-and-out curative service. Something more like a gardener's attention to the process of nature is required in the care of someone who is dying.

Home or hospital?

As a warden with knowledge of local services and of the personalities of those involved, your opinion as to where a dying resident can best be looked after may be helpful in making the decision about whether to move someone to hospital. While personal wishes should be respected whenever possible, sometimes when community resources are scarce and the resident needs a lot of help, there is no alternative to hospital care. When this is so, neither the relatives nor you should feel guilty, but should concentrate on finding ways in which the dying person's life can be lived as richly as possible until its end, within the limits of the situation. Do not be afraid to ask for extra visiting privileges or outings because you feel that they may disrupt ward routine. You are likely to find ward staff more approachable and flexible than you think, provided the care of other patients is not jeopardised.

Hospice care

The modern hospice movement was started because of the difficulties of caring for dying people in either a home or a hospital setting. Hospice staff can concentrate on the patient's total needs without the distraction of operating lists or the pursuit of unlikely cures. Technical knowledge and ability is still essential – staff need to understand the advantages and disadvantages of particular drugs and other types of treatment in controlling troublesome symptoms such as pain, cough or difficulty in breathing.

Two objections are sometimes made to hospice care. Firstly, many hospices are religious foundations, and some people fear that they will find the spiritual climate oppressive. However, this rarely seems to be a problem in practice. Secondly, some people expect a hospice to be gloomy and forbidding. In fact there usually seems to be a feeling of peaceful competence, often made livelier by staff children in playgroups.

The more a hospice can be integrated into the community, the more comfortable people will feel about it, and about death and dying. If you have a hospice near your scheme, try to find out more about its services and facilities. This knowledge should help you to come to terms with your own fears and make you more able to help your residents when they are dying or have a relative or close friend who needs hospice care. Hospice places are not always available, but their number is increasing; find out more from the Hospice Information Service.

People's reactions to the prospect of death

Some people die quickly after a brief illness, and the question of adjustment does not arise. Others, however, have to face a period when they suffer an illness and know or suspect that they will die before long. They react to this situation in various ways, often showing the feelings described below. Some people progress through them in stages, but more often they move back and forth between them. For instance, someone who one day seems to have accepted what is happening may be angry all over again on the next day, or may even be denying that they are seriously ill.

Denial

Sometimes the seriously ill person avoids the truth, does not ask questions, and does not want the facts to be spelt out. If the doctor or another carer tries to talk about the illness and its outcome the patient will be deaf to the information, and may later strenuously deny that anyone has raised the subject. You should be aware of this stage of denial whenever a seriously ill resident tells you that 'no one told me anything'. This may be a true account of his or her perceptions, but will not necessary mean that no one has tried to explain what is going on.

Those around the dying person may collude in this behaviour. If a man who is dying and his wife both deny the truth about his illness, each of them has to cope with it alone – a sad ending to a relationship that may have involved 40 years of mutual help and comfort. Again, relatives sometimes try to persuade the doctor to concoct a tale of likely recovery because 'Mother would never be able to take it'. Mother almost certainly can, but the family are wondering whether they can bear the stark reality of helping mother to die. However, you should remember that denial is a useful defence until the hearer is ready to take in the truth; it is useless and unkind to try to break it down.

Anger

People may not expect a terminally ill person to be angry, and it can be very difficult for carers and relatives to cope with and understand. A religious person may direct the anger at God, and a minister of religion may be the best person to help. More commonly the anger finds a human target, often chosen at random. The victim may be a carer or doctor whose kindness and competence may come under attack, or a relative may be picked on.

The anger stage can be worked through if the person can express their feelings to someone who can tolerate them as a sign of pain, rather than being hurt or offended or withdrawing love and attention. For the person on the receiving end of the anger – and it may be you – this is not at all easy. Perhaps you may find it helpful to think of the person's feelings as a bit like pus bursting from a boil – until the nastiness is out, the sore cannot heal.

Withdrawal

Denial and anger may be followed by withdrawal, when the dying person gives up hope, stops fighting and comes close to despair. If relatives and carers conspire to protect the person from this stage, they will have to face it alone, when instead they need support from someone who understands the situation but is not overwhelmed by it. All the helper can do is to be with the dying person in their misery.

Unpleasant physical symptoms are especially distressing for someone going through this stage, so try to make sure these are being treated. People sometimes gain comfort from making practical arrangements for relatives who will be left behind. You may like to suggest this, though great sensitivity is likely to be necessary if, for instance, the resident has not yet made a Will. You could also encourage them to think about the amount of meaning and purpose there has already been in their life. It will also help if they can be reassured that they will die peacefully and also will not be left alone.

Regression

Some dying people become babyish and demanding. Their carers may find this irritating, and then feel guilty. On the other hand, they may enjoy 'babying' the dying person, who then comes to resent their attitude. Dying people should be treated as adults and expected to behave as such, within the limits of their illness.

Acceptance

This is not necessarily a miserable or depressing stage, and you can help the dying person through it with dignity.

Feeling helpless is a recipe for depression: even the smallest effort to keep up a good appearance helps lift the spirit. Three days' growth of beard ruin a man's self-respect. Most women like to wear their own attractive day or night clothes and to have their hair set or tinted, even in the last weeks or days before death. Personal possessions reflect our personalities, so the clutter on the bedside table can be very reassuring.

Patients who accept their approaching death are often eager to be used as 'teaching material' to help doctors and nurses learn more about terminal

illness. Many people say that this enables them to find some meaning in
their experience.

Talking with someone who is dying

Most – though not all – doctors try to tell their terminally ill patients as
much about their illness as they are able to take in. A dying person may
have been told everything, but have blocked it out during the denial
stage. If you think your resident is ready to be told more, you should tell
the GP. This will of course be much easier if you have built up a good relationship with the doctor, so that your judgement of the situation will be
valued.

There may be times when you will want to opt for the easy way out by 'jollying along' a dying resident. For instance, if they say 'I'm not getting any
better, in fact I seem worse', and you reply, 'Now cheer up – you'll be as
right as rain by Easter', this makes their situation lonelier and more difficult, whilst an inarticulate but sympathetic grunt or repetition of what
they said would allow them to continue to talk and be reassured about not
being left alone.

Another difficulty may arise if relatives try to involve you in a conspiracy
to keep the truth from the dying person. This places you in a quite impossible position, and you should state clearly that you think the deception is
both useless and unkind.

No one should have the impression that dealing with dying people
involves learning the right thing to do, as there are no right answers.
What matters is the quality of your relationship with the person who is
dying and how well you communicate your concern and common
humanity. Words may be unimportant; listening and just being there are
what really matter.

You may find it helpful to read an excellent book called *I Don't Know
What to Say – how to help and support someone who is dying* (see p 227).

What to do at the death bed

When a resident is about to die, you should encourage the relatives to sit
with and help look after them. Remember that hearing is the last sense to
be lost; even people who appear to be unconscious may be aware of what

is said around them. Perhaps a priest or other minister of religion may be able to comfort the dying person or the family by prayer or other means. However, great sensitivity is required in this situation, as considerable distress may be caused, for instance, if Christian symbols and practices are used for someone of another faith. Get advice about this if you are unsure about the procedure for a resident from a different religious or ethnic group from your own. (Also see Further Reading.)

The spiritual and emotional aspects of the situation need to be underpinned with common sense. Relatives and friends watching beside a death bed need comfortable chairs; they may welcome a drink being brought into the room and perhaps a sandwich. They will also need access to a nearby lavatory.

An expected death is rarely gruesome – the person gradually stops breathing, and becomes pale and cold, quite peacefully. If those present feel able to, they should remove excess bedding, leaving just one pillow and a covering sheet. The body should be straightened with the arms by the sides, and heating in the room should be turned off. The eyelids should be gently shut, the mouth held closed by a pillow or book under the chin, and the doctor should be notified. After the death certificate has been filled in, the relative who is going to organise the funeral should get in touch with the undertaker, who will usually remove the body.

HELPING BEREAVED PEOPLE

However well relatives and friends seem prepared for the death of a loved one, it will still come as a shock when it happens. The conventional British stiff upper lip is not particularly healthy behaviour at this time; if those from other cultures and traditions want to express their feelings more openly, no attempt should be made to stop them

Because other people do not know what to say to someone who has been recently bereaved, they may avoid meeting them altogether. In fact, what is said is much less important than just being there. Simply say how sorry you are, and do not worry if you shed a few tears. However, avoid wallowing in emotion; visitors to a bereaved household should never expect the mourners to comfort them.

Informing others about a death

To prevent rumours circulating through a scheme, it is best to give out simple details about a resident's death, without invading the privacy of the mourners.

Children should be told truthfully about a death in language they can understand, with emphasis on the dead person being 'all right now'. They should not be excluded from family grief; if Granny is weepy or irritable, an explanation that she is sorry about Grandad dying is better than allowing them to imagine that they are to blame. However, grief should not be forced upon them – if they are playing happily, they should not be expected to sit in silence.

Organising the funeral

The funeral is usually arranged by a close relative of the dead person. Age Concern England produce a useful Factsheet on this subject. Residents who wish to do so should of course be encouraged to attend. Do not discourage them as a well-meaning but misguided attempt to stop them becoming upset. Religious services and family gatherings are important rites of passage which enable the survivors to adjust to the fact of death and to express their grief.

In British society a funeral service seems to help mourners most when it includes references to the dead person's life and personality. This is of course difficult for clergy to achieve if the deceased has not entered the church doors since their marriage 50 years ago. However, you may be able to pass on useful personal details and suggestions about favourite hymns or pieces of music that will help make the service more personal.

If you need to advise other residents about the rituals usually followed by a particular faith that is unfamiliar to you, get advice from someone who knows. For instance, Orthodox Jewish mourners sit 'shiva', a seven-day period of mourning in the home; visits from gentiles during this period are welcomed, though men should take along a hat to wear during prayers, while women, however liberated, should be prepared to be self-effacing.

You may find the book *Caring for Dying People of Different Faiths* useful (see p 227).

The process of mourning

Immediately after the death, bereaved people are commonly numbed, and may even be surprised not to feel more sadness. They may behave like robots while performing the necessary duties of registering the death, arranging the funeral and so on. This stage usually lasts a few days, often until after the funeral, to be replaced by attacks of acute grief interrupting a constant feeling of sadness. These bouts are often brought on by chance reminders as, for instance, when a widow receives a letter addressed to 'Mr and Mrs'.

This stage of grieving feels very like fear or acute anxiety. Some mourners are unable to eat or sleep, and lose weight, though others grow fatter through 'comfort eating'. They may complain of palpitations, headaches and an upset stomach, and may be irritable and nervous. All these symptoms will be worse during grief attacks. Bereaved people are often unable to concentrate on anything and wander aimlessly indoors and out. They may constantly scan people's faces as though searching for the dead partner or friend.

A mourner may call aloud for the dead person, and think constantly about the time immediately before the death, saying, 'I go over that morning again and again'. Hallucinations of the dead person's presence are very common – for example, a widow may 'hear' her husband's key in the lock at his normal time of homecoming, or even his voice. Strangers in a crowd may be mistaken for the dead person and approached, with embarrassing results. Remember that behaviour like this is normal; if necessary, reassure mourners that they are not 'going mad'.

Gradually, attacks of grief occur less frequently, and bereaved people gradually start to enjoy life again. If they feel guilty about this, try to tell them that the dead person would not have wanted them to go on grieving for ever.

After some time – often a year or more in a close relationship – the survivors begin to put together a new life, and should be encouraged to do so. Eventually reminders of the dead person are no longer painful and will evoke happy memories. Nevertheless, relapses of grief are to be expected at the anniversary of the death and at other significant times, such as Christmas and birthdays; they may also be stimulated by new losses.

Though grieving may seem acceptable behaviour in a widow or widower, you should accept as normal similar behaviour in close friends of the dead person, or anyone to whom the loss is significant – including yourself. There is no need for you to hide your sorrow about a death in the scheme from the other residents. They may be comforted by realising how much you value them.

Giving support after the funeral

Support for bereaved people often dwindles as relatives and friends return to their homes after the funeral, though mourners badly need a listening ear. Do not blot out their need to express grief by making continual neutral conversation, or by jollying them along. Do not feel guilty if something you say stimulates tears, or if you start crying – shared tears may do a lot to reduce feelings of isolation.

Sorrow will not be the only emotion a mourner experiences and needs to talk about; anger is very common. Carers and relatives may be 'blamed' for the death, and the mourner may also be angry with the dead person themselves, especially if the death was sudden and the deceased's affairs were not in order. The mourner may feel that the clearing up has been left to the usual dogsbody.

Feelings of guilt are also common. Mourners may feel guilty about real, imagined or magnified faults in the relationship that has ended, especially if there were disagreements during a long illness and the bereaved person felt irritated or now feels angry. Natural relief that caring is over may also be accompanied by guilt. Try to reassure mourners that they did all that was humanly possible in the circumstances, if this is true; if not, maintain a tactful silence.

Sometimes dead people are spoken about almost as saints, and 'shrines' are set up in their honour with photographs, flowers and candles. Resist the temptation to point out how far this rosy picture is from the truth; these feelings too must be allowed to run their course. Just occasionally, idealisation is used to cover anger that the mourner is unable to express; when you suspect this, try introducing a little reality into the situation.

It often seems to comfort the survivors if another person somewhere has benefited from their loss. The fact that someone else has received a transplanted organ, or that useful medical information has been gained from a post-mortem examination can help the bereaved person. Even the amount of memorial donations to a favourite charity provides comfort.

Well-intentioned friends often urge bereaved people to attend doctors' surgeries asking for 'something for their nerves'. In general this is unwise, as the suppressed grief will emerge later in one form or another, and may then be even more difficult to endure. Sometimes a mourner becomes exhausted, and then an occasional hypnotic to provide a restful night may be useful and harmless. If you are worried about the mourner's mental or physical health, consider getting in touch with the GP; if suicide is mentioned, do this without delay.

Some mourners benefit from bereavement counselling, and the local Age Concern or hospice will know what is available in your area. Organisations such as Cruse – Bereavement Care and the National Association of Widows may also be useful contacts.

This chapter has been about the loss of another human being, but the other losses common in old age will be grieved for in the same way – when a pet dies, for instance, or when a part of the body is 'lost' following a stroke, a mastectomy or an amputation. Do not forget that everyone coming into sheltered housing has been bereaved of a previous home, with all the memories it holds.

Grief is the price we have to pay for loving, committed relationships; mourning is sad, but it would be even sadder to have nothing and no one to mourn.

7 Getting Help from Other Agencies

The services provided by statutory and voluntary agencies can help to improve the quality of life of residents in sheltered housing. Remember that both the amount of help and the charge made for it vary considerably around the country. Make sure that your residents know what help is available, and support them in getting it. However, your residents should decide whether or not they want a particular service; ideally they should make the contact and arrangements for themselves.

CO-ORDINATING LOCAL SERVICES

As you will be dealing with a variety of people, it will help to brush up on your interpersonal skills. Make as many personal contacts as you can in your local health and social services, and find out and use the names of people you come across regularly. When other professionals visit your scheme, seize the opportunity to explain how you work and to outline your residents' needs, perhaps over a cup of coffee. Consider broadening your own experience by arranging a visit to watch your doctor's receptionist or home care organiser in action. When others have been especially helpful, send a card at Christmas, or an invitation to a social event: people are more likely to put themselves to extra trouble when they feel their efforts are valued.

Try to remain polite and pleasant in your dealings with people providing services, even when they seem unhelpful and your problems are overwhelming. Though difficult, this is the best way to ensure that the vulnerable elderly residents who depend on you receive the help they require.

Older people often have very complex problems. Try to help them break these down into their components – for instance, a need for help with personal care, for hot meals or for social contact. The resident, if necessary with your help, can then ask clearly for the service required.

Compiling your own list of local services may make it easier to get help quickly. When there seems to be an urgent need for a missing service – a day centre for mentally frail people, for instance – you could ask why, and press for its introduction. The secretary of the local Community Health Council may be able to help you with this when a health need is not being met. When a resident's need for social care has been recognised but help is not forthcoming because of shortages, the resident may be glad of your help in using the social service department's complaints procedure, which also deal with appeals like this.

Although wardens have people all around them, professionally speaking they are often isolated. It can be very useful for them to meet, both for mutual support and to identify unmet needs. Meetings could be organised for wardens employed by the same organisation, or for those from different organisations based in the same area. This approach is encouraged by the National Wardens Association.

USING THE HEALTH SERVICE

General practitioner

Everyone is entitled to be on the list of a family doctor. You can obtain a list of GPs from main post offices, public libraries, the local telephone book or directly from the Family Health Services Authority (FHSA), formerly the Family Practitioner Committee (FPC). The Community Health Council (CHC) (see below) can also help with addresses and with the administrative procedures used to find or change a GP. The CHC can also supply you with a very useful free leaflet called 'Patients' Rights – a summary of the responsibilities of users of the NHS'.

Some family doctors are especially interested in older people and their medical problems; you could find out whether any GPs nearby have this special interest. It helps if the GP works as part of a primary health care team, at a health centre that offers a range of resources. The surgery premises should be easy for residents to get to independently, and the practice staff helpful.

Apart from attending to a resident's day-to-day health needs, the GP provides access to other medical services such as hospital specialists and can also refer patients for help from other members of the primary health care team. A GP who understands the needs of a sheltered housing scheme can improve the health and independence of residents and make your job as warden considerably easier.

Make sure that residents are registered with a GP when they enter your scheme. It may be possible for a newcomer to keep the GP they have already, but check with the resident that the doctor is aware of the change of address, and that it is within the practice catchment area. If this is not done, difficulties may arise if the resident needs to call the doctor out for a home visit. When a new GP has to be found, the choice of doctor is of course up to the resident; you may, however, be asked for advice, and should be prepared with suggestions.

The GP's relationship with the residents

Encourage residents to deal directly with their doctors; if confidential information comes your way, be careful to keep it private. You may sometimes feel it would help if you knew more about a resident's medical condition, but if they wish to keep this information private, they have every right to do so. You may wonder whether you should confide your worries about a resident's health to a doctor, nurse or other health care professional without the resident's consent. This can be very difficult to decide. Mentally intact people have a right not to consult the doctor if they do not wish to do so. In such cases, you may try to persuade the sick resident to seek help, but have no right to over-ride their decision to manage unaided. At other times you may fear that the resident's judgement is so clouded by illness that they are unable to make sensible decisions. The best course then is to notify the doctor and explain the situation. The doctor can then decide what to do next, usually visiting the sick resident to make a skilled assessment of their health, especially the mental state.

When the doctor is seeing a resident in their flat, you should be present during the consultation only if asked to be. Otherwise, give whatever information is necessary and explain how you may be reached if needed.

For routine medical attention, it is best for the resident to attend the surgery or health centre whenever possible. Facilities for diagnosis and treatment are readily on hand there, and expensive medical time is not wasted in travelling to the scheme. Some residents, however, may find it difficult to get to the surgery; also, a home visit by the doctor may give a useful all-round picture of the patient's problems to help in organising treatment appropriately.

A doctor 'on site' makes it easier for housebound patients to be seen regularly. When a number of frail residents are on one GP's list, the doctor may make regular visits at a pre-arranged time. This will enable you to explain how someone's health and independence are being maintained from day to day, and the doctor can alert you to warning signs or allay your unnecessary fears. Any decline in a resident's condition is more likely to be spotted early, and repeat prescriptions for drugs properly reassessed. Regular attendance at a scheme helps the doctor too, as any non-urgent problems can often be held over until the next visit. You may be able to work with the doctor and avoid an upset for a resident by spotting a potential emergency; for instance, if a resident seems unwell before a long weekend or public holiday, you can make sure the doctor sees them beforehand rather than waiting to see what happens.

The GP's duties

Patients have a right to see a doctor – not necessarily their own GP – at the surgery during surgery hours. People who have not made an appointment may be offered one at a later surgery. If they think their problem will not wait till then, they should say so, politely but firmly. Many practices keep a space in surgery appointment lists for genuine emergencies. However, to minimise disruption to other patients, those with urgent problems will have to see whichever doctor is available, and may have to wait to do so.

A GP is not obliged to make a home visit whenever asked to do so; the decision as to whether or not this is necessary is up to the doctor. If you think that a resident's condition warrants an early visit but the GP's receptionist seems reluctant to arrange this, ask when you can discuss the matter directly with the doctor. Be prepared to ring back at a time when the doctor is free to take such calls.

When telephoning the doctor in an emergency, try to have the reason for the call clear in your mind. There are three ways in which doctors help sick people: by working out what is wrong with them, by curing the illness or relieving its symptoms, and by telling patients and those around them what to expect to happen next. If the resident needs help in any of these ways, your call is justified. However, you should try to avoid emergency calls that are either trivial or inappropriate. For instance, a lonely older person may have a real need for social contact, but a brief visit from a doctor who may be a stranger will do little or nothing to help. When you are in doubt as to whether or not an emergency visit is necessary, try to arrange for the resident to talk to the doctor directly. Of course, you should always err on the side of caution: you are not expected to make medical decisions.

Make sure that you give adequate basic information as to who the patient is and where they are. At night it is a great help in finding an address if someone puts lights on at the front of the building.

Put out emergency calls between the hours of, say, midnight and 7.00 am only if it is absolutely necessary to do so. Of course, illness, accident and mishap are no respecters of the clock or the calendar, and there is sometimes no alternative to asking for help in these unsocial hours. Doctors usually have to do a full day's work the day before and the day after a night on call. They will be more likely to respond quickly and cheerfully to an emergency call if they know that the person on the other end makes such calls only when absolutely necessary. While you should never take chances in a real emergency, you may be able to avoid the night hours. If someone seems unwell at 9.00pm, for instance, it is better to notify the doctor before he or she retires to bed rather than to wait and see what happens. In the same way it may be possible to keep a call until 7.00am rather than to put it out an hour or so earlier.

No patient is automatically entitled to a second opinion from a hospital specialist unless the GP thinks it is necessary. There are two reasons for this: firstly, it is often difficult for a patient to understand on the basis of their symptoms which hospital doctor is required; without the GP's general medical knowledge, the patient may not be directed to the correct specialist, and treatment may be delayed. Secondly, a few people make repeated, unnecessary demands for referral. They may be suffering from depression, or have other social or psychological problems. The GP can make sure that they can get appropriate help, rather than making a wearying and useless round of hospital specialists.

GPs now offer all patients over 75 years old an annual consultation, either at the surgery or at home (see p 46).

Practices now produce information leaflets describing the services they offer. You may like to collect these and display them on the scheme notice board.

Nurses

District or community nurses

They may visit a resident to change dressings or a catheter, to give injections or to help with bowel problems. They will also teach nursing skills to relatives and other carers, and are a vital source of advice and support. In some areas nursing auxiliaries may perform the simpler nursing duties, and help with bathing, personal hygiene or getting someone up. A district nurse is usually attached to the GP's practice, and the receptionist or practice manager will put you in touch with one.

Practice nurses

Many doctors also employ a practice nurse, who may see patients independently of the doctor. They often run preventative health care services such as screening clinics, and may help with weight loss and stopping smoking. They may also monitor long-standing conditions such as high blood pressure and diabetes, dress wounds, give injections and syringe ears.

District and practice nurses will be likely to know which of the specialised nurses described below work in your area, and how you can reach them.

Community psychiatric nurses (CPNs)

These have special qualifications in mental health nursing. They care for people of any age who have mental health problems, and also for confused older people. They are useful sources of advice on ways of coping with confused residents who wander, neglect themselves or show other sorts of challenging behaviour. If you have difficulty in getting medical help for someone who seems to have a psychiatric illness, it is sometimes useful to ask if a CPN can visit, as his or her opinion that psychiatric help is needed may be more likely to be listened to than yours.

You may be able to get in touch with a CPN directly at the headquarters of a community mental health care team, or you may need to work through the GP. To find out what the arrangements are in your area, ask the GP's receptionist or practice manager, the community or practice nurse or the secretary of the Community Health Council.

Continence advisers

These nurses are specially trained to help with faults of bladder or bowel function. They work in continence clinics in hospitals or health centres, but also visit patients at home.

The GP or practice nurse may know if there is a continence adviser working locally. You could also get in touch with the Continence Foundation, which has information about all services round the country.

Incontinence pads and pants may be available free or at low cost from the health authority, but sometimes the range is limited. The continence adviser or district nurse will be able to say whether something more suitable is available. If the health authority is unable to fund this, the resident should seek further advice from the Continence Foundation. The social services department may run an incontinence laundry service, and you may want to ask about this.

A Factsheet called *Help with Incontinence* is available from Age Concern England (see p 233).

Cancer nurses

These have special training in helping with symptom relief and also with the emotional needs of cancer sufferers and their families. The Macmillan Fund (National Society for Cancer Relief) and the Marie Curie Memorial Foundation both operate a community nursing service and also have homes for respite care; the GP and district nurse have access to these. Also, your local hospice may have an outreach team to look after people at home; the Hospice Information Service can provide further details.

Stoma care nurses

These work in hospitals and in the community, helping patients to adjust to the change in their bodies and to cope with day-to-day care of the stoma. Residents who have had a colostomy or ileostomy for years may have lost contact with the stoma care nurse; the district nurse will know how to get in touch with one.

Night nursing, sitting services and respite care

In some areas nurses will visit patients in the evening to provide late night treatment and help with getting to bed; the district nurse will know about this, or you could ask at the Community Health Council.

Night-sitting to relieve a carer can sometimes be arranged through a Crossroads Care Attendant Scheme, the Red Cross or another agency. A day-time sitting service may be available, as may a period of respite care in a hospital or residential home. The district nurse, social services department or local branch of Age Concern will be able to tell you what is available in your area.

Private nurses

These can be obtained through agencies, but services tend to be expensive.

Health visitors

These are nurses who have had an extra year's training in preventive medicine, psychology, public health and sociology. They will usually be part of the primary health care team based at the health centre or GP surgery.

'Geriatric health visitors', who specialise in the care of older people, are invaluable. They are trained to recognise the early signs of illness and the social circumstances that predispose to it, and are often involved in the Over-75 check. Health visitors should know the full range of health and social services available to your residents.

Physiotherapists

These work in hospitals, including Day Hospitals, and increasingly in the community, sometimes treating patients at home. They specialise in movement and its disorders. Physiotherapists can help to strengthen weak muscles, loosen stiff joints and help people with disabling conditions such as stroke or Parkinson's disease to make the best use of their remaining abilities. They can also give carers practical advice on how to lift and handle a disabled person.

NHS physiotherapy is sometimes in short supply, and it is possible to get treatment privately. It is wise for a resident considering this to ask the doctor if physiotherapy is likely to be helpful, and, if so, to write a referral letter. Suitable physiotherapists will be state registered and members of the Chartered Society of Physiotherapy, with the letters SRP, MCSP after their name.

Dentists

Since October 1990, patients can register with a dentist for continuing care in the same way as with a GP. Dentists do not have to take on everyone who applies to them, and some older people have difficulty in finding a dentist who provides NHS care. They can ask for help from the Family Health Services Authority, the Community Health Council, the local branch of Age Concern or the district dental officers of the Community Dental Service, reached via the health authority.

If older people have difficulty in getting to the surgery, the dentist may visit them at home. Some sheltered housing schemes include a room where dental work can be done. The Community Dental Service may provide clinics and in some case takes mobile caravans to rural areas. Alternatively, it may be possible to arrange special transport to the surgery, for instance via Dial-a-Ride.

People who have registered with a dentist for continuing care will be able to get telephone advice in an emergency arising outside surgery hours, and if necessary will be given urgent treatment.

Further information can be found in Factsheet 5 *Dental Care in Retirement* from Age Concern England.

Chiropodists

These can diagnose and treat foot disorders, which are a common cause of mobility problems. It is especially important that people with diabetes get regular chiropody, preferably from someone with a special interest in this sort of work.

Chiropody is available free on the NHS, and a doctor's referral letter is not necessarily needed. In some areas the service is in short supply, and residents may decide to have private treatment. Health centre staff or the district nurse may be able to recommend someone suitable. (See also p 45.)

It is not always possible to see the chiropodist or foot care assistant often enough to keep the toenails properly cut, and if the resident is unable to do this for him or herself, it can be very difficult to find help. The district nurse, the Community Health Council or local branch of Age Concern may know whether there is a nail-cutting service in your area; if not, you may want to press for more adequate foot care to be provided locally.

Community Health Councils (CHCs)

Community Health Councils were introduced in the 1970s to bridge the gap between the organisations providing health services and the patients who used them. CHC members were supposed to keep the local NHS under review by visiting hospitals and clinics to see how services worked and then suggesting possible improvements. They were also expected to comment on how well health and social services worked together in 'grey areas', and to make sure that services corresponded to what was needed locally and roughly conformed to national norms.

Despite NHS changes that have affected their powers, CHCs remain an invaluable source of information as to what local health services are available and how best to use them. The Secretary and staff were in a good position to collate and pass on facts about unmet needs to organisations that could do something about them. They are still able to help with complaints about health services and the staff who operate them. This sort of work is often best done informally, but when a formal complaint is necessary, CHC staff can give it the best chance of success by making sure it passes through the proper channels in good time.

CHCs often have High Street premises and are usually open during office hours. Their meetings are open to the public and the Secretary and staff are useful contacts for the warden to make.

Unfortunately, recent legislation has limited the role of CHCs to some extent. For instance, though a Regional Health Authority must consult the CHC on proposals to establish an NHS trust, once the trust has been set up it does not need to consult the CHC before altering service provision. The role of CHCs is now limited at meetings of health authorities and NHS trusts: members will not necessarily be supplied with the relevant papers beforehand, they may speak only if invited and may be excluded from non-public parts of meetings. These changes seem likely to make it more difficult for CHCs to fulfil their previous role in the long run, and health services are likely to become less responsive to those who use them.

USING SOCIAL SERVICES

Effects of community care legislation

Recent legislation affects the way social services departments work. Some of the important features are set out below.

The intention of the Government is that domiciliary day and respite services should all aim to help people who wish to do so to remain in their own homes whenever this is possible and sensible. This may mean that some frail or disabled residents who would previously have moved on to residential care will now remain in sheltered housing. This is probably what most people would prefer, provided adequate home care is available; however, if home care is insufficient, the residents' quality of life may be worse than if they had moved into a residential home.

Social services departments have a new duty to assess the needs of people who ask for community care services. In that assessment, they should take into account the client's needs, what the client wants to happen and what the carers' wishes are. Then the social services department must decide what – if any – services they will provide or arrange. Age Concern England's Factsheet 32 *Disability and Ageing – your rights to social services* explains rights to services for disabled and older people.

When a person's needs are complicated, or when a great deal of support is needed, a care manager may be responsible for making sure that all services work together well.

Local authorities must encourage the development and functioning of independent organisations providing services. This means that social services may arrange for a service to be given by such an agency – personal care at home, for instance – rather than employing personal carers and running its own service.

Most people agree with the ideas behind community care. Older people who need some help with daily living are likely to have better lives if they can get that help at home and have more choice in how it is given. However, some people have doubts as to whether enough money will be available for the system to work properly. It will not help older people to discuss what their needs and preferences are if the services they are shown to require are not there.

You can find out more about the new system from Age Concern's publication *The Community Care Handbook* (see p 230).

Occupational therapists (OTs)

Occupational therapists help people to maintain independence and daily living skills. They visit people with an illness or disability at home to find out whether equipment such as walking aids or modified cutlery would help them, and, if so, to arrange for it to be provided. The OT can also suggest adaptations that could usefully be made to the home. These might include ramps for wheelchair access, extra handrails or the resiting of kitchen equipment.

Unfortunately, in some areas there are very long waiting lists both for the OT's original assessment visit and, after it, for equipment to be provided or work to be done. Faced with these problems, residents may decide to obtain what they need more quickly from another source. Disabled Living Centres can advise about what is available, and residents can make appointments to try out equipment. This is not on sale at centres, but can be ordered from the manufacturers. The Disabled Living Foundation in London can direct you to your nearest Disabled Living Centre.

Other sources include branches of the Red Cross, which may lend home nursing equipment such as bath seats and commodes; a small charge may be made. Alternatively, some equipment is on sale at large chemists such as Boots.

Personal care and help at home

Most home care services now concentrate on helping clients with washing, toileting, dressing, meal preparation and going to bed at night. There may be a special short-term intensive service for people recently discharged from hospital. The helper may be called a home care assistant, personal carer or have another, similar title. In some cases private agencies may provide this service, but access to it will still be via the social services department.

Arrangements for help with bathing are very variable round the country. In some areas bath aides or nursing auxiliaries visit clients at home, whilst in others clients are transported to a bathing centre. In many places an assisted bath can be offered only about once a fortnight, whilst most older people would like to have one at least once a week or more frequently. Some sheltered housing providers have tried to help by putting in a communal shower with a seat, or installing a modified bath which is easy to use. If you think something like this would help the residents of your scheme, you could raise the topic with your managers.

In some areas home care assistants still do shopping and collect pensions. Help with domestic work such as cleaning may need to be arranged privately. However, practical assistance in the home is a service to which disabled people who need it should be entitled under the provisions of the Chronically Sick and Disabled Persons Act 1970 (see Age Concern Factsheet 32 *Disability and Ageing – your right to social services*; Factsheet 6 *Finding Help at Home* explains the full range of services that may be available).

Help with meals

Services for people who have difficulty in cooking for themselves vary round the country. The best known form of help is Meals on Wheels, when a hot midday meal is delivered to the person's home at reasonable cost. The Meals on Wheels service may be run by the social services department, by voluntary organisations such as the WRVS or Age Concern or by another agency. Kosher, Asian or Afro-Caribbean foods may be available, as may diets for special health needs, such as diabetes. How often meals are available, how much they cost and whether there is a service at weekends varies from place to place.

Whilst the Meals on Wheels service is often valuable, it has its limitations. It is difficult to provide much choice as to what is on offer and what time it arrives. There is an inevitable delay between cooking and eating, so food may become less appetising and loses some of its nutritional value.

An alternative on offer in some areas is a supply of oven-ready meals in a small freezer. Sometimes the client is also lent a microwave oven. Some sheltered housing schemes operate their own system, selling freezer meals to residents at cost. Residents then have more choice of menu, and can cook the meal at a time to suit themselves. Such a system may be very useful to mentally alert people with purely physical disabilities, or to those who are reluctant to cook during a period of convalescence. However, mentally frail people may not be able to manage such tasks without help.

Some older people prefer to attend a luncheon club, enjoying the social contact as much as the meal. These are sometimes run by local authorities and sometimes by voluntary agencies. Some are held in sheltered housing schemes, where both residents and older people who live nearby can attend. There is usually a charge for the meal, and transport is sometimes available.

It is worth remembering that some people will become independent of these services and able to cook for themselves if their health problems are attended to and appropriate kitchen aids are provided.

Day centres

These are run by the social services department, voluntary groups or in residential homes. Day centres may form part of 'resource centres', which provide a range of services and information for older people. They are usually open from mid-morning to mid-afternoon, with tea, coffee and a hot mid-day meal provided. As with luncheon clubs, there may be a charge for attendance and for transport. They can be an excellent source of social contact for older people who enjoy activities such as dancing, indoor bowls and crafts. In addition, services such as chiropody or help with bathing may be on offer.

Some day centres cater specially for dementia sufferers. These can give valuable stimulation to the mentally frail person and a welcome respite to carers. Unfortunately, there is often a long waiting list for places.

Clubs

These can be useful in relieving isolation and providing social contact, particularly for residents suffering from a particular condition such as multiple sclerosis or a stroke, or from a disability such as a hearing loss. Churches run clubs for older people, and voluntary organisations such as Age Concern may offer a range of activities such as tea dances, ballroom dancing or 'pop-in' centres. Fitter retired people may like to get involved in running club activities.

Many older people continue to attend the Women's Institute, Rotary Club or other special interest group after retirement, and they may prefer to mix with a variety of age groups in this way.

A shy newcomer may feel more comfortable being introduced to a club by a resident who is already a member. However, not everyone is a 'joiner': older people should not be expected to take part in activities that are not to their taste.

Residential and nursing care

Some people who live in sheltered housing may choose to move on to a residential or nursing home, perhaps because they are finding it more difficult to look after themselves. Despite the emphasis on care in the community, residential care is still supposed to be available to those who want and need it. Local authorities still run some homes, but have transferred some of their stock to other agencies such as housing associations or 'not for profit' trusts. Private homes are run by individuals for profit, and voluntary homes by charities. Local authorities may use places in any of them, and these are allocated through the social services department. Most residential homes, whether private, voluntary or local authority, are now inspected by a separate unit of the local authority. They may continue to care for residents only if they satisfy registration requirements.

Nursing homes must have qualified nurses on the staff. They are inspected and registered by the District Health Authority. Some homes are 'dual registered' as both residential and nursing homes.

If, after assessing the older person's needs, the local authority agrees to arrange a place in a residential or nursing home, the authority becomes responsible for paying the full fee. It will then aim to claim a sum of money back from the resident as a contribution to the charges. This amount will be based on a detailed assessment of the resident's ability to pay. It will include any social security benefits the resident is entitled to, as he or she will be expected to claim these. The resident will then be left with a certain amount of money each week for personal expenses. If they so wish, the resident's relatives can make a contribution to enable their elder to afford a more expensive home.

Age Concern's Factsheet 30 *Local Authority Charging Procedures for Residential and Nursing Home Care* explains the complicated charging system in more detail.

People sometimes move into a home they know of already or find one by personal recommendation. The Registration Officer for Residential Homes at the social services department and the Registration Officer for Nursing Homes at the District Health Authority both keep lists of the homes they register. Local organisations such as Age Concern, the Citizens Advice Bureau or Community Health Council may be able to advise, as may social workers in the community or in hospital. Helpful national organisations include Counsel and Care and Elderly Accommodation Counsel. Age Concern England's Factsheet 29 *Finding Residential and Nursing Home Accommodation* will also be useful.

Social workers

These can be reached at the area or team office of the social services department. Social workers may be available to advise and counsel residents on medical or social problems. Sometimes they will arrange for the different sorts of social care described above, and may work as 'care managers', making sure that more complex care packages are delivered efficiently. Social workers may also advise residents about financial help; in some areas a Welfare Benefits Officer specialises in this sort of work. Some social services departments employ staff who specialise in the care of people with a visual handicap or hearing impairment.

Residents who are admitted to hospital and who need help after discharge should have an assessment of their future care needs. This may be carried out by a hospital social worker.

VOLUNTARY SOCIAL SERVICES

These vary in different areas, but where available give useful back-up to the services arranged by the local authority. They may include day centres, voluntary visiting services, help with practical jobs, a transport service such as Dial-a-Ride, recreational activities and holidays for older people.

Organisations for people with particular diseases (eg stroke, Parkinson's, Alzheimer's) or disabilities (eg deafness) may provide social contact for sufferers and their carers and practical help of various kinds. You can find out where they are from the local telephone book, or by getting in touch with the head office listed in the Useful Addresses section.

Voluntary organisations are now playing a more prominent role than ever before. Many are planning to provide services through contracts with local authorities under NHS and Community Care legislation. Your local branch of Age Concern, Citizens Advice Bureau or Council for Voluntary Service should be able to tell you about all the voluntary organisations in your area.

HELP FROM RELIGIOUS ORGANISATIONS

Many elderly people who have attended a place of worship regularly will want to go on being part of the congregation as they grow older. Others return in old age to beliefs and practices that they may have abandoned for a while. Some have never joined any organised religion, or may continue to hold humanist or atheist beliefs.

Meeting the religious needs of these different groups while respecting the wishes of people with no interest in religion may be a difficult job. You may also have beliefs of your own, and it hardly needs saying that you must avoid imposing these on your residents. Whenever necessary, ask advice from community or religious leaders from ethnic or religious groups other than your own.

Clergy are as variable in their personalities and talents as residents of sheltered housing, and the enthusiasm of their congregations will also be unpredictable. What you can expect in terms of spiritual support and pastoral care for your residents will vary widely from place to place. It is a good idea for clergy to become sufficiently 'part of the scenery' around the scheme so as not to be regarded with alarm as heralds of approaching death. Housebound residents who are unable to attend their old place of worship may welcome a service being held in the scheme, whatever the denomination.

Clergy and church officials may be reluctant to intrude on a scheme if they fear that their visit will be unwelcome, and they may be unaware of the special needs of someone who has fallen sick or has been bereaved. It is therefore important for you to make tactful enquiries if you think a resident would like to see a minister of religion. You may also wish to try to involve a local church, synagogue, mosque or other religious organisations in the life of the scheme by inviting a congregation to a social evening.

Useful Addresses

Age Concern Greater London
54 Knatchbull Road
London SE5 9QY
Tel: 071-737 3456

Age Exchange Reminiscence Centre
11 Blackheath Village
London SE3 9LA
Tel: 081-318 9105/3504

Alcohol Concern
305 Gray's Inn Road
London WC1X 8QF
Tel: 071-833 3471

Alcoholics Anonymous
PO Box 1
Stonebow House
Stonebow
York YO1 2NJ
Tel: 0904 644026

Alzheimer's Disease Society
Gordon House
10 Greencoat Place
London SW1P 1PH
Tel: 071-306 0606

Anchor Housing Trust
Anchor House
269a Banbury Road
Oxford OX2 7HU
Tel: 0865 311511

Arthritis and Rheumatism Council for Research
PO Box 177
Chesterfield S41 7TQ
Tel: 0246 558033

ASH (Action on Smoking and Health)
109 Gloucester Place
London W1H 3PH
Tel: 071-935 3519

Association of Community Health Councils for England and Wales
30 Drayton Park
London N5 1PB
Tel: 071-609 8405

Association of Teachers of Lipreading to Adults
c/o S Gaston
3 Halons Road
Eltham
London SE9 5BS
Tel: 081-850 4066

BACUP
3 Bath Place
Rivington Street
London EC2A 3JR
Tel: 071-696 9003

Boots Monitored Dosage System
Tel: 0800 886655

Braille National Library for the Blind
Cromwell Road
Bredbury
Stockport SK6 2SG
Tel: 061-494 0217

Breast Care and Mastectomy Association
15–19 Britten Street
London SW3 3TZ
Tel: 071-867 1103

British Association for the Hard of Hearing
7–11 Armstrong Road
London W3 7JL
Tel: 081-743 1110

British Colostomy Association
15 Station Road
Reading
Berkshire RG1 1LG
Tel: 0734 391537

British Diabetic Association
10 Queen Anne Street
London W1M 0BD
Tel: 071-323 1531

British Gas plc
326 High Holborn
London WC1V 7PT
Tel: 071-242 0789

British Heart Foundation
14 Fitzhardinge Street
London W1H 4DH
Tel: 071-935 0185

British Lung Foundation
8 Peterborough Mews
London SW6 3BL
Tel: 071-371 7704

British Tinnitus Association
105 Gower Street
London WC1E 6AH
Tel: 071-387 8033

British Wireless for the Blind Fund
34 New Road
Chatham
Kent ME4 4QR
Tel: 0634 832501

Broadcasting Support Services
252 Western Avenue
London W3 6XJ
Tel: 081-992 5522

Cancerlink
17 Britannia Street
London WC1X 9JN
Tel: 071-833 2451

Carers National Association
20–25 Glasshouse Yard
London EC1A 4JS
Tel: 071-490 8818

Centre for Policy on Ageing
25–31 Ironmonger Row
London EC1V 3QP
Tel: 071-253 1787

Centre for Sheltered Housing Studies
Dog Lane Mews
Dog Lane, Bewdley
Worcs DY12 2EF
Tel: 0299 402722

Continence Foundation
2 Doughty Street
London WC1N 2PH
Tel: 071-404 6875
Helpline: 091-213 0050

Counsel and Care
Twyman House
16 Bonny Street
London NW1 9PG
Tel: 071-485 1566

Crossroads (Association of Crossroads Care Attendants Schemes Ltd)
10 Regent Place
Rugby
Warwickshire CV21 2PN
Tel: 0788 573653

Cruse – Bereavement Care
Cruse House
126 Sheen Road
Richmond
Surrey TW9 1UR
Tel: 081-940 4818

DAWN (Drugs, Alcohol, Women, Nationwide)
Boundary House
91–93 Charterhouse Street
London EC1M 6HR
Tel: 071-250 3284

Disabled Living Foundation
380 Harrow Road
London W9 2HU
Tel: 071-289 6111

DSS Leaflets Unit
PO Box 21
Stanmore
Middlesex HA7 1AY

Elderly Accommodation Counsel
46a Chiswick High Road
London W4 1SZ
Tel: 081-995 8320
081-742 1182

EXTEND (Exercise Training for the Elderly and Disabled)
1A North Street
Sheringham
Norfolk NR26 8LG
Tel: 0263 822479/824355

Gay Bereavement Project
Vaughan M Williams Centre
Colindale Hospital
Colindale Avenue
London NW9 5HG
Tel: 081-200 0511

Health Education Authority
Hamilton House
Mabledon Place
London WC1H 9TX
Tel: 071-383 3833

Help the Aged
16–18 St James's Walk
London EC1R 0BE
Tel: 071-253 0253

Hospice Information Service
St Christopher's Hospice
51 Lawrie Park Road
Sydenham
London SE26 6DZ
Tel: 081-778 9252

Institute of Housing
Octavia House
Westwood Business Park
Westwood Way
Coventry CV4 8JP
Tel: 0203 694433

Keep Fit Association
Francis House
Francis Street
London SW1P 1DE
Tel: 071-233 8898

Marie Curie Memorial Foundation
28 Belgrave Square
London SW1X 8QG
Tel: 071-235 3325

Medic-Alert Foundation
12 Bridge Wharf
156 Caledonian Road
London N1 9UU
Tel: 071-833 3034

MIND (National Association for Mental Health)
22 Harley Street
London W1N 2ED
Tel: 071-637 0741

National Association of Widows
54–57 Allison Street
Digbeth
Birmingham B5 5TH
Tel: 021-643 8348

National Society for Cancer Relief (Macmillan Fund)
Anchor House
15 Britten Street
London SW3 3TZ
Tel: 071-351 7811

National Wardens Association
24 Clifford Lawton House
3 Whiston Road
London E2 8BN
Tel: 071-729 6516

Parkinson's Disease Society
22 Upper Woburn Place
London WC1H 0RA
Tel: 071-383 3513

Partially Sighted Society
Low Vision Adviser
62 Salusbury Road
London NW6 6NS
Tel: 071-372 1551

Royal College of Psychiatrists
17 Belgrave Square
London SW1X 8PG
Tel: 071-235 2351

Royal National Institute for the Blind (RNIB)
224 Great Portland Street
London W1N 6AA
Tel: 071-388 1266

Royal National Institute for Deaf People (RNID)
105 Gower Street
London WC1E 6AH
Tel: 071-387 8033

SPOD (Association to Aid the Sexual and Personal Relationships of People with a Disability)
286 Camden Road
London N7 0BJ
Tel: 071-607 8851

Stroke Association
CHSA House
123–127 Whitecross Street
London EC1Y 8JJ
Tel: 071-289 6111

Surgichem Ltd (NOMAD Monitored Dosage Systems)
Surgichem House
Milton Court
Horsfield Way
Bredbury Park Industrial Estate
Stockport SK6 2TD
Tel: 061-406 8710

Talking Newspaper Association
National Recording Centre
Heathfield
East Sussex TN21 8DB
Tel: 0435 866102

Terence Higgins Trust
52–54 Gray's Inn Road
London WC1X 8JU
Tel: 071-831 0330
Helpline: 071-242 1010
12.00 noon–10.00 pm

Winslow Elderly Care 1992
Telford Road
Bicester
Oxon OX6 0TS
Tel: 0869 244733

Women's Nationwide Cancer Control Campaign
128 Curtain Road
London EC2A 3AR
Tel: 071-729 1735
Helpline: 071-729 2229

Further Reading

You can ask for books produced by commercial publishers at your local bookshop or library. Books or leaflets produced by national organisations can be obtained from the addresses on pages 220–224. When a leaflet is free, it is wise to send a large sae with your request.

Good health in later life

Keeping Well – a Guide to Health in Retirement (1991) Anne Roberts, Faber & Faber, London. Available from Centre for Sheltered Housing Studies.

Good eating

Eat Well, Stay Well – Healthy eating for people over 60 and *Eat Well, Stay Well for Afro-Caribbean Pensioners*. Available from Age Concern Greater London.

Easy Cooking for One or Two (1988) Louise Davies, Penguin Books, London.

Sensible drinking

Alcohol and Older People – Safer Drinking for the over-60s. Avaiable from Alcohol Concern or Age Concern England.

Smoking

'Give Up' pack – free from ASH; write to the address on page 220 for publications list.

Stopping Smoking Made Easier. Free from Health Education Authority.

Exercise

The Magic of Movement – A tonic for older people (1988) Laura Mitchell, Age Concern England.

Sex, loving and relationships

Living, Loving and Ageing – Sexual and personal relationships in later life (1989) Wendy Greengross and Sally Greengross, Age Concern England.

Various SPOD publications, including *Sexuality and the Physically Disabled – An Introduction for Counsellors*. Write to the address on page 224 for a publications list.

Loneliness – How to overcome it (1988) Val Marriot and Terry Timblick, Age Concern England.

Body maintenance

The Foot Care Book – An A–Z of fitter feet (1988) Judith Kemp, Age Concern England.

Leaflets, including *Cervical Smear Test: when did you have your last test?* and *Everyone's Having the Smear Test* from Women's National Cancer Control Campaign (address on p 224).

Common illness in later life

Various books and leaflets by appropriate organisations, such as Stroke Association, Parkinson's Disease Society, BACUP, etc. Write for publications list to appropriate addresses on pages 220–224.

The eyes and sight problems

All about glaucoma; All about macular degeneration; All about diabetic retinopathy; All about cataracts. Free leaflets from RNIB: write for publications list.

Learning to live with it – Ageing Maculopathy and *Coping with Sight Loss at 80 plus.* Among other In Touch Care Guides, from Broadcasting Support Services.

The ears and hearing impairment

Understanding Hearing Aids; *Installation Guidelines for Induction Loops in Public Places*; *Questions about Tinnitus*; *A Layman's Guide to Tinnitus and How to Live with it*. All available from RNID.

Difficulties with continence

In Control – Help with incontinence (1990) Penny Mares and Factsheet 23 *Help with Incontinence*. Both from Age Concern England.

Confusion and dementia

Caring for the Person with Dementia; *Advice Sheets* and *Information Sheets*. Available from the Alzheimer's Disease Society: write for a publications list.

Aggression; *Wandering*; *Screaming and Shouting*; *Inappropriate Urination*. All by Graham Stoke, Winslow Press, London.

Dementia and Mental Illness in Older People (1993) Elaine Murphy, Papermac (2nd ed).

The 36-hour Day – Caring at home for confused elderly people (1992) Nancy L Mace and Peter V Rabins, Age Concern England.

Medicines

Medication in Sheltered Housing, a research study undertaken on behalf of the Abbeyfield Society, Anchor Housing Association and Hanover. Available from Anchor Housing Trust.

Know Your Medicines (1991) Pat Blair, Age Concern England.

Looking after dying people

I Don't Know What to Say – how to help and support someone who is dying (1988) Dr Rob Buckman, Papermac.

Caring for Dying People of Different Faiths (1987) Julia Neuberger, Austin Cornish.

Rights and risk-taking

Your Rights (published annually) Sally West, Age Concern England.

Rights and Risk, Alison J Norman. A discussion document on Civil Liberty in Old Age, available from Centre for Policy on Ageing.

Living Dangerously – risk taking, safety and older people, Deirdre Wynne-Harley. Available from Centre for Policy on Ageing.

Speak Up for Yourself – putting advocacy into practice. A guide available from Age Concern England.

The Law and Vulnerable Elderly People (1986) Sally Greengross (ed), Age Concern England.

The Right to Take Risks. Available from Counsel and Care.

About Age Concern

A Warden's Guide to Health Care in Sheltered Housing is one of a wide range of publications produced by Age Concern England – National Council on Ageing. In addition, Age Concern is actively engaged in training, information provision, research and campaigning for retired people and those who work with them. It is a registered charity dependent on public support for the continuation of its work.

Age Concern England links closely with Age Concern centres in Scotland, Wales and Northern Ireland to form a network of over 1,400 independent local UK groups. These groups, with the invaluable help of an estimated 250,000 volunteers, aim to improve the quality of life for older people and develop services appropriate to local needs and resources. These include advice and information, day care, visiting services, transport schemes, clubs and specialist facilities for physically and mentally frail older people.

Age Concern England
Astral House
1268 London Road
London SW16 4ER

Tel: 081-679 8000

Age Concern Wales
4th Floor
1 Cathedral Road
Cardiff CF1 9SD

Tel: 0222 371566

Age Concern Scotland
54a Fountainbridge
Edinburgh EH3 9PT

Tel: 031-228 5656

Age Concern Northern Ireland
3 Lower Crescent
Belfast BT7 1NR

Tel: 0232 245729

Publications from ◆◉◉ Books

A wide range of titles is published by Age Concern England under the ACE Books imprint.

Health and Care

Taking Good Care: A handbook for care assistants
Jenyth Worsley
Written for all those concerned with caring for older people, this book covers such vital issues as communication skills, the medical and social problems encountered by carers, the role of the assistant, the resident's viewpoint and activities and group work.

£6.95   0–86242–072–5

Good Care Management: A guide to setting up and managing a residential home
Jenyth Worsley
This companion volume to *Taking Good Care* has been written for care home proprietors and managers, present and prospective. Topics covered include setting up a home, contracts, budgetary planning, staff management and training, the management of care and quality control.

£9.95   0–86242–104–7

The Community Care Handbook: The new system explained
Barbara Meredith
The delivery of care in the community has changed dramatically as a result of recent legislation, and continues to evolve. Written by one of the country's foremost experts, this book explains in practical terms why the

reforms were necessary, what they are, how they operate and whom they affect.

£11.95   0–86242–121–7

CareFully: A guide for Home Care Assistants

Lesley Bell

Recent legislation places increasing emphasis on the delivery of care to older people in their own homes, thereby underlining the crucial role of the Home Care Assistant. This accessible guide provides practical advice on the day-to-day tasks encountered and addresses such issues as legal responsibilities and emotional involvement.

£9.95   0–86242–129–2

Money Matters

Your Rights: A guide to money benefits for older people

Sally West

A highly acclaimed annual guide to the State benefits available to older people. Contains current information on Income Support, Housing Benefit and retirement pensions, among other matters, and provides advice on how to claim them.

Further information on application

Managing Other People's Money

Penny Letts

The management of money and property is usually a personal and private matter. However, there may come a time when someone else has to take over on either a temporary or permanent basis. This books looks at the circumstances in which such a need could arise and provides a step-by-step guide to the arrangements which have to be made.

£5.95   0–86242–090–3

Policy

Age: The unrecognised discrimination

Edited by Evelyn McEwen

Comprising a series of discursive essays by leading specialists on evidence of age discrimination in British society today, including the fields of employment, healthcare, leisure and the voluntary sector. This book is an important contribution to the growing debate.

£9.95   0–86242–094–6

The Law and Vulnerable Elderly People

Edited by Sally Greengross

This report raises fundamental questions about the way society views and treats older people. The proposals put forward seek to enhance the self-determination and autonomy of vulnerable old people while ensuring that those who are physically or mentally frail are better protected in the future.

£6.50   0–86242–050–4

To order books, please send a cheque or money order, payable to Age Concern England, to the address below. Postage and packing are free. Credit card orders may be made on 081-679 8000.

ACE Books (DEPT WG)
Age Concern England
PO Box 9
London SW16 4EX

INFORMATION FACTSHEETS

Age Concern England produces over 30 factsheets on a variety of subjects. Among these the following titles may be of interest to readers of this book:

Factsheet 5 *Dental care in retirement*

Factsheet 6 *Finding help at home*

Factsheet 10 *Local authority charging procedures for residential and nursing home care*

Factsheet 23 *Help with incontinence*

Factsheet 27 *Arranging a funeral*

Factsheet 29 *Finding residential and nursing home accommodation*

Factsheet 32 *Disability and ageing: your rights to social services*

To order factsheets

Single copies are available free on receipt of a 9″ x 6″ sae. If you require a selection of factsheets or multiple copies totalling more than five, charges will be given on request.

A complete set of factsheets is available in a ring binder at the current cost of £34, which includes the first year's subscription. The current cost for annual subscription for subsequent years is £14. There are different rates of subscription for people living abroad.

Factsheets are revised and updated throughout the year and membership of the subscription service will ensure that your information is always current.

For further information, or to order factsheets, write to:

Information and Policy Department
Age Concern England
1268 London Road
London SW16 4ER

Index

abdominal pain: first aid *115–16*
acupuncture *109*
acyclovir *102*
advocacy *11–12, 18, 19, 187*
aggression *168–9;* coping with *133–4*
agitation *61, 175, 184*
AIDS *80–2*
aids and equipment *25, 60, 151, 183, 213–14*
alcohol and its abuse *25–6, 28, 39–42, 71, 105, 184–5;* safe limits *40*
allopurinol *104*
alternative medicines *76–7, 107–10*
aluminium hydroxide *95*
Alzheimer's disease *164–5, 166–70, 184*
ambulance, calling an *113–14*
amiloride *92*
anaemia *29, 69, 99, 142;* pernicious anaemia *28, 69*
analgesics *see* pain killers
angina *49, 50;* first aid *120–1;* medicines for *91–2*
ankles, swollen *51, 92*
antacids *94–5, 96*
antibiotics *93*
anticholinergics *101*
anticoagulant drugs *29, 99–100*
antidepressants *100*
antipsychotics *100–1*
anxiolytics *101*
arterial disease *52–3;* medicines for *92*
arthritis *70–1, 109–10;* aids and equipment *25, 183, 213, 214;* of the neck *142;* treatment for *70, 103–4, 105*
aspirin *50, 54, 102–3, 108*
atenolol *92*

bathing *181–3, 214*
bendrofluazide *92*
benorylate *103*
bereavement *37, 197–201*
beta-blockers *50, 92*
bile acids *97*
biopsies *75*
Bisacodyl *97*
bismuth preparations *95*
bites, animal: first aid *116*
bladder: cancer of *78;* catheterisation of *152–3;* infection *147;* unstable *148*
bleeding: abnormal (from vagina) *78;* from bladder *78;* from bowel *77;* from cuts *123–4;* from open fractures *130;* from gums *117;* from nose *117;* from scalp *131;* from varicose veins *117–18*
blindness *see* visual handicap
blisters *118*
blood disorders *68–9*
blood pressure: checking *48;* high *52;* medicines for *92, 142*
bones and joints, disorders of *70–2;* broken (first aid) *129–30*
bowel: cancer *31, 58, 69, 77–8;* problems *see* constipation; diarrhoea; incontinence, faecal
Braille *157*
breast cancer *48, 77;* hormone treatment for *106*
bronchitis *54*
bronchodilators *93–4*
bruises: first aid *118–19*
burns: first aid *119–20*
buserelin *106*

Calcitonin *104*

calcium *29, 71*

calcium channel blockers *91, 92*

cancer *75–9;* coming to terms with *76;* tests for *75;* treatment of *76, 106; see also* specific cancers

cancer nurses *208*

carbenoxolone *95*

carbimazole *99*

carbohydrates *27*

carers, needs of *179–80*

cataracts *44, 63–4*

catheters, urinary *152–3*

Caved-S *95*

cervical cancer *78*

cervical smears *47–8, 226*

chemicals: burns from *120;* in eyes *126*

chest: diseases and infections *54–5;* medicines for *93–4;* pains in (first aid) *120–2*

chiropody *45–6, 211*

chiropractic *108–9*

choking: first aid *122*

cholecystitis *58–9*

cimetidine *95*

clothing *144;* hygiene and *181, 182, 183;* for incontinence sufferers *149–50, 151*

clubs *216;* for deaf people *161;* luncheon *25, 31, 215;* stroke *61*

codeine *96, 102*

codeine linctus *94*

colds *54*

colostomies *58, 78, 96*

Community Health Council *203, 211–12*

community nurses *207;* community psychiatric nurses *207–8*

confusion and confused people: acute confusion *133, 163;* and alcohol *184–5;* books on *227;* coping with *170–189;* depression mistaken for *164;* due to physical illness *55, 163;* and medicines *183–4;* due to poor sight and hearing *163, 174–5;* moving to residential homes *186–7;*

moving in to sheltered housing *185–6;* varying levels of *169; see also* Alzheimer's disease; memory; multi-infarct dementia; risk-taking

conjunctivitis *66*

constipation *31, 56, 96–7, 115–16, 149, 154*

continence advisers *146, 208*

coronaries *see* heart attacks

coughs *54–5;* medicines for *94, 154*

cramp *122–3*

crime, street *24*

cuts: first aid *123–4*

cycling *23*

cytotoxic drugs *76, 106*

day centres *215–16*

day-sitting services *180, 209*

De-Nol *95*

deafness *see* hearing, impaired

death: expected *197;* sudden *137;* informing others of *138, 198; see also* funerals

dehydration *30–1, 150*

dementia *164–189; see* Alzheimer's disease; confusion; multi-infarct dementia

dental problems *44, 117*

dentists *210*

dentures: care of *44;* and speech *162*

depression *25, 33, 61–2, 164, 168;* medicines for *100*

diabetes *31, 73–4, 92, 93;* first aid for *124–5;* and eyes *43, 63, 65;* other problems *52, 150;* treatment for *98, 184*

diarrhoea *125, 155;* as cause of confusion *163;* treatment for *96, 125*

diclofenac *103*

Didronel *104*

diethylstilboestrol (DES) *106*

digestive system: problems with *55–9*

digoxin *91, 108*

diltiazem *91*

diphenoxylate *96*

Disabled Living Centres *213*

disorientation *167, 172–5*

district nurses *207*

diuretic drugs *92–3, 142, 150*

diverticular disease *31, 55–6, 69*

doctors *see* general practitioners

drugs *see* medicines

dying people: attitudes to death *193–6;* benefit entitlements *191;* books on caring for *227;* home care for *190–2;* hospice care *191, 193;* hospital care *192;* talking with *196*

ears: disorders of *66–8; see* hearing, impaired

eating *see* food

eczema *108, 109*

education, adult *21*

electroconvulsive therapy *62*

emergencies *111–139;* taking charge in *112–113;* getting help in *113–14, 206;* learning from *138–9; see* ABC of *115ff.*

emotional outbursts *168; see also* aggression, coping with

emphysema *54*

epileptic fits *128, 165;* first aid *128–9;* medicines for *102, 109*

Epsom salts *97*

ethnic minorities: advocacy for *11–12;* depression among *62;* food and *11–12, 24;* and illness *29, 50, 52, 54;* and medicines *90, 107, 109*

exercise *22–3;* and arthritis *70;* and heart disease *50;* and osteoporosis *71*

expectorants *94*

eyes: disorders of *63–6;* emergencies *125–7;* testing *43; see also* visually handicapped people

fainting *127*

faith healing *109*

falls *141–3;* first aid *127–8*

Family Health Services Authority *203*

fats (in diet) *27*

feet *see* foot care

fibre *30, 31;* and constipation *97, 154*

first aid *111–137;* kits *111–12*

fits *see* epileptic fits

'flu *54;* injections against *55*

fluid intake *30–1;* incontinence and *150–1;* constipation and *154*

food: eating habits and *11–12, 24–6;* essential *26–31;* and hygiene *31–2;* from social services *214–15*

foot care *45–6, 211;* in diabetes *73–4; see also* blisters

forgetfulness *see* memory, loss of

fractures: first aid *129–30*

fruit (in diet) *30*

frusemide *92*

funerals, organising *198*

gallstones *31, 58–9;* treatment *59, 97*

general practitioners *203–7;* annual consultations with *46–8;* emergency calls to *113, 206;* and residents *11–12, 18–19, 107, 204–7*

giant cell arteritis (GCA) *65–6, 72;* treatment for *105*

glands: disorders of *73–4*

glaucoma *43, 64–5, 100*

glyceryl trinitrate (GTN) *91, 120*

goitre *74*

goserelin *106*

gout *72, 93;* treatment for *104*

GPs *see* general practitioners

grazes: first aid *123–4*

grief, coping with *197, 199–201*

gums *44;* bleeding from *117*

haemorrhoids *31, 58, 154*

hallucinations: coping with *173–6*

headaches *130–1*

head injuries: first aid *131*

health services *203–12*

health visitors *209*

hearing, impaired *66–8, 159–62;*
    aids *159–61;* books on *227;*
    mistaken for confusion *163;* talking
    to people with *161–2;* testing for *159*

heart attacks *50–1, 142;* first aid *120–1;*
    medicines for *91–3*

heart failure *51*

heart rhythm disturbance *51*

heating: costs *144–5;* and safety *144*

Heimlich manoeuvre *122*

herbal medicines *108*

hernia, inguinal *57*

hiatus hernia *57–8, 69;* medicines for *96*

hips, artificial *71*

HIV *80–2, 109*

hoarseness *162*

home care services *8, 191–2, 213–15*

homes: nursing *217;* residential *186–7,*
    216–17

homeopathic preparations *108*

homosexuality *37;* and AIDS *82*

hormones *73;* for cancer treatment *76,*
    106

hospice care *191, 193*

hospitals: and care for dying people *191,*
    192; compulsory admission to
    187–8

housing managers *13*

HRT (hormone replacement
    therapy) *71*

hygiene: food *31–2;* personal *181–3*

hypertension *52*

hypnotics (sleeping tablets) *100*

hypoglycaemia *98, 124–5*

hypothermia *101, 131–2;* prevention
    143–5; first aid *131–2*

ibuprofen *103*

idoxuridine *102*

ileostomies *58*

impotence *35–6*

incontinence, faecal *155;* advisers on *208;*
    books on *227*

incontinence, urinary *145–6;* advisers on
    146, 208; books on *227;* causes of
    147–53; helping people with *150–3*

indigestion *115;* medicine for *94–5*

inhalers *93–4*

inhibitions, loss of *37–8, 168–9*

insomnia *32–4, 61; see* sleeping pills

insulin *73;* injections *74, 98*

iron *28, 29, 69;* tablets *99*

isosorbide dinitrate *91*

joints *see* bones and joints

kaolin preparations *96*

Kaposi's sarcoma *81*

lactulose *97*

laundry services *151*

lavatories: and incontinence *150, 151–2*

laxatives *96–7, 154, 155*

leukaemia *79;* treatment for *106*

levodopa therapy *28, 101*

Librium *101*

lighting: and sight problems *44, 156–7*

loperamide *96*

luncheon clubs *25, 31, 215*

lungs *53;* cancer of *77;* common
    problems of *54–5;* and pleurisy *121*

lymphoma, treatment for *106*

Macmillan nurses *76, 191, 208*

macular degeneration *64*

Madopar *101*

magnesium trisilicate *94–5*

malabsorption *26, 59*

malnutrition *25–6*

mammography *48*

mastectomy 77

masturbation, public 37–8, 168

meals, oven-ready 215

Meals on Wheels 214–15

medicines: wardens administering 9–10, 83–6; alternative 76–7, 107–10, books on 227; and confusion 183–4; containers for 89; ethnic minorities and 90, 107, 109; labelling of 88; 'memory boxes' for 85, 90; monitored dosage systems for 85; naming of 86–7; over-the-counter 107; unwanted effects of 87; see also specific medicines; swallowing 89

melanoma, malignant 79

Melleril 184

memory: loss of 166–7; stimulating 176–8

Menière's disease 68

Mental Health Act 187–8;

mental illness: medicines for 100–1; see also Alzheimer's disease; confusion; deprssion; multi-infarct dementia

methylcellulose 96, 97

metoclopramide 96

MID see multi-infarct dementia

minerals (in food) 29

morphine 96, 103

mourning 197–201

multi-infarct dementia 92, 164, 165–70

nail cutting 45, 211

nervous system: disorders of 159–62

nifedipine 91

night sitting and nursing 179, 191–2, 209

nitrates (medicines) 91

Non-Steroidal Anti-Inflammatory agents (NSAIs) 103–4

nose bleeds 117

nurses 207–9; agency 209; cancer 191, 208; community 207; conmunity psychiatric 207–8; continence advisers 146, 208; district 207; health visitors 209; Macmillan 76, 191, 208; night 191–2, 209; practice 207; stoma 58, 209

occupational therapists 25, 151, 183, 213

osteoarthritis 70–1, 149

osteomalacia 105

osteopathy 108–9

osteoporosis 71

otosclerosis 67

OTs see occupational therapists

overdoses 133; see poisoning

overprotection; and falls 142–3; see risk-taking

oxprenolol 92

pacemakers 51

Paget's disease 72; treatment for 104

pain killers 102–3, 191

palpitations 51

paracetamol 54, 102–3

paraffin, liquid 97

paralysis (from stroke) 60, 135, 136

Parkinson's disease 61, 148, 149, 162; medicines for 28, 101–2

penicillin 93

peptic ulcers 54, 56, 69; medicines for 95; and smoking 38

personality change 168

pharmacists, help from 87, 88–90

phenobarbitone 102

phenytoin 102

pholcodine 94

physiotherapists 71, 151, 210

piles see haemorrhoids

placebos 110

plaque, removal of 44

pleurisy 121

pneumonia 55

poisoning: first aid 132

polymyalgia rheumatica (PMR) 72; medicines for 105

practice nurses 207

presbyacusis 67–8

prescriptions, repeat 88

privacy, residents' rights to 14

probenecid *104*

promazine *184*

propranolol *92*

propylthiouracil *99*

prostate gland: cancer of *78–9, 106;* and incontinence *148–9*

proteins: in diet *26–7*

psychiatric emergencies *133–4*

psychotherapy *62*

questioning, repetitive *167, 180–1*

radiotherapy *76*

ranitidine *95, 96*

'Recall' packs *21–2*

religious needs, meeting *218–19*

reminiscence sessions *21–2*

repetitive questionning *167, 180–1*

respite care *179–80, 209*

restlessness *184; see also* 'wandering'

retinal detachment *65*

retirement, making most of *20–3*

risk-taking *17, 170–3;* books on *228*

road safety *24*

ruptures *see* hernias, inguinal

safety *24; see* risk-taking

scalds: first aid *119–20*

schizophrenia, drugs for *100–1*

'screening' *47–8*

Section 47 of National Assistance Act *188*

sedatives *see* sleeping pills

'senile dementia' *165*

senna tea *97*

Senokot *97*

sex *34–8;* books on *226;* difficulties with *35–6, 153;* unacceptable behaviour *37–8, 168;* and warden's role *36–7*

sheltered housing: types of *8–9;* helpful designs *177*

Shiatsu *109*

shingles *62;* medicines for *102*

sight, impaired *see* eyes; visually handicapped people

Sinemet *101*

skin cancer *79, 81*

sleep *32–4, 61; see also* sleeping pills

sleeping pills *34, 100;* hazards of *142, 183, 184*

smoking *38–9;* hazards of *52, 71, 166, 225*

social services *212–18*

social workers *217–18*

Sparine *184*

spectacles, care of *43*

speech, impaired *60, 162–3*

splinters: first aid *134*

sport *23*

stealing, accusations of *178–9*

steroid therapy *105*

stings: first aid *134–5*

stoma *58;* nurses *58, 209*

stomach: pains *see* abdominal pains; upset *see* diarrhoea; vomiting

strokes *60–1;* disability from *152, 162;* and multi-infarct dementia *165;* first aid *135–6*

sucralfate *95*

suicide attempts *133; see also* poisoning

sulphinpyrazone *104*

sunburn *136*

suppositories *97*

swimming *23*

tamoxifen *106*

theft, accusations of *178–9*

thiamine *28, 105*

thioridazine *184*

thrush *93*

thyroid disease *74;* medicines for *92, 98–9, 184*

timolol *92*

tinnitus *68, 174–5*

'tranquillisers' *100–1;* unwanted effects *142, 183, 184*

transient ischaemic attacks *60;* first aid *136*

triamterene *92*

ulcers: peptic *see* peptic ulcers; skin *79;* varicose *53*

unconsciousness: first aid *114, 131, 137*

urinals, bottle *153*

urinary infections *147*

urine: colour *30; see also* incontinence

urostomies *78*

Valium *101*

varicose veins *31, 53;* bleeding *117–18*

vasodilators *91–2*

vegetables, cooking *30*

vidarabine *102*

violence, coping with *133*

vision, sudden loss of: first aid *64, 65, 66; see also* eyes, emergencies

visually handicapped people: aids and entertainment *156, 157–8;* guiding *158–9;* lighting and *44, 156–7;* labelling of medicines *88;* registration of *155;* services for *156;* talking to *158; see also* eyes

vitamins *27–9, 104–5;* A *27, 28, 105;* B group *28, 69, 99, 105;* C *28, 30, 105;* D *27, 28–9, 31, 71, 105;* K *27, 29, 105*

voluntary social services *218*

voluntary work (by residents) *22*

vomiting: first aid *115–16, 125*

walking (as exercise) *23*

'wandering' *172–3*

wardens: role *9–11, 13–14, 140;* and residents health *14–19;* and local services *202–3;* training of *10, 12–13*

washing (personal hygiene) *181–3*

water pills *see* diuretics

womb, cancer of the *78*

wounds: first aid *114, 116, 123–4*